MINOR OFFENCES

IRELAND'S CRADLE OF CRIME

TOM TUITE

Gill & Macmillan

**For legal reasons, juveniles' real identities
cannot be used, therefore names and certain
personal details have been changed, but the
cases, crimes and stories featured are real.**

Gill & Macmillan Ltd
Hume Avenue, Park West, Dublin 12
with associated companies throughout the world
www.gillmacmillan.ie

978 07171 4265 1

Typography design by Make Communication
Print origination by Carrigboy Typesetting Services
Printed by Creative Print and Design, Wales

This book is typeset in Linotype Minion and Neue Helvetica.

The paper used in this book comes from the wood pulp of
managed forests. For every tree felled, at least one tree is
planted, thereby renewing natural resources.

A CIP catalogue record for this book is available from the
British Library.

5 4 3 2

CONTENTS

ACKNOWLEDGEMENTS

Over the years, many people have helped me in my work; without their collective assistance, guidance and advice, it would not have been possible to write this book.

To them all I wish to express my sincere thanks. In particular, I am indebted to: Pól Ó Murchú, Sarah Molloy, Michelle Finan, John Quinn, Catherine Ghent, Niall Nolan, Dr Ursula Kilkelly, Tina Haughton, Brendan Rice, Simon Ball, Kitty Harvey, Rose Sweeney and Jim McGuirk.

My publisher Fergal Tobin provided enthusiasm which was gratefully received and I thank him for helping to make this book become a reality.

Special thanks are due to my colleagues Ray Managh, Tomás Mac Ruairí, Sean MacGowan, Bronagh Murphy and Sonya McLean who have all helped me in numerous and valuable ways.

On a more personal level, I am infinitely grateful to my parents and, most of all, to my wife Claire without whom I would never have finished this book.

INTRODUCTION

Some of the biggest crime stories to emerge in Ireland over recent years have involved young offenders and how they were dealt with by the courts. A child, or minor, as defined in Irish criminal law, is a person under the age of 18. A minor offence is one deemed fit to be dealt with at District Court and, where juveniles are concerned, Children's Court level. For many years, the Children's Court in Dublin, the setting for most of this book, sat in the upper yard in Dublin Castle. However, Dublin Castle was not a suitable venue for the Children's Court, so it moved, first to Morgan Place, in the Four Courts, for a number of years. Later it moved to a three-storey, red-brick building in Smithfield and, after a number of years, the Children's Court was rehoused in its own specially commissioned building in Smithfield, in the early 1990s. Its location now is supremely ironic. Booming and rejuvenated Smithfield, resplendent with new offices, apartments and hotels, has become an emblem of prosperous Dublin, Ireland even. Sticking out like a sore thumb, the tracksuit-clad and shaved-headed youths who hang around outside the courthouse at the edge of Smithfield Square mostly come from disadvantaged parts of Dublin, where poverty and drug abuse are rife and criminality is an easy inclination. The contrast is astonishing in a modern-day tale of two cities, two Irelands.

The first step a child takes along the journey to the juvenile justice system is his or her arrest for a criminal offence. The next step is a referral to the Garda Juvenile Diversion Programme. It operates under the supervision and direction of the Garda National Juvenile Office, based in Harcourt Square, and is implemented throughout all Garda divisions by about 90 specially trained gardaí, known as Juvenile Liaison Officers (JLOs). Numbers admitted to the programme have increased steadily over the decades, and especially since 1990, when the programme was extended from Dublin countrywide. Though the system has been around since the early 1960s, the Juvenile Diversion Programme was placed on a statutory footing only with the commencement of parts 4 and 5 of the Children Act 2001. Section 18 of the Act states that 'unless the interests of society otherwise require, any child who has committed an offence and accepts responsibility for his criminal behaviour shall be considered for admission to a Diversion Programme.' The programme is operated under the supervision of the Superintendent, Community Relations Section, who is known as the Director. At local level, it is operated by Garda JLOs who are trained in restorative justice principles and mediation skills. In order for a juvenile to be eligible for the programme, the following criteria have to be met: the offender is under 18 years of age at the time of the commission of the offence and must admit involvement in the crime in question; the parents, guardians or person acting in *loco parentis* must agree to the terms of the caution. Further detail on the programme can be found in Appendix I.

Every year, thousands of children are steered away from offending through the Garda Juvenile Diversion Programme. Those who come before the courts on a regular basis represent a hardcore where the task of diverting them from crime is much more difficult. In reality, the juvenile justice system in Ireland is in chaos, despite the introduction of the much-vaunted and yet not fully implemented 2001 Children Act. A small number of persistent offenders are getting into more trouble; young people awaiting trial or sentencing often accumulate new charges; many are playing the system; there are few sanctions available, and the courts are forced to cope with and resolve inadequacies elsewhere in the system and in other services.

Anecdotally based, this book attempts to capture a snapshot of the lifestyles of some of the young people who come before the courts and what happens to them. It also tries to demonstrate how juvenile crime is not a black-and-white issue and how many children end up being put through the rigours of the criminal justice system for a multiplicity of reasons. While it is easy to show contempt for the parents of young offenders, an understandable response in many cases, many of them, despite their best efforts, have seen their children give themselves over to crime and thus waste their lives and often ruin those of other people. This book is a portrait, not an official history. It concentrates on episodes that seem especially significant and individual experiences which illustrate wider truths. For legal reasons, juveniles' real identities cannot be used, therefore names and certain personal details have been changed, but the cases, crimes and stories featured are real.

Gangland crime and anti-social behaviour have become major political and social issues and juvenile crime is closely linked to both. Scratch under the surface of the backgrounds of many repeat young offenders in Dublin and there can be found clear links to organised crime. Crime bosses and their goons become figures of almost idolatrous reverence for many of the disenfranchised young people who come before the Children's Court. Many of them have lives in which crime is as normal to them as going to school is for most children—such youngsters spend more time in courtrooms than in classrooms. They form part of a counter-culture that seems to be in open conflict with law and order, wherein a first court appearance is regarded almost as a rite of passage. Much of this young generation, in worst-case scenarios, serves as a recruiting ground for the ranks of the serious crime gangs; youngsters, ripe for grooming, stand to attention, ready and willing to answer the call-up.

The problem is complex and there are no quick-fix, magic solutions. But what is clear is that political willpower and support are required to bring about the vitally needed approach where prevention, not detention, is recognised as being better than the cure.

TOM TUITE
28 September 2006

I. REASONS

01 | WHY? PARALLEL LIVES

In 2004, an extensive study by the Irish Association for the Study of Delinquency (IASD) pointed out the similarities in backgrounds of young people who come before the Children's Court in Dublin. The study was based on a thorough inspection of court files and data made available by a number of agencies in relation to a sample of 50 young people whose cases were finalised in the Dublin Children's Court from January to October 2004. Some 751 young people had their cases ended throughout that period. Out of the 50 youngsters, 42 were male. Altogether, the sampled group had 551 charges brought against them. According to the report:

> 19 had less than five charges; 13 had between five and nine charges; and 18 young people had ten or more charges. The number of charges against a person can be closely related to the speed with which a case is concluded. Some young people experienced significant delays in the courts system. For example, ten young people made their first court appearance more than six months after the date of the offence. 11 young people had their cases concluded more than one year after their first court appearance, and in two of these cases, more than two years. Theft and robbery offences accounted for 27% of the 551 charges, followed by public order offences (23%), traffic offences (18%) and criminal damage (10%).[1]

Out of the 36 young people convicted by the court, half received detention sentences.

> Nine were committed to St Patrick's Institution for Young Offenders because they were aged 16 or over at the conclusion of their court proceedings. Nine young people were committed to detention schools because they were under 16 at the conclusion of their court proceedings. Non-custodial sanctions (probation bonds, suspended sentences, community service orders, fines and peace bonds) were applied to the other 18 young people convicted on charges. A further ten young people were not convicted on any of the charges against them, while four were sent forward for trial to the Circuit Court.

The IASD's study also highlighted facts that often emerge during juveniles' cases.

> Many young people in the study sample first came into contact with An Garda Síochána at an early age. 20 young people first had offences referred to the Garda National Juvenile Office before the age of 12.

This report also showed that many young people appearing in the Dublin Children's Court had a troubled family background. Problems cited included:

> Absence of at least one parent for significant periods of the young person's childhood (26 out of the 38 for whom family background information was available); breakdown of relationship between parents (14); young person living without either parent (12); criminal record of family members (14); housing problems (11); large family size (17); parents with serious substance misuse problems (8); and in a small number of cases, self-harm (7), physical (2) or sexual abuse (2) indicators. Many young people (18) were strongly influenced by an anti-social peer group.

The other common denominator among the majority of juvenile defendants, educational problems and lack of schooling, was evident in the study.

> Educational disadvantage was a significant problem for young people appearing before the Dublin Children's Court. 28 of 34 young people for whom educational information was available left school before the legal age of 16 and without completing their Junior Certificate. 13 young people were assessed as having significant literacy problems.

All of the 18 young people who were sentenced to detention had experienced family, educational, alcohol or substance-abuse difficulties. Examples of how young people can end up on society's margins and then turn to crime are seen in the courts on a daily basis. In the worst cases, traditional family structures have broken down; such structures might have acted as a net to catch those at risk of falling through the cracks in society. Many, some in their early teens, end up homeless for a multitude of reasons and rely on emergency hostel accommodation. This entails the young person turning up at a garda station. Social services are then contacted by the gardaí to find out which hostel has vacant beds. The hostels work on a 'first come, first served' basis. The child must go from the garda station to the hostel, alone, in the hope that the bed has not been snapped up in the meantime. Those lucky enough to get a bed in one of the hostels can find themselves in a hostile environment with offenders who are often much older and highly criminalised. Many in the hostels have chronic addiction problems and histories of violent crime, following years of living from day to day on the streets. Bullying is rife, with older youths victimising the younger new arrivals. Frequently they are forced to commit thefts such as muggings, pickpocketing or mobile-phone snatches, and then hand over the goods to the ring leaders, in order to stay in the hostel without the fear of being picked on.

In summer 2004, there were four Dublin boys from different areas of the city but about the same age; they probably didn't know each other, but to an uncanny extent their lives were parallel. Within four weeks, they all sat on the same seat, a court dock, and pleaded guilty to criminal offences, some minor, some of a more serious nature. The common denominator between them was that they were out of school and their lives had spiralled out of control into a web of criminality and often chronic drug addiction, as part of the fallout from the complete breakdown of their families. These factors are indicative of the lifestyles and backgrounds of the many who make up the endless throng of troubled teenagers who walk through the doors of the Children's Court in Dublin, on a daily basis. In wealthy, modern Ireland, the word 'Dickensian' can still apply to countless teenagers brought up in a world rarely shown on television.

The first of these boys was just 16 years old, and already a veteran of street life. He had started sleeping rough when he was 13, having run away from home to escape from a vicious, abusive stepfather. His crime: stealing a sandwich and other pickpocketing efforts to support his heroin-addicted life on the streets. Once, when arrested for stealing a wallet, he explained that he had been compelled to do it because, he 'was starving'.

His tragic story, told by his lawyer, outlines the horrific sequence of events. The judge heard how he had had to learn to survive on the streets, where he was at the mercy of drug dealers and was uncertain as to where he would sleep from one night to the next. His stepfather had been violent to the boy's mother. As the boy got older, he had tried to intervene and protect her from the nightly beatings. But he too had been viciously beaten by the abusive stepfather. At 13, and with nowhere else to go, he had fled to the streets, which had nothing to offer him other than heroin addiction. For the sake of his welfare, he had been put in a detention centre on foot of a High Court order. This period in a stable environment allowed him to quit heroin. But within weeks of his release, he was addicted again. Efforts had been made to get him into a care home but staff in the unit feared that his drug use could adversely influence other young people living there. He had then started to live in a hostel where one of the staff members had once saved him from an overdose. But three years after he fled home, there was a small ray of light at the end of the tunnel; the boy's social worker had arranged for him to be provided meals daily and had organised a place on a heroin addiction treatment programme for him. She was trying to find him a placement in a day centre for troubled children, which could occupy his time.

Once the boy started to provide clean urine samples, to show that he had stopped taking heroin, it would then be possible for him to return to the care home. The boy spoke once and briefly at his hearing, quietly telling the judge: 'I'll do it, I'll try my best.' The judge imposed a suspended sentence. And so that the efforts to restore some normality into his life would be tracked, she ordered that the case be brought back to court every three weeks.

Six months later, he was back at square one. Just before Christmas, he asked to be held in custody to help him quit drugs. His request was granted but after he was released, he fell back into the same situation. His struggle continues.

The second boy in this quartet of childhood misery and neglect also resorted to heroin after his family life deteriorated. On the night of 26 March 2004, he found himself in a Malahide video shop, armed with a knife. He was aged 17, a heroin addict and now armed robber, having come a long way from the child who loved to spend his time playing Gaelic football. He had turned to hard drugs after his parents had split up. He no longer saw his mother, and his father had started a new family. In the video store, he produced a knife and threatened the cashier before taking a sum of money from the shop till and fleeing the scene.

Somehow, a control mechanism managed to kick in and he found himself in revulsion at the depths to which he had descended. Two days later, he turned himself in to Coolock Garda Station to own up to the offence, and in court from the outset he admitted robbery of the shop. In criminal cases involving juveniles, a parent or guardian is required by law to attend the proceedings. But the woman sitting in the back of the tiny courtroom supporting the teenager was not his mother but a family friend who had given him a home.

This woman said that she was more than happy to look after the boy. Since moving in to her home, he had been helpful with daily chores and she had grown to trust him enough to mind her children when she went out on errands. Having found this new home, he had also managed to stay off drugs and 'detoxed' on his own. The boy hoped to start a training course that could lead to an apprenticeship in carpentry. The judge described the offence as extremely serious but was impressed by the boy's acknowledgment that he needed help. She released him on a probation bond to continue his efforts to become a carpenter and to reside with the lady who had stepped in and offered him a home. He became one of the luckier ones and never came back to the Children's Court.

The third boy was aged 16, from north inner-city Dublin and a good and supportive home. He was diagnosed as having Attention-Deficit Hyperactivity Disorder (ADHD), when he was aged seven years. Despite having him assessed, his concerned parents found little help available for their son's behavioural and learning problems. He was sent to a treatment centre where it was hoped he could be helped, but his condition did not improve. To add to his troubles, his parents separated while he was still in his early teens, at which point he started to take cocktails of cocaine and assorted tablets. These were the factors which had led to his being arrested for a string of offences over the previous two years: 17 convictions for theft and motoring offences alone.

A six-month term in St Patrick's Institution on a charge of driving a stolen car was handed down, but his welfare and progress were to be kept under supervision after his release by means of a probation bond for two years.

The fourth boy who appeared in court that week had admitted taking part in a burglary of a primary school. The 16-year-old had been badly affected and unsettled by the drastic breakdown of his family and home life, which had deteriorated completely around the time of the school burglary. According to the boy's solicitor, the boy's father said that he had been going through a rough period and had been living on the streets. After his parents' separation, he had been living with his mother who also had difficulties; she had put him and his siblings on the streets, where he remained, sometimes staying with his grandmother. Amazingly, during that chaotic period, he managed to keep going to school, and completed the Junior Certificate.

Having been told that the boy's father was now trying to rebuild his relationship with his wife and that they had got back together again, the judge adjourned sentencing the teenager and granted bail to allow time for the preparation of a probation report. He then asked the boy if he understood that he could be facing a sentence; the teenager shyly whispered back: 'Yes.' As the case was adjourned, both the boy and his father, who had been instrumental in reconstructing their home life and central to his son's admission of guilt, thanked the judge for the chance, as they left court together. Later he was released on a probation bond.

These four stories all feature remarkable similarities: family break-up, dropping out of school and drug abuse. Commenting on these cases and other similar ones that come before the Children's Court on a daily basis, Pól Ó Murchú, one the country's most experienced child law solicitors, said that backgrounds of broken homes, poverty and drug abuse are significant factors in the profiles of many children who find themselves caught up in the juvenile criminal justice system. Early intervention and greater support for families experiencing difficulties are the key to preventing children from coming before the courts at all, he explains: 'The real lesson is to support young mothers and fathers and to support kids at risk.' And greater support is needed for schools to help prevent truancy and identify children with behavioural problems. 'The children in the courts are out of school on average for about a year and a half.' Many of them exhibit behavioural difficulties when they are as young as five or six. Then they start dropping out of school and find themselves before the courts. 'Parents, schools and their principals need support. They really need to have more help at community level.'

Ó Murchú tells the following story:

When we first met Ben he was about five or six years old. His older brother was up in court that day. Ben was full of life and friendly. Everybody spoke to him. As the Children's Court moved location, we kept seeing Ben. . . . Unfortunately, by the time he was 13 or 14, he was a very regular attender in the Children's Court. At 14, he received two years' detention in Trinity House. At 16, he received two years' detention in St Patrick's Institution. Regrettably he had become part of the criminal justice system.[2]

Ó Murchú has set out a number of reasons why society needs to be more attentive to the area of juvenile justice. 'Violent gang crime is already a feature of many housing estates,' he states.

These estates are controlled by gangs. No one will dare cross them, no one will dare give evidence against them. None of us really know what is going on. Fr Peter McVerry[3] sees 13- and 14-year-olds growing into gang members, like watching seeds grow in an incubation chamber. They sell cocaine by day and control their territory by night. They murder and maim those they disagree with. Those who owe them money will find that their parents' home, or their girlfriend's home is smashed up or their children will have a leg broken. No one will report these crimes to the gardaí. They will not be reported in the media because people are too scared. You have to live in these estates to know what is going on. These gangs are untouchable either by the community or by the law until they cross another gang which is prepared to be even more violent. These young people who have been excluded and from whom hope has been eradicated have nothing to lose. Armed robberies and drug dealing are their only route, a very successful route to sharing in the benefits of the Celtic Tiger.

Most young offenders come from disadvantaged areas where crime is rife. Many come from failed families and have parents who were very young, sometimes children themselves, when they became parents. The two important issues of housing and supports for young parents need to be addressed, according to Ó Murchú:

> Fr McVerry firstly states we must develop socially integrated housing and as long as those who are poor and excluded are physically segregated in low-income ghettoes, then we are sowing seeds of strife and division and maintaining an environment in which crime and its associated violence are seen as a perfectly rational option. Secondly, we must radically reform the structure of the education system to ensure equality of access to education and equality of opportunity within the educational system to all young people. In addition, there must be very extensive community supports available to young mothers and to young fathers to parent and nurture their children adequately.

The current Child Psychiatric Services in Ireland are totally inadequate and greater consideration of the complex problems of young people is vital, he argues.

> The Department of Health has, for many years, consistently ignored many reports recommending properly structured child and adolescent psychiatric services with adequate funding. Because of inadequate services the real losers are children who require psychiatric intervention, and their families.

Like many professionals who work with troubled children, he says that full implementation of the much-lauded Children's Act is vital.

> Our own Government is due to seek approximately 15–20 amendments to the Children's Act, 2001, as a package of reform measures for the juvenile justice system. This will include plans to raise the age of criminal responsibility from seven to 12 years of age. New ways of dealing with children causing problems in the community will be introduced including Good Behaviour Contracts, Community Sanctions and Anti-Social Behaviour

Orders (ASBOs). If the child continues to behave in an anti-social way, the child can be referred to the Garda Diversion Programme and, if the problem remains, gardaí will then be able to apply to the court for an ASBO. Adequate and proper resources will be required to ensure that these most vulnerable children and their families will be adequately and properly supported.

Education is a key to helping to tackle the crisis. Ó Murchú cites figures from the National Educational Welfare Board which show that almost one in five second-level students missed more than 20 days in 2004; in the country's most disadvantaged areas, more than one-third of second-level school students are in this situation; at primary level, 47,000 pupils (one in ten) were absent at least 20 days in 2004, while the proportion in this category in the poorer areas is almost one in five.

Regrettably some of these children end up in the Children's Court. Many of the children attending the Children's Court have been out of school for approximately two or three years before coming to the attention of the Children's Court. Early intervention is urgently required.

The number of children in care in Ireland is rising steadily.

The proportion of children in care has doubled over the past 15 years from 2,756 in 1989 to 5,517 in 2001. The children's charity, Barnardos, says that the numbers showed that greater investment in family support structures are needed. Again, early intervention and support to vulnerable families is urgently needed.

According to Ó Murchú, society and policy makers must examine how young offenders are to be rehabilitated when many juveniles are locked up with older and frequently more highly criminalised youths—in flagrant breach of international standards of practice in the western world. About 150 children and teenagers were placed in adult prisons in 2005, and a total of 166 children (aged between 15 and 17 years) were in adult prisons during 2004. He explains further:

> The Ombudsman for Children, Emily Logan, has confirmed that adult prisons were highly inappropriate settings for children and these children are amongst the most vulnerable in the State. She adds 'It's clear that an adult prison cannot meet the needs of children.' Mr Justice Dermot Kinlan (Inspector of Prisons and Places of Detention) has confirmed that St Patrick's Institution is a most inappropriate place for 16- and 17-year-olds. He says it should be destroyed immediately. His report, published in April 2005, indicated that the workshops are closed, inmates are locked in cells for long periods of time and bullying seems rife. There is inadequate education, care, welfare and rehabilitation available to young people in St Patrick's Institution.

There are people in society who have the thankless task of dealing with the human wreckage that is washed up on our streets. Ó Murchú says that their advice should be taken on board and a more concerted approach should be taken to the substantive issue of poverty.

> Barnardos launched a seven-step campaign which, it says, could lift thousands of children out of poverty if the Government implements the measure. Latest figures published this year showed 14.6% of children (i.e. 148,000 children) were in consistent poverty.

That seven-step campaign includes the following: raising incomes for families with children living in poverty; improving educational outcomes for all children; introducing preschool schemes or early childhood education and care; eradicating health inequalities so that every child has access to health care; improving housing standards for children at risk; making work pay enough so that families can escape poverty traps; and ensuring that policies relating to children have a positive impact through 'joined-up' government structures.

Children's rights have to be recognised and the health authorities should be compelled to attend the Children's Court cases involving minors who are in their care, he says. And that opinion has also been expressed in a report published by the Law Society of Ireland, entitled *Rights Based Child Law*. This report confirms that, apart from the right to an education, children have no defined rights under the Irish constitution.

At the moment, children who are dependent on the State for their care, education, health and protection are vulnerable to having second best choices made for them. Some children are seriously disadvantaged by the absence of the provision in the Constitution protecting their interests. The Law Society Report proposes using the model of the South African Constitution which contains an express list of children's rights. Only when the Constitution is amended will the State be able to cherish all its children equally. This report recommends that the exclusion of the Health Service Executive (HSE) from the definition of 'Guardian' in Section 3 of the Children Act, 2001, be deleted and recommends that the Act be amended to require the HSE to send a representative to a court hearing at the request of the defendant, his family, legal representative or the court.

Poverty is the most important common denominator in cases of children who start out on the path of criminality. Sometimes their offending stems from the need to fund an addiction; more often, young people get involved in crime as a result of negative influence from other youths who come from dysfunctional families that have little regard for law and order. Many young people come from families that over generations have become dynasties of criminality where illegal pursuits are not just tolerated but actively encouraged. One Dublin family in particular is able to trace its ancestors through the court records back to the foundation of the state. And it is believed that the family's antecedent generations can also be found in pre-independence court records going back to the early 1800s.

Children often find themselves roped into 'gangland' at an impressionable age; by the time they realise the danger they are in, they are too late to break out of its clutches. Often, vulnerable teenagers are sucked in by professional gangsters who have massive street credibility in their communities and, safe in the knowledge that they are almost untouchable by the law, prey on the vulnerable. They target the young, frequently befriending them at amusement arcades or on the streets; they gain their confidence and gradually groom them into becoming integral yet often disposable parts of their gangs. It can start off with a young teenager being offered drugs 'on tick' with a nod and a wink that they can pay later. When the dealer decides that he wants his money, he knows full well that the child cannot pay, and other arrangements will be made in lieu of hard cash. Under the threat of physical violence, a child can end up working for the dealer. Terrified at what recriminations could result, the child is not going to make a report to gardaí.

A small, meek-looking boy was brought before the Children's Court on 13 May 2004. He was 13 years old and, despite his tender years, was firmly in the clutches of gangland. As he sat in the defendant's bench, looking downward, it was explained that he had already become deeply involved with criminals who punished his family whenever he tried to leave their gang. He had been drawn into 'a web of crime' and was in 'way over his head'. He had also become violent towards his mother but social services could do little to help.

Gardaí had been called to the family home following a domestic row in which the boy had allegedly tried to choke his mother. His mother said that this had been an ongoing situation for years. Unable to get help from social workers, she had decided to go ahead with the prosecution.

The garda who had been called to the scene and had arrested the boy reported that the defendant had 'been hanging around with men who are in their twenties and they have drawn him into a web of crime. . . . When he tries to dissociate himself from them, they punish his mother by smashing in her windows. He is caught up in something way over his head.' The boy's family was petrified.

Strict bail was granted, compelling the boy to obey a curfew from 8 p.m. to 8 a.m. He was also to reside with a relative while on bail, and his solicitor said that she would write to social services immediately regarding the family's concerns.

It was believed that the boy's actions stemmed from confusion and mixed messages. His mother often managed to convince him to stay away from the gang. But when they got their hands on him, they were able to reverse brainwash him into thinking that it was she who was wrong and that he must not obey her.

During the following week, the boy's mother was targeted by the vengeful criminals, angered at her efforts to break their grip on her son. The family home was ransacked and all of the windows smashed. In a later court hearing, it was reported that a burglary on the family home was a 'repercussion of him being in court'. The gardaí were 'keeping a close eye' on the boy's home to protect his family, but one of the gang members was a suspect in a serious assault on a garda, who had nearly been killed. Having heard that social workers were putting a plan together to help the boy, the judge remanded him on bail for four weeks and gave him a strict warning to meet with the social workers and not to associate with the gang. The criminals were persistent. For the previous three years, they had enjoyed controlling the boy who, being young and impressionable, was easily persuaded to do tasks for them. These involved delivering and storing drugs as well as money.

The mother's fear was compounded by the fact that she was deaf. Frequently the gang broke into her house through an upstairs windows, while she sat downstairs oblivious to their presence. They smashed up rooms and destroyed personal property, not even having to worry about making too much noise in the process.

Within the following weeks and months, social services intervened and the boy was placed in a programme to assist troubled children, where professionals would work with him on a one-to-one basis. A placement in a new school was found and he was also moved from his area to live with relatives. The gangsters'

grip was finally broken as a result of a brave mother's determination not to lose her son, garda involvement, monitoring by
the court, intervention by social services, a new school and
relocation. He was one of the lucky ones.

Another distraught mother told the Children's Court on 19 May
2004 that she had repeatedly approached social workers, telling
them that her son, then aged 16 years old, was involved with
dangerous criminals and that he had twice tried to kill himself.
Her son, she explained, had a number of personal difficulties.

The woman had been driven to spending nights searching
Ballymun, 'hounding' her son to keep him away from drug
dealers. Eventually she had sought help from the Garda Síochána
who had advised her to report her son if he was involved in any
public order breaches. This had resulted in his being arrested and
detained in the Finglas Child and Adolescent Centre where he had
started to study for his Junior Certificate. However, the boy had
wrecked a room in the detention centre and the staff in the centre
were reluctant to have him. The mother pleaded for bail, afraid
that if her son were remanded to St Patrick's Institution, he would
be criminalised and unable to continue his education. The mother
was in a Catch-22 situation. Her fear was that her son would be
further criminalised by going to St Patrick's Institution. But if he
were released, and in the absence of therapeutic intervention, the
same would happen. The judge adjourned the case and granted
bail.

The mother's fear that criminal elements in her community
would win her son over were well founded. On 19 January 2005, he
was arrested in Santry. A garda probe into a planned drugs
delivery led to a bust, with the boy getting caught red-handed in
possession of €35,000 worth of cocaine. Today, he is behind bars,
having received a lengthy sentence in Dublin Circuit Criminal
Court.

02 | EXTREME LEARNING DISADVANTAGE:
'WHAT DOES NEGATIVE MEAN?'

The two brothers had a wretched existence: they could not read, write or tell time and they did not understand dates, months or seasons. 'He had no active engagement with society apart from through the courts,' it was said of the younger of the two. The elder boy, meanwhile, would be described as 'feral', a concept that is almost impossible to comprehend in modern Ireland.

The brothers, Peter and Joseph, could have been lifted from the pages of a Charles Dickens novel such was the hardship they had endured all of their lives. The elder brother, Peter, had been convicted of sixteen offences between 1 January 2002 and 17 February 2004. By then he was completely out of control and had been that way since the age of 12 when he had first left his caravan home and opted for life on the streets. Peter's family lived in a caravan parked on the side of a small road used by heavy vehicles. 'I'm living next door to Hell,' his mother said. The family had no toilet or washing facilities and the nearest tap with running water was 40 metres away. Home life was completely unstable, with Peter and his siblings repeatedly witnessing episodes of domestic violence.

Always hungry looking, with bloodshot eyes and cheeks flushed from solvent sniffing, he walked with his head stooped forward, and he looked decrepit. His body was scarred from heroin injections. In fact, the only time he looked remotely healthy was after he had spent time in custody where he would have had a bed for the night and regular meals every day, things that were alien to his street urchin life.

On 5 March 2004, Peter was detained in St Patrick's Institution for five months for a spate of crimes which took place over twenty-five months while he was living on the streets of Dublin. Previously he had been barred from entering the city centre after his distraught mother had said that she could not prevent him from going there. At an earlier hearing, she had told the court that she had frequently spent nights searching the streets of Dublin for her son and often did not know where he was or who he was with. She was terrified that he was exposed to drug abuse and said that she had done her best to keep him at home. The mother was not present on the day he was sentenced for offences which involved fifteen prosecuting gardaí.

Over the previous four years, Peter had been out of school, and had repeatedly broken court-imposed curfews, city-centre bans and orders from judges to stay out of trouble. Shortly before his sentence hearing, a place was found for him in a hostel for troubled teenagers, run by the Probation and Welfare Services. However, Peter, who was now more used to sleeping rough than in a bed, had already gone missing from the hostel for a week. He continued to sleep rough on the streets of Dublin and, as a result, the Probation and Welfare Service's supervision broke down.

On 17 February, he burgled a flat on Dublin's Middle Abbey Street and stole a Playstation games console and four compact discs. The stolen property was snatched from the hands of a small and frightened child who lived with his family in the flat. Peter's solicitor said that the probation report that was obtained by the court had shown that there had been continued difficulties but Peter was anxious to get bail. However, Judge Mary Collins said that while Peter's circumstances were tragic, it would be in his interests if he were sentenced instead of having the case adjourned again. 'I have given you every opportunity, put it back and put it back and have listened to the same story. It has got to the stage where there are serious problems,' she said. 'It is better for you if I deal with it today.' She sentenced Peter to four months for the burglary and a further one-month consecutive sentence for the connected theft charge, with all other charges taken into consideration.

Peter's criminal record showed that on 1 January 2002, he had stolen a gold necklace worth €100 in Dame Street; on 2 February, at College Green, he had attempted to pickpocket a man; on 26 July 2002, he had stolen €70 from a man during a mugging on South Great George's Street; on 28 July, on Dame Street, he had stolen a wallet; on 22 August 2002, he had stolen a mobile phone from a man on Dublin's Westmoreland Street; on 27 August 2002, a bench warrant had been issued for his arrest for skipping court; on 14 December 2002, on Dame Street, he had been caught begging; on 23 December, at College Green, Dublin 2, he had stolen a wallet worth €30. On 17 June 2003, he had failed to comply with a garda's direction to leave a vicinity where he was at risk of causing a breach of the peace; on 9 August, a bench warrant had been issued for his arrest for skipping court; on the same day, at Essex Gate, he had stolen a man's mobile phone worth €150; on 24 September and 11 December further bench warrants had been issued for his arrest for skipping court; on 11 December, he had been caught with stolen property—a mobile phone. On 17 February 2004, he had committed the burglary at the flat on Middle Abbey Street.

A few weeks later, Peter pleaded guilty to the last remaining charges against him.

Judge David Anderson heard that, on 19 February 2004, Peter had been observed by gardaí as he was trying to break a shop's front-door lock. Peter's solicitor explained that his client had recently been given a five-month sentence for a number of offences, and hoped to put offending behind him after his time in custody. Judge Anderson said he would not substantially prolong Peter's time in custody and imposed a four-month sentence for the attempted burglary.

Peter's life after custody continued in much the same way as it had before he was detained. In October 2005, having just turned 18, Peter pleaded guilty to attacking a man on Lord Edward Street, Dublin, and stealing his wallet, and to possession of a stolen bank card. He also admitted obstructing a garda during a drug search on Thomas Street. He had swallowed a number of tablets as a garda was about to search him under the Misuse of Drugs Act. Peter then had 22 previous convictions, had been refused bail and held in custody over these charges. He had also been held on a High Court order on welfare grounds.

Now the court heard the shocking details. Peter was an illiterate drug addict who had spent most of his teens living on the streets with no state assistance. Homeless and refused accommodation by state services, he had developed a chronic heroin addiction, leading to his case being brought to the High Court that year, when he was 17, seeking a childcare order to detain him for his own safety. This move, his solicitor explained, was taken 'in a situation in which State agencies failed to intervene'. At this stage, she said, the teenager had been injecting heroin and cocaine into his groin and everyone believed he would live for just two weeks. She also said that Ireland had done Peter 'a great wrong by leaving him on the streets'.

Throughout his period on the streets he had been helped by Focus Ireland, the voluntary agency for the homeless, whose staff had felt that he was severely at risk. His heroin addiction had deteriorated while his involvement in criminal activity, fuelled by a need to feed his drug problem, had escalated. Peter had been refused homeless payments despite the fact that he had been homeless since the age of 14. Psychological assessments had been ordered, but these services had been put in place only as he was approaching his eighteenth birthday and after his case had been brought to the High Court.

One psychological report on him stated that he: 'had a level of illiteracy rarely found in the general population, with limited comprehension of time, dates and seasons.' Another psychological report said that the teenager's ability to engage with the services put in place for him was limited. During a meeting with a psychologist, Peter was asked if he had been tested for HIV or Hepatitis C. Peter replied that he had tested negative for them both. He then asked the psychologist what the word negative meant.

However, following on the High Court case, the health services put support measures in place for him. These included accommodation in a hostel, a placement on a drug rehabilitation course and involvement of care workers. A six-month suspended sentence was also imposed for a period of eighteen months on one of the charges. Judge Murphy released the teenager on bail on other charges, stressing to him that, for the first time ever, he had support services to help him.

She explained that he had to reside at the hostel and abide by the directions of its staff and attend a drug treatment centre. She also stressed to him that he would have to dissociate himself from his former peer group if he wanted to deal with his heroin addiction successfully. He was warned that should he fail to keep these conditions, a six-month detention term would be imposed. Peter, who remained silent throughout most of the proceedings, agreed that he would be co-operative and abide by the bail conditions. The court remanded him to appear again later that month. The judge wished him good luck and advised him to 'make the most of this opportunity'. At the subsequent court appearance, he was released on a probation supervisory bond. At time of writing, he is living in hostel accommodation for the homeless.

In a not unusual repetition of history, as Peter left the juvenile justice system to go out into an uncertain future, his younger brother found himself in similar circumstances. Joseph had first come before the courts when he was aged 12, and over the following year alone had been arrested for eight offences. The boys' father had left the family home when Joseph was aged 12, and after that he lacked significant parental guidance. Like his older brother, Joseph had also witnessed domestic violence and alcohol abuse in his home. When he was aged nine, his family had moved to England; on their return three years later, he was enrolled in a school, but was expelled after twelve days. After that he had no education and was functionally illiterate.

By the age of 15, he was associating with older drug addicts who were heavily involved in crime. He started abusing heroin and, like his brother before him, became addicted. Joseph was placed in a non-secure care home but the placement broke down because of his use of drugs.

In April 2005, he was remanded in custody to the National Remand and Assessment Centre, in Finglas. The centre, as it had done two years previously, highlighted that he needed multi-agency intervention. 'The reason he was offending was because he felt he was going nowhere,' his solicitor said. A report from Focus Ireland, the voluntary agency for homeless people, which had been providing him with help, said that he had 'no active engagement with society apart from through the courts'. He had no reading age, no comprehension of days, dates or months, and there were difficulties in getting him into a school setting.

In early 2006, efforts were made to force intervention by the Health Service Executive. A placement was sought in the Ballydowd Special Care Unit in Lucan, and pending the decision on whether he would be admitted, he was held in custody. By 9 February 2006, he had been appointed a guardian and was in interim full care of the Health Service Executive. He also pleaded guilty to fourteen offences for trespassing, public order violations, failing to appear in court and obstruction of a garda during the course of a drug search. An appeal of his refusal for admission to the Ballydowd Unit was launched. His addiction had been cited as a reason for his being refused a place in the centre for troubled young people in west Dublin.

A representative of the HSE proposed that a step-down placement in Joseph's previous non-secure care unit would be provided to follow a detention period of three months in the Ballydowd facility. Judge William Hamill expressed concern that a placement in the secure Ballydowd Special Care Unit was contingent on a step-down placement and said that since the one proposed had been previously unsuccessful, he feared that Joseph would again be refused entry. He remanded Joseph in custody to Oberstown Boys' Centre for a further two weeks, pending a decision on the requested placement in the Ballydowd Special Care Unit.

On 27 March, when the case was next back in court, Judge Catherine Murphy said that most of the offences were 'directly referable to the circumstances outlined'. 'I can say that I believe a great deal more should have been done for you at an earlier stage,' she added. She remanded the teen in custody pending a decision on the Ballydowd Special Care Unit.

On his next appearance in April, all the charges against him were dropped when word came though to the Children's Court that a three-month placement in the Ballydowd unit had been ordered by the High Court. Most of his offences stemmed from the lifestyle he had led, Judge Murphy reiterated. The judge categorised his offending thus: 'In effect they really seem like a frightening number of charges but in a sense they boil down to a small core of offences. Not turning up to court: that can be explained in the context of your lifestyle. . . . Minor thefts, trespassing because you had nowhere to go. I am happy in relation to the charges to make no further order.' Joseph was then transferred to Ballydowd with the hope of making a fresh start. After his stint in Ballydowd, he was put in a care home from which he would later be moved, like his older brother, into hostel accommodation for the homeless.

03 | SEVERE PSYCHIATRIC PROBLEMS:
CIRCUMSTANCES VERGING ON UNIQUE

P aul truly believed that he had to get out on bail. After all, he was expected at Old Trafford football stadium, for his trial to play with his heroes, Manchester United.But Paul was brain damaged and that was a truth in his own mind only. He would shuffle into the courtroom with his mouth hanging open. He had difficulty in gauging space and would often have to be helped through doorways. Intense legal issues involving him would be discussed while he sat on one side of the courtroom silent and with no idea what was happening.

From Paul's early childhood until he reached his teens, his case had been brought to the High Court thirty-two times in efforts to give him the care and welfare he needed. The boy came from a shattered family background, and had suffered from behavioural problems since the age of five. However, his problems were drastically exacerbated when he was 14, following a tragic sequence of events.

In October 2000, Paul took a lift in a car which was being driven by a joyrider at high speed through Dublin city centre. The car crashed, injuring two gardaí and Paul in the process. The part of Paul's brain which controlled cognitive functions was damaged. The injuries he sustained also compounded existing emotional problems. As a result, he was placed in the Ballydowd Special Care Unit, in Lucan, from 2001 to 2002, for his own welfare. After his release, which coincided with the death of his mother from cancer, an unsuccessful after-care plan was put in place by the health board. His subsequent placement in a home for boys broke down after he returned to the family home in the south inner city.

There, he ended up living with his older sister, a chronic heroin addict. She also shared her inner-city flat with a drug dealer and with Paul's two younger siblings. Paul's father was an alcoholic who lived on the streets.

This unsafe and hostile environment, together with Paul's limited cognitive ability, had led to his involvement in a number of minor offences such as engaging in a breach of the peace, attempted theft of a moped, assault and criminal damage. In turn, these would lead him into the criminal justice system.

On 30 October 2003, three years after the accident, the first of what would become a series of gruelling court appearances spanning several months took place. Paul was then aged 17 and efforts to get help for him had been undertaken by his family but not by the health services to whose care he had been entrusted. One of the health service's psychiatric reports had found nothing wrong with him. However, his family firmly believed that his mental health had suffered greatly as a result of the accident and had sought a neurosurgeon's report on his condition to demonstrate how critical the brain damage was and also how necessary it was for Paul to be sent to an appropriate therapeutic environment. His concerned relatives, including two aunts, had battled long and hard to get their nephew into a rehabilitation programme.

Judge Connellan said that Paul was 'at risk' and accused the health board authorities, who he said were responsible for him, of 'passing the buck'. He adjourned the case with bail pending a neurosurgeon's report and directed that representatives for the health board also attend court on the next date.

Three weeks later, Paul's fate took a turn for the worse when Judge Mary Collins reluctantly remanded him in custody to Cloverhill Prison. It was revealed in court that the health board had planned that after his placement in Ballydowd had finished, Paul would be sent to a 'secure step-down care unit' but this had not happened. Instead he was let out and ended up back at his sister's home where there was a worrying level of drug abuse. Arrangements had also been made for him to attend a day-care centre which he had refused to do.

A representative for the health services told Judge Collins that since his release Paul was no longer in their care. 'I cannot provide anything,' the representative said. Judge Collins said that the prison service now had 'to step into the health board's shoes' which, she added emphatically, was 'clearly inappropriate.'

She said that the teenager needed a 'structured environment and not prison'. However, the only option available to her was to remand him in custody, to prevent him from 'roaming the streets'. He was remanded in custody to Cloverhill Prison pending the neurosurgeon's findings.

Five days later, the case was back and the presiding judge, Angela Ní Chonduin, demanded action, saying that in this exceptional case funding was not an excuse. 'I do not want to put this young man in custody for one night longer than is necessary,' she said, adding that somebody would have to take responsibility in assisting the youth on 'humanitarian grounds'.

The court heard that the health board had considered referring Paul to a care facility in England but had declined to pursue this route. By now, an independent psychiatrist had held that because of his intellectual problems which had been compounded by his head injuries, he was not fit to plead.

Judge Ní Chonduin issued a witness summons and subpoenaed Paul's social worker to attend court, indicating that the case would be brought back to court every day until some progress was made. Meanwhile, Paul returned to Cloverhill Prison.

The next day, counsel for the health board submitted that the Children's Court did not have the power to summons its social workers to court for this purpose. 'There is little else we can do, we can only bring things forward as far as resources allow,' the health board's counsel said.

However, Judge Ní Chonduin again asked for the youth's social worker to attend court the following day to account for the efforts to find an appropriate facility for him. 'It is the welfare of this child I am concerned with. It is a matter of priorities,' she said. She also released the teenager into the custody of his aunt. Counsel for the health board said that the board was now willing to re-examine the case, but that it could take several months before any of its efforts to get him into a suitable facility would come to fruition.

Judge Ní Chonduin granted bail on condition that Paul present himself at a garda station every evening to see if any of the city's hostels could provide him with a bed for the night. After his next court appearance, three days later, it was decided that he was to remain in hostel accommodation, and the case was adjourned for another two weeks to see what progress the health board had made.

Judge Ní Chonduin then heard that the health board had agreed to finance the teenager's referral to the rehabilitation centre in England and that he was willing to go. However, Paul's doctor needed to make the referral to the hospital, and so the case was adjourned until early in 2004, pending the referral. In the meantime, the youth would have to stay in hostels, which, it was felt, was 'less detrimental' than placing him in custody.

In January, the hostel arrangement broke down because Paul kept returning to his sister's flat. The probation and welfare services intervened and offered a placement in a special unit in Chapelizod. But they needed specialised support staff from the health board, in the form of care workers, who could give Paul individualised attention. The health board was willing to 'explore' the issue of financing to provide the probation unit with the care staff it needed. However, in the meantime, Paul would have to spend more time in prison where he would be under 24-hour suicide watch because he had threatened to harm himself.

On 22 January, Judge Catherine Murphy agreed with Paul's solicitor that the case was unique and that the health board had not done enough to prioritise it. She said that Paul was 'extremely vulnerable to exploitation as a consequence of his medical and psychiatric history and subsequent brain injury' and recommended that the case be brought to the High Court to compel the health board to release the required funding. The boy's solicitor pointed out that by the time the case went to the High Court, the teenager might have reached his eighteenth birthday, at which stage he would no longer be a minor and the health board would no longer be obliged to help him.

However, in the absence of any practical alternative, Paul was remanded in custody to Cloverhill Prison for a week.

The teenager had remained quiet throughout the bulk of that day's complex proceedings. But as it became apparent that he would face the next week in jail, he was overcome with terror and begged to be released. 'I do not want to go to jail. I don't want to go to them places. I don't need any help, I can look after myself. I'll be okay on the streets,' he pleaded. Judge Murphy explained that Paul, like all people, needed help at times, at which the confused and upset teenager turned and walked out of court to await transfer to Cloverhill.

The efforts to find him suitable interim accommodation with the required supports, were then caught up in red tape. On 28 January, Judge John O'Neill heard that while the health board was now ready to provide a team of care workers, the Probation and Welfare Services were now reluctant to take Paul into their hostel in Chapelizod. Despite earlier indications that they could give him a home, in which he would be specifically looked after by the health board team, the unit's management had decided to reconsider the matter.

A meeting of the managers of the hostel was scheduled to take place five days later but in the meantime, Paul had to go back to Cloverhill Prison.

Paul's solicitor, Sarah Molloy, decided to call for political intervention. She wrote to a number of TDs and government ministers, asking them to demand that the required resources be allocated to release Paul from custody. She firmly believed that the state had failed in its duty to one of its most vulnerable citizens.[1] In her letter, she said:

There is no Garda objection to bail, but he is currently home-less, brain-damaged and unable to look after himself. All concerned parties fear for his safety for these reasons. Due to his medical condition, sending him to a conventional detention centre has been deemed as unsuitable. Meanwhile his aunts have ensured that the family's rent is paid to the Dublin City Council and that there is food in the flat for the children.

However, because of their own family commitments, Paul's aunts could not take the teenager into their own care and the medical reports on his condition indicated that they were unequipped to look after him anyway. The best available alternative seemed to be the Lionsvilla Probation Hostel in Chapelizod, with additional care workers provided by the health board. The boy's solicitor explained:

> His needs are enormous and are compounded by the fact that there is no stable adult residing in his home. Living conditions are cramped and outbreaks of violence are a regular occurrence.
>
> Due to the continued difficulties in the flat he became homeless before Christmas and was using 'out of hours' hostel services. Inevitably due to his vulnerability and unsuitable accommodation he came to the attention of the gardaí. It was hoped that during this time suitable accommodation and support might be located for him. There is currently an application for a placement in a rehabilitation centre in York, England, as there are no appropriate facilities to help him in Ireland.
>
> However we are also seeking an interim placement pending this application.

On 4 February, Paul arrived at the courthouse in Smithfield, dressed in a white boiler suit, having torn his own clothing to shreds in prison, the previous night.

In a bizarre twist, it emerged that instead of being held in prison, he could have been sent to a hospital for interim treatment. However, the South Western Area Health Board had not checked whether facilities existed for him in Ireland. Judge Catherine Murphy heard that the Probation and Welfare Services had brought these facilities, including Stewart's Hospital in

Dublin, to the health board's attention. Rehabilitation was dealt with by a separate bureaucratic division of the health board.

A report from the health board stated that the teenager should not be held in prison. But commenting on the report Judge Murphy said, 'How come they [the health board] said that they do not think Cloverhill is an appropriate venue and they are quite aware of the reasons for him being there?'

Speaking directly to Paul, Judge Murphy said: 'I am very sorry about this; there will have to be another week in custody before we can be given further developments.'

The teenager simply answered, 'Yeah, I heard you', before being led out of the courtroom to be transferred to Cloverhill for yet another week.

Paul's aunts were shocked to learn that there were facilities in the state where he could have been given some attention. 'I find it much better that there is a place for him in Ireland where we will be able to visit him more often,' one of the exasperated women said. 'But I am very much upset that it took this long to find it for him. We have been talking to social workers day after day; before this they said there was literally nothing for him in Ireland; it leaves me bewildered.'

On 11 February, the court was told that the South Western Area Health Board was making every effort to provide the required facilities within ten days. Legal representatives of the health board said that a suitable private health-care agency had recently been found which could provide the teenager with interim care.

However, the health board itself had not made this discovery; it had been found through an RTÉ Radio interview conducted with the teenager's solicitor, Sarah Molloy, after which the solicitor had been contacted by the unit. She had then notified the health board of its existence. Counsel for the health board told Judge Bridget Reilly that the board had become aware of the full extent of the teenager's conditions only within recent weeks. However, as the boy's solicitor later pointed out, this information had been available to the board since the previous November.

The health board's barrister explained that: 'The complexity of his needs presents a cocktail of circumstances verging on the unique.' A child-care expert was to travel to Cloverhill Prison that day to assess Paul and to determine if he was suitable for admission into the unit. The health board would also have Paul assessed by a neuro-psychologist the following day.

It was envisaged that in March, Paul, with health board care workers, would travel to the UK to be assessed by the rehabilitation centre there with a view to more long-term care.

Crucially, a commitment was also given that the health board would continue to give Paul the care and attention he needed once he became an adult, that summer. Paul, who was dressed in a baggy jumper, cords and runners, became distressed and begged to be let out of prison, repeatedly pleading with the court that he wanted to go home.

Commenting on the progress in the case, the boy's solicitor said that the health board seemed to be using a 'carrot and stick' approach to the teenager. She also rejected suggestions made by the health board that confidential material and documents relating to the child's medical condition had been leaked to the press without authorisation. Ms Molloy said that it had been the news media's coverage of Paul's case over the previous three months that had resulted in the health board's offering more proposals than it had offered over the previous nine months.

Judge Reilly adjourned the case, sending the teenager back to Cloverhill Prison for a week, after which the health board was to provide some answers to the question of appropriate accommodation for Paul. Counsel for the health board asked to be excused attendance at the next appearance, saying that the board was not compelled to attend court in criminal as opposed to child-care proceedings. One of Paul's relatives expressed her dismay at the lack of progress in the case. 'I am not impressed and I have concerns over his health. They [the SWAHB] have given us these promises before and have not fulfilled them.'

On Wednesday, 18 February 2004, in the tiny courtroom of the Children's Court, the delighted 17-year-old boy's face broke into a smile, the first that had been seen in months, after he was told that he would not be sent back to Cloverhill Prison, where, by now, he had spent five weeks in a suicidal state. Smiling excitedly, he gazed around the courtroom, at his solicitor and family members, and then replied, 'Thanks very much.'

Paul was granted bail and sent to the Ballydowd Special Care Unit, where he would be under the supervision of a dedicated 'multi-disciplinary team of therapists, psychiatrists and psychologists', for three months. However, Judge, Ní Chonduin sought information on what the health board planned for Paul after he had finished his interim placement in the Ballydowd Centre.

Neuro-psychologists for the health board had assessed Paul during the previous week, and their report seemed to put the blame on the teenager for his problems, which they attributed to his 'laziness and lack of willingness to co-operate'.

But Judge Ní Chonduin said that she was more influenced by a separate independent neurosurgeon's diagnosis that Paul had suffered 'massive injury'. She described the new proposals to place the teenager in Ballydowd as 'last-minute' arrangements made after the health board had been pressurised into prioritising the case.

She feared that after Paul finished his placement in Ballydowd, he would soon reach his eighteenth birthday and the health board would 'drop' him into a psychiatric hospital for the rest of his life.

Judge Ní Chonduin adjourned the case until 29 March 2004, for an update on the health board's long-term plans for him. She granted bail on condition that the teenager reside in the care unit.

On 29 March, the health board pledged to care for Paul after he reached adulthood. Judge Ní Chonduin adjourned the case for another two months pending further reports on Paul's fitness to enter a plea on the charges.

On 20 July, Paul walked free from the court and out of the criminal justice system after it was revealed that he had been found unfit to plead. Judge Ní Chonduin ordered that the charges against him be dropped, having received assurances about his future care. Different accommodation had been arranged which had seen the teenager moving into an apartment, paid for by the health board. A care worker would visit the youth on a daily basis to teach 'life skills' and to show him how to manage living on his own.

The possibility of finding Paul a placement in a rehabilitation centre in Leeds, in England, was still being pursued. However, some of Paul's relatives were worried over the level of care being offered to him. One of his aunts said that the plans 'were not as rosy as they seem'. She said that the youth did not stay in the apartment at night and was drinking and smoking cannabis. She also said that nothing had come of proposals to find him a training course.

The judge advised the two aunts to continue to raise their concerns with the health board, telling them to 'camp on their doorsteps' if necessary. Closing the case and dropping the charges, she spoke to the youth and said: 'A lot of people have gone to a lot of trouble for you; you have to stay in that flat.' The youth nodded and agreed, saying, 'Okay.'

About a year later, and nearly five years after the accident which had left him in such a debilitated state, Paul was placed in the specialised hospital in Leeds, where he remains and is under the care of rehabilitation experts.

DARREN

On 2 February 2005, Darren, a 17-year-old boy with a history of untreated psychiatric problems, set fire to his home and then took his nephew's pet turtle and cut off one of its legs and decapitated it in front of the young child. His case would highlight the dearth of assistance available in Ireland for young people with severe mental health problems.

At an earlier Children's Court appearance, on 13 January 2004, then aged 16, Darren had been charged with an assault, which he admitted. Judge Bryan Smyth heard how Darren had attacked a man on Grafton Street after he saw him beating up a woman. The teenager had been passing by a nightclub the previous July when he witnessed the attack. He intervened to defend the woman. However, by the time a patrolling garda arrived, the man was being held to the ground by Darren who was repeatedly punching him in the face. Judge Smyth adjourned the case, with bail, until 9 March, for a report on the victim's injuries.

On that date, the court first learned about Darren's mental difficulties and how he had taken a cocktail of prescription drugs, cocaine and ecstasy, causing him to suffer a paranoid psychosis. The mental breakdown had led him to racially abuse and threaten to kill a foreign national, on 24 November 2003, at Parnell Street, in Dublin. Having approached the man and repeatedly called him a 'black bastard', the boy told him he would kill him, and then produced a knife, which he gestured threateningly at the victim. Judge Smyth was told that the man was left shocked by the encounter as were his three young children who were sitting in his parked car nearby.

During the incident, Darren was observed to have been under the influence of an intoxicant and his behaviour was 'completely erratic,' the court heard. Describing the events as appalling, Judge Smyth adjourned sentencing until 1 June, for an updated probation report. He granted bail but imposed strict terms, forbidding the boy to consume alcohol or illegal drugs, and ordering him to obey a nightly curfew.

This court case ended with Darren being released, but his difficulties continued. Following the arson attack on his home, he was remanded in custody because his distraught parents, who had grave fears for his wellbeing, could not cope with his problems. They had sought the prosecution in the hope that it would lead to their son's getting help. However, those hopes were to be dashed. He was held in St Patrick's Institution for a psychiatric assessment. After several further remands, he appeared again on 30 March where the court was told that he had been held in a detention centre's cell for nearly two months despite a psychiatrist's findings that he needed urgent hospitalisation.

It had been recommended that Darren be transferred from St Patrick's Institution to the Central Mental Hospital (CMH). However, nearly two months had passed and he was still in custody waiting for a placement there. The boy's solicitor had contacted several government ministers over the case and was awaiting their response.

Judge Smyth adjourned the case for two weeks to see if there were any developments on the placement. The boy asked the court if he would be allowed on bail but was told that he would have to stay in custody. Later, Darren was transferred from the detention centre to the CMH. It was hoped that this would be an interim measure, pending attempts to identify a facility where he could be treated.

At a subsequent hearing, on 29 July, the boy, now aged 18, sat in the defendant's bench with little understanding of what was happening around him. The judge was told that he had a learning disorder, and demonstrated signs of schizophrenia and paranoia. According to his solicitor, the CMH was not an appropriate facility for his problems and, furthermore, while there he was at risk of 'sexual exploitation' by other patients with serious criminal histories of murder and rape. A recent assessment report on the youth stated that Darren had the 'interpersonal age equivalence' of an infant aged one year and nine months. Other assessments put him on the level of a child aged four.

A consultant psychiatrist at the CMH told Judge Collins that the teenager had been suffering hallucinations and exhibiting signs of paranoia, believing that attempts were being made to poison him. He had been talking to himself and was prone to inappropriate fits of laughter. The doctor agreed that there were concerns for the boy's safety and that he was at risk from the other patients.

It was planned that other mental health specialists would be contacted with a view to holding a case conference to establish what facility would be best suited to treat the troubled youth. The court heard that there was no facility in the state that could help Darren but that the UK had units for cases involving people with chronic mental health problems, and that the National Health Service funded placements in appropriate private clinics. The boy's solicitor said that if suitable treatment could not be found in Ireland, the Health Service Executive (HSE) should provide funding for a placement outside the jurisdiction. Previously, the HSE had placed him in the Mater Child Guidance Clinic but he had absconded and attempted suicide.

Judge Collins said that the case did 'not come in the crime arena' and adjourned the case, pending the planned case conference.

Darren, who claimed that his house had been broken into on the night he had torched it, said that he wanted bail but was remanded back in custody to the CMH.

On 15 September, Judge Angela Ní Chonduin heard that the teenager had undergone medical treatment and now needed a 'step-down' placement. However, this follow-on placement should be provided by his local service, the Mater Hospital, and the Mater did not have a bed for him at the time.

His distraught family was told that because the teenager had been discharged from the CMH he would now have to be returned to a detention centre, because the Mater did not have a bed for him. The alternative was to grant bail but the judge feared for the boy's own safety and that of others, if he were released. Concerns were also raised that his family would not be equipped to look after him and that if he failed to take his medication, he could suffer a relapse.

Judge Ní Chonduin made a direction that a representative of the Mater Hospital attend the teenager's case to explain what help they could give to him, the case concluded for the day and Darren's family left the court weeping.

The following morning, the court was told that the teenager needed a placement in a disability service and not a psychiatric service. Moreover, the Mater Hospital was not a secure environment and the doctor representing the Mater recommended that the Daughters of Charity Hospital would be a more suitable hospital for the teenager. Judge Angela Ní Chonduin remanded the teenager in custody until the following week to allow efforts to be made to contact this hospital and to canvass its views on the matter.

As the case was adjourned, the teenager's family hugged him and whispered words of comfort as he was taken from the courtroom to be transferred back to St Patrick's Institution.

On Friday, 23 September, the court heard that the teenager was 'too intelligent' to be placed in the hospital. Judge Ní Chonduin observed that the youth had 'fallen between two stools'. 'Basically the psychiatric services are saying that he needs a disability service. The disability services say he needs a psychiatric service,' she said.

She ordered the HSE's director of disability services to attend the court case on the following Tuesday to outline what facilities could be offered to Darren.

On Tuesday, 11 October, Judge Ní Chonduin was told that the HSE was arranging for assessments of the teenager to take place to establish what hospital was best suited to his needs; it could take another three to four weeks to establish which facility would be required.

Judge Ní Chonduin adjourned the case until early November. Again, having been given no alternative, she remanded him further in custody to St Patrick's Institution.

'I am concerned about the contents of the reports on him,' she said. 'It clearly says that if he was released by the court he would become non-compliant with his medication, there would be a deterioration of his mental state and increased risk of harm to himself and to others.' It was the twenty-sixth time that the case had been before the court since the teenager's arrest.

On Tuesday, 1 November, Judge Timothy Lucey heard that Darren was not well enough to come to court and he put the case back for a week. By then, the teenager had been sent back to the CMH.

On the case's twenty-ninth day in court, on Monday, 5 December, it was disclosed that Darren's condition had deteriorated further. The case was put back for another two weeks, pending efforts to source a suitable therapeutic placement for him. He would remain in custody over Christmas. On Monday, 16 January 2006, the case was adjourned for another week, with no evident progress. The boy had not been released by the CMH to come to court. On 24 January, the case was adjourned because a special meeting had been scheduled for the following day to establish what services could be provided. Adjourning the case for a week, Judge Catherine Murphy said that she was not happy with the situation.

The case was back on 2 February, exactly a year after Darren had first been remanded in custody and the initial efforts made to establish the extent of his problems and to source a suitable hospital. The young man was not brought to court.

Judge Murphy described as a 'scandal' the fact that no suitable treatment placement had been found. She put the case back a week and directed that the boy's local health officer attend the proceedings to assist with information on what measures were to be put in place for him in the community.

On Friday, 10 February, the case was in court for the thirty-fourth time. Judge Murphy released the boy, saying that the time he had spent in custody was far in excess of any sentence that would have been imposed for the offences. She stressed that Darren would need support from the HSE and that if he failed to take his medication, he could suffer a relapse and would then pose a risk to himself, his family and members of the community. The HSE told the court that at present a hospital that had been identified as most suitable was not prepared to take him. It could still take up to three months until the appropriate measures were ready to enable that hospital to receive him. A team of specialists from the UK had been brought in to assist in meeting his complex needs.

Judge Murphy said that reports on the teenager had highlighted that he needed to be held in a secure facility. She was told that at present the teenager would be offered outpatient psychiatric services from the Mater Hospital. The teenager and his mother would also receive support from care workers to ensure that he took his medication. However, it could still take over two weeks before suitably experienced care workers could be employed to assist the boy.

On being told that he would be released, Darren thanked the judge. His face broke into a smile and his mother and aunt burst into tears as they hugged him and brought him out of the courtroom.

However, a curious thing happened minutes after he walked out with his mother. A car pulled up to bring him to the Mater Hospital. The mother believed that this was for the outpatient psychiatric services mentioned minutes before in the court. Darren was taken to the Mater and then brought to the other hospital where he was sectioned, although the court had been told that morning and on several dates previously that the other hospital was not equipped to take him.

04 PROSTITUTION: 'I WANT TO LIVE'

On 4 January, two gardaí patrolling the Benburb Street area—a notorious red-light district—found Emer down an alleyway. She was engaged in a sexual act with a man who was in his fifties. Also present, standing at a nearby corner, were her mother and her younger sister who was six years old.

Throughout her childhood, Emer had witnessed domestic violence and lacked stability and guidance. Into this vacuum stepped a young man who became her boyfriend. It was he who held her down and forced a heroin-filled syringe into her veins, when she was 16 years old. So began her addiction and around that time she frequently disappeared and her name would appear on garda missing person lists. Once, when she was 16, her boyfriend brought her to England. On her return, she started to live with her mother and sister in accommodation paid for by the health services. Her mother too had become a chronic drug addict. From her mid-teens, Emer had started to come to garda attention, mostly for petty theft offences. As a result of these, she received some intervention from the Probation and Welfare Services. In one of their reports, they concluded that Emer was seriously at risk of becoming involved in prostitution.

The activities predicted by the Probation and Welfare Services turned into reality. By early 2005, gardaí in the Bridewell Station, in Dublin, had received numerous phone calls about Emer. The anonymous calls claimed that she had been working as a street prostitute while her mother was present. Some of these calls came from other street prostitutes, who were disgusted to see the teenager being pimped by her mother and felt compelled to report her to gardaí.

Emer appeared in the Children's Court three days after her arrest, looking emaciated and jaundiced. She was accompanied in court by her mother. Judge David Maughan remanded her on bail for three weeks to allow her to consider her plea. Her bail conditions included a requirement that she reside at her current address, a B&B, and obey a curfew from 10 p.m. until seven o'clock the following morning. She was also to stay away from the Benburb Street area.

However, a few days later, a garda attached to Bridewell Garda Station found Emer down a laneway, and arrested her for being in breach of the curfew. He had called to the B&B during curfew hours and been told by her mother that she had gone out to buy drugs. Meanwhile, Emer's mother was being investigated over her involvement in her daughter's prostitution. 'We would have to stress that there is a file going to the DPP in relation to the mother and another child being involved. We followed the accused and her mother and another child down a lane, with a man aged 50. We believe that her mother was involved with her, and a child aged six,' said the garda.

In court before Judge Catherine Murphy, a distraught Emer begged the judge for bail: 'I want to go home to my mother and sister. I learned my lesson; I don't want to go back to prison.' In relation to her mother being present while she was engaged in the alleged acts of prostitution, Emer said: 'She was minding me, making sure I don't get pregnant.'

Judge Murphy noted that in a probation report in 2004, concerns had been raised that Emer was at risk of getting involved in prostitution.

'It is a very sobering report indeed and the concerns anticipated seem to have materialised,' she continued, 'This is a matter for the health board to become involved very quickly.'

She remanded Emer in custody to Mountjoy for a week, saying she was doing so for the teenager's own safety. 'I would be putting you at huge risk if I were to let you out today,' she told the weeping girl. Emer sobbed: 'I love my mother; I just want to go back to my mother.'

Three days later, she was brought back to court. In the intervening time, the health board had been contacted with a request to attend Emer's court case. However, there was no representative from Emer's health board present when the case was called. Judge Angela Ní Chonduin adjourned the case for two weeks to allow the health board time to intervene. She also ordered the attendance of the health board and Emer's social worker at the court case to outline their plans for her. Emer, who was weeping during the proceedings, begged for bail, saying, 'My mother wants me home.'

However, Judge Ní Chonduin would not allow her home. 'She can't have you, she cannot mind you and you cannot mind yourself,' she told Emer.

On Thursday, 27 January, Judge Ní Chonduin again refused to grant bail, saying that Emer was at serious risk of re-offending and would be in danger if released. 'The offences are tragic and sad for a little girl her age,' the judge said. 'That child has been exposed to a lot and subjected to a lot; that really concerns me.'

In the meantime, care proceedings had been initiated and a guardian was appointed to Emer. Judge Ní Chonduin further remanded Emer in custody for another week and directed that she receive medical attention for her drug problem. By now, Emer's six-year-old sister had been taken into care.

Their mother had been tracked down by a Sunday newspaper and in an interview with a reporter had denied allegations that she had been 'pimping' her daughter. She also denied that she was a drug addict, something which gardaí strongly disputed.

Back in court on 3 February, the teenage girl was released from custody but she was not permitted to live with her mother, who was present during the proceedings. A team of specialised care workers had intervened and a placement in a care home had been provided where Emer could be monitored around the clock.

She was granted bail for two weeks on condition that she remain in the care home from 7 p.m. until morning time. She was to be given counselling for drug abuse, together with educational assistance, and a psychological assessment might also be undertaken. 'I want to retrieve what I can of her young life and get it back on track,' Judge Ní Chonduin said as she released the teenager.

It was also indicated that if Emer progressed positively in the care home and accepted the assistance offered to her, the criminal charges might be struck out. 'I do not want her to have a criminal record for that charge; it would be to her detriment in the future,' the judge said. 'I am going to keep a tight rein on the case.' She also warned that if Emer broke the bail conditions, she would be put back into custody.

The intervention offered a ray of hope to the young girl. Further to the therapeutic and drug rehabilitation assistance, the social workers were also given the difficult task of shadowing Emer 24/7 to ensure that she would not begin to regress. However, within days, her progress was sent into a tailspin due to her chronic addiction which she was finding nearly impossible to overcome. A fortnight after her release from custody, she was in breach of the stringent bail conditions that had been set down, and gardaí were seeking an arrest warrant. A report from the centre said that while she had been in the care home, under the watchful eyes of care workers, Emer had still managed to break out to get heroin. She had tested positive three times for 'opiates' —meaning that she was still on heroin. And the report also highlighted that on one occasion she had managed to slip out for just 'two minutes', during which time she had been able to buy heroin and inject it into her veins.

The arrest warrant was duly issued, which meant that once more Emer would be facing more time in jail. Coincidently, on that day, Emer went missing from the care home in which she had been ordered to reside.

On Monday, 21 February, Judge Mary Collins was told that gardaí were seeking a bench warrant for Emer's arrest over her failure to appear in court. The garda applying for the warrant said,

'We believe she is in the company of her mother. Her grand-mother said that she and her mother were with her for two nights.' The authorities had been searching for Emer for three days by then. Judge Collins issued a bench warrant for Emer to be brought back before the court, adding that she hoped the teenage girl would be found quickly.

Having been missing for a week, the teenager was found, as gardaí suspected, with her mother, staying at a relative's house. Gardaí had called to the house in the north of the city and interviewed the mother who was adamant that she had not seen her daughter, and was equally unwavering in her claims that she had nothing to do with her disappearance.

However, as the gardaí were about to leave, one of them noticed a jacket hanging on the back of a chair and recognised it as being like one Emer had often been seen wearing. The gardaí turned and dashed through the house and out into the back garden where they found Emer trying to climb a wall in an effort to get away. She was arrested and brought back into court.

Gardaí had objections to bail on the grounds that there was a strong belief she was likely to re-offend and because she had been in breach of bail by absconding from the care home. She had also tested positive for heroin use three times after she had been released from custody.

Emer's solicitor explained that the teenager had many difficulties and had been trying her best to abide by the bail conditions, but that the care home was located near a drug rehabilitation treatment centre and an area frequented by drug addicts. 'When she went outside the door, people were constantly offering her drugs,' the solicitor said. Emer wanted to be placed in another care home not so close to a drug treatment centre.

A representative for the Health Service Executive (HSE) explained to the court that the care home that Emer had been residing in was the only one available at that time. Judge O'Donnell refused bail and remanded a tearful Emer in custody for a week. He also agreed to direct the HSE to hold a case conference for Emer to examine possible alternative placements for her. Her mother was not present during the case.

On 2 March, Emer was released from Mountjoy Prison after the court heard that she was being bullied by other inmates and had been supplied with heroin there.

Her solicitor said that Mountjoy was an inappropriate place for her to be detained. 'When I visited her in Mountjoy she said that she had been bullied by other detainees. One threatened to cut her up. She has been offered drugs and was under pressure from others to take drugs. The pressure is so heavy that if she is sent back there she will take drugs. Her addiction to heroin is causing her huge problems. I would be fearful that if she was sent back to Mountjoy, it would not be in her best interests. Because of her addiction matters are out of control.'

Judge Ní Chonduin was also told that the only alternative was to send Emer back to the care home from which she had gone missing and which was located in an area frequented by other addicts. The judge agreed that it was 'the best of a bad option'.

The court was assured that Emer would be constantly 'shadowed' by care workers, who planned to help her get drug treatment, psychological assessments and educational assistance. Promises were also given that if Emer absconded from the care home, the gardaí would be notified immediately. Her mother was to be allowed two supervised visits a week.

Judge Ní Chonduin also ordered that the teenager's mother be tested for drugs twice a week. She was to be allowed to visit her daughter only if she tested negative for drugs.

In mid-March 2005, the HSE made a commitment to continue its involvement with Emer after she reached adulthood, at which time there would be no statutory obligation on it to provide her with care and welfare. Judge Murphy adjourned the case until April and also congratulated Emer on her efforts to quit heroin; the latest urine samples showed that she had remained drug-free since her last appearance in court.

The judge relaxed one of the bail conditions on Emer by changing a curfew and allowing her to be out of the care home for an extra hour every day. This was to allow the care workers who were monitoring her constantly to take her to recreational activities.

A care plan was then devised for the teenager who was now making valiant efforts to beat her heroin addiction. Judge Catherine Murphy adjourned the case for a month, on 5 April, to allow Emer's solicitor to scrutinise the proposed care plan. Adjourning the case, Judge Murphy commended the teenager for the efforts she had made to beat her addiction: 'Keep up the good work, you are doing extremely well. It is not easy but you will get there with support. Everyone is very pleased with you and is admiring the success you are having and how hard you are trying.'

On 31 May, Emer, now looking like a different person from the gaunt, skeletal addict she had been just months before, told the court she was determined to build a better life for herself. 'I want to live,' Emer told Judge Murphy, also saying that she had developed a new understanding that she could have a better quality of life than she had previously experienced.

A weekend trip with care workers, in the west of Ireland, had given her a new insight into how she could change her life. 'It was relaxing, very nice, and I know that there are much better things in the world. I have learned so much.'

Emer, who was supported in court by a care worker, also added that she was now learning life skills, some rudimentary for most people, like how to budget money. Previously, when given a weekly allowance, she habitually spent it all at once. The concept of queuing at a counter in a shop was unknown to her.

Emer's mother was also in addiction recovery and taking methadone, the substitute drug used to wean addicts off heroin. The younger sister was still in care.

Judge Murphy adjourned the case for a further three weeks for another report on the teenager's progress.

Alas, in spite of Emer's optimism, genuine as it was, things started to go awry over the following weeks. In July, the court was told that she had started to disengage with the care programme and she was suspected of stealing. Judge Ní Chonduin adjourned the case, with bail, ordering Emer to continue with the course and also to obey a nightly curfew commencing at 7 p.m. She warned the teenager that she had to re-engage with the team of care workers and the supports put in place to help her.

More fears were raised that the teenager had become less co-operative as a result of recent contact with her mother. Judge Ní Chonduin urged her to continue with the training course, stressing that learning a trade was the only way that she would be able to live independently. She reminded her that custody was still an option.

The situation worsened and, on Tuesday, 9 August, Judge Thomas Fitzpatrick heard that Emer, now aged 18, had tested positive for use of cannabis and valium and had broken the court-imposed curfew. When she was arrested for breach of the bail conditions, she had become aggressive, shouted threats at the arresting garda and social workers and also lashed out and assaulted the garda. Judge Fitzpatrick revoked bail and remanded the teenager in custody to Mountjoy Prison. Emer, who had been in tears, pleaded for bail, claiming that she was pregnant and that she would be in danger from another detainee in the prison.

The case was adjourned for a week when she was released subject to the conditions that she obey the curfew rules and become involved in the comprehensive care plan. She was due back in court on 19 September but failed to appear and a bench warrant was issued. Care workers now had grave concerns for her wellbeing and believed that she had started abusing heroin again. She was also believed to be living with a man.

Judge Ní Chonduin issued the bench warrant saying that she wanted Emer to be 'picked up as soon as possible'.

On 27 October, after she had been missing for nearly two months, Emer was remanded back into custody. She had handed herself over to gardaí that morning and was then brought to court. She had tested positive for cocaine, heroin and cannabis use, and gardaí objected to bail. Several attempts, involving huge amounts of garda manpower, had been made over the previous two months to locate her.

Emer's social worker told the court that she had been in phone contact with the teenager while she was missing and had repeatedly encouraged her to present herself to gardaí. The social worker also said that while the accommodation Emer had previously been offered was no longer available, efforts would be made to find alternative accommodation for her. Emer told the court that she had been living with her fiancé and pleaded not to be held in custody again.

Judge Murphy remanded the girl in custody to Mountjoy Prison for a week, saying that this would 'serve as a breaking point of the last two months of chaotic lifestyle'. It would also allow plans to be proposed for Emer's future accommodation.

The teenager was released on bail on 3 November, having pleaded not guilty. A hearing date for the case was set for the following March, but the case was to be reviewed again in early December to monitor her adherence to the bail conditions. It was the last time she appeared in court, having drifted off with her fiancé although still making occasional contact with her social workers.

By 1 December, she was missing again and another bench warrant was issued. The hearing date in March came but there was still no appearance, leaving the case hanging over her. There were fleeting glimpses of Emer and she still made occasional contact with her social workers, but she was back on heroin. She also had a new boyfriend.

05 | PAEDOPHILIA: A SECRET LIFE

Sexual exploitation is a risk that faces many young people who come before the Children's Court. One girl ended up being used as a sex-toy for extended family members. Due to a chaotic family background she was put into care at a young age. In her new setting and with the support and guidance of a loving foster family, she started to develop as a normal young girl. However, having lived happily with the foster family for years, she initiated contact with her biological family when in her early teens. At first, it seemed that this could be good for her. However, she soon came under the influence of older members of her extended biological family who started to control her and give her alcohol. Increasingly vulnerable and confused, she found herself being used to gratify them sexually.

Psychologically damaged, she was later put into a care home, from which she repeatedly absconded, and she started to engage in underage sex. She attempted suicide and attacked care staff when it was recommended to her that she needed psychiatric assistance. Later, when she was 15, she met a 40-year-old man, became his girlfriend, and ran away with him. Only when found by gardaí did she learn that the man was a convicted sex offender. At that point, she ceased to have any contact with him.

Another girl who came from a troubled family background was sexually exploited by youths from her neighbourhood, starting when she was in her early teens. Older boys paid her £5 to perform sexual acts on them. After the introduction of the Euro, the girl, unaware of the difference in value of the two currencies, still charged a fiver and the boys, while continuing to use and abuse her, laughed at how they were now getting her to gratify them for less.

In another case, a boy, aged 13, from a troubled family background, had been put in care. However, he started absconding from the care home and associating with older teenagers. He was brought before the Children's Court charged with theft and burglary. Concerns over his frequent overnight disappearances from the care home mounted. After one such instance, gardaí found him wearing a new tracksuit that he had not owned the previous day, and there was an unexplained amount of cash in his pockets and also a packet of condoms. At time of writing, his case is still pending.

It was 3.30 in the early hours of 12 July 2004. A detective garda on the night shift, doing a routine patrol on Ranelagh Road, spotted a 15-year-old boy out walking. The garda pulled over his unmarked car to ask Robert what he was doing. Robert replied that he was going to Leeson Street to seek a prostitute.

It was decided that Robert should be taken back to his home for his own safety. At that stage, he was not under arrest. But as the car neared Robert's home, the lad suddenly went berserk and started to struggle. His violent behaviour continued and he kicked the detective repeatedly, leaving him with bruising on his legs. Worry over the reaction he anticipated at home having been discovered out at odd hours for such a bizarre reason had prompted him to lose his temper and attack the garda.

The prostitutes he was seeking were his associates. Robert would later be described as having reached a crossroads in his life; although he had achieved good results in his exams, his non-attendance at school had become a massive worry. He sometimes had problems with his nerves, had difficulties in controlling his temper and lacked a male role model in his home. Also at this time he was in debt to a drug dealer, associating with prostitutes, selling drugs at school and had taken to carrying a knife around late at night.

Before being found that morning, Robert had been known to several gardaí in south Dublin. They believed he had been abused, and, what was more sinister, was working as a rent boy and involved in a child prostitution ring, operating in south Dublin. It was believed that a prominent businessman was the mastermind behind the prostitution ring and that Robert had been paid for sexual services from his early teens. Robert refused to give enough details for the gardaí to act and bring about a prosecution.

It was believed that he had been seriously traumatised. He would often turn up at south Dublin garda stations and, in an effort to get attention, would make outrageous claims he would later admit were fictitious. However, he refused to divulge the truth of what he was involved in. By this stage he had been sent to counselling which broke down after a short time without any real breakthrough.

His first Children's Court appearance, for attacking the garda, was on Monday, 27 September 2004. Robert, who was supported in court by his mother, had pleaded guilty to the assault on the garda and had no previous convictions. He had also pleaded guilty to using a stolen credit card to make a €700 withdrawal from an ATM machine, which occurred in July 2004.

In mitigation, it was said that Robert's mother was fraught with worry over her young son. Judge William Early was told that the mother believed her son could benefit from guidance from the Probation and Welfare Service. The judge agreed to adjourn the case pending a probation report. The teenager was granted bail with strict conditions compelling him to obey a nightly curfew from 9.30 p.m. to 7.30 a.m. and he was also ordered to attend school daily. The case was adjourned until the following November.

On Robert's next appearance, Judge Michael Connellan noted that the probation report had raised numerous serious issues about the teenager. There was also a new charge before the court over Robert's recent arrest for possession of a knife. And the court heard that there were fears for the boy's safety.

Pleading for bail, Robert's solicitor said that there were plans for Robert to start specialised counselling for children who were 'at risk'. However, Judge Connellan refused, saying that the probation report detailed horrifying facts about Robert's life. 'He is running wild, his mother is doing her best; she gave up her job to look after him. He is associating with prostitutes, carrying a knife, selling drugs at school and owes money to drug dealers. . . . I am concerned that something might happen to him,' he said as he remanded the teenager in custody for a psychological assessment. Judge Connellan also criticised Robert's estranged father, comparing him to 'a butterfly that hops from one flower to another'.

A week later, a bail application was heard. Judge Angela Ní Chonduin agreed to release the teenager on strict conditions including a curfew compelling him to remain indoors at his home at night. She adjourned the case for a week, at which time there were further adjournments, with bail.

However, on 24 January 2005, bail was rescinded and Robert was put back into the detention centre for his own safety. His solicitor described Robert as being 'confused' and added that he needed help and 'to be taken out of the locality where he has been living'.

Robert was supported in court by his mother and had agreed to be placed in custody for the assessment. A welfare report on Robert, furnished by a probation officer, was also negative, Judge Early was told. Judge Early ordered that the schoolboy should have a psychological assessment in a detention centre; however, he expressed concern that a week might not be long enough for the teenager to receive the help he needed.

His solicitor said that the week in custody would allow time to 'get the train in motion'. 'It would be safer,' she added.

After a week, Robert changed his mind and wanted to get out again. He instructed his lawyers to make a bail application; however, his worried mother was not in favour of the request. Judge Bridget Reilly remanded Robert in custody for a further two weeks, pending the psychological assessment, and also urged him to accept the help offered. In a sudden outburst, the normally soft-spoken teenager called her decision 'a load of bollocks' and then threatened to break out of the detention centre.

Judge Reilly advised him that it was 'easy to pretend to be tough, but much manlier to take the help that is being offered.'

More disturbing details emerged when the case was back on Monday, 14 February 2005. By now, Robert had been the subject of a comprehensive psychological assessment which had taken place while he was in custody. In relation to the contents of the report, Judge Catherine Murphy said: 'I read the report; what struck me was that I did not know if I was reading a story book or to take it seriously. That is an important part of this case; it seems that there is a history of him having told stories that did not add up.'

An investigation was ongoing into the story that before being held Robert had had a suspicious income of €300 a week. The teenager had also been the subject of an investigation where he could be viewed as the victim although he had not made a complaint to gardaí. Judge Murphy adjourned the case and remanded Robert in custody, telling him that she was doing so not to penalise him but rather to explore what measures could be taken to protect him. She also asked for the psychologist who had written the report to come to court.

Robert's mother said that she was worried for her son and added that she could not confine him to their home if he were released. But Robert pleaded for bail, saying that he could reside with relatives outside Dublin where he would be safe. Judge Murphy told him: 'This is more serious than you realise; you've been embroiled in serious activities; you need structure in your life, to go back to school and to know where you will be living.' Therapeutic intervention was also needed, she said. 'I will not let you out until that is available. I would be worried that if I let you out on bail today that the influences would be too great for you to withstand and you would be back involved in the same level of activity again.'

On Tuesday, 22 February 2005, Robert was described as needing more psychological counselling, support from social services and, most importantly, to be taught other ways of making money.

'That is vital. I cannot overemphasise that these easy ways of making money are not right,' Judge Mary Collins explained to him as she adjourned the case pending endeavours to put in place a range of psychological and therapeutic supports for him. She also said that he needed to return to education and to cease the activities in which he had been involved. Judge Collins explained to Robert, who had asked for bail, that she was keeping him in custody for his own welfare, at which Robert indicated that he understood. She said: 'The problems have to be looked at so that you can go home, have your schooling set up, set up services to make sure you go to someone for therapy. It is not appropriate today to grant bail; the priority is to get other services involved.'

The case, however, fell into a rut where little was achieved. On 28 February, his solicitor said that Robert was willing to comply with any terms set down by the court if he were released on bail. She said that psychologists who had assessed Robert had become 'very concerned about his activities'.

'He needs a lot of support and help. The detention centre say that he is not suitable to be staying there and he is not typical of the type of people held there. Everyone is concerned for his safety and welfare given his case history,' she told Judge Angela Ní Chonduin.

'I really want to get out today. I don't care if I have to go to meetings. I'll go back to school,' Robert told the court.

His mother said: 'I would be nervous, but willing to give him the chance. But I'd be afraid that if he went against my wishes, I would not be in control. If he does, I'd go straight to the garda station.'

Judge Ní Chonduin admitted that holding Robert in custody was not the solution but added that she was concerned about releasing him. She decided to remand the youth in custody and made a direction for his social worker to attend the case to explain what care plan was proposed for him.

On 3 March, Robert's solicitor told Judge Ní Chonduin that she was seeking to have his social services file 'reopened' and for them to intervene and follow recommendations psychologists had made to help Robert.

'We will do our utmost to implement the recommendations,' the solicitor for the HSE told the court. The HSE also asked for time to bring the matter to the attention of the social workers in Robert's locality. Judge Ní Chonduin adjourned the case but refused to grant bail. However, on his next court appearance, on 22 March, he got bail.

By this date, the case had taken another twist. Judge Ní Chonduin was told that while Robert had been in custody, it had been discovered that a third party had been lodging money into his bank account. The lodgments were made in cash and his creditor was never traced by the authorities who suspected that the payments were a bid to buy his silence.

In a separate case in late 2004, a Dublin man was jailed for sexually abusing young children. Apart from the allegations that led to his incarceration, several others had been made against him that never went to trial.

About a year before he was jailed, a young boy suddenly went out of control. The youngster started abusing alcohol, and soon he was using heroin. By the age of 14, he was getting arrested for public order and assault offences. According to his mother, he had been seeing a psychologist because of his experiences with the same jailed sex abuser. Her impressionable son and several of his friends, all aged about 11, had been befriended by this man. Having gained their confidence, he had started to invite them to his apartment. Later, she alleged, he plied them with alcohol and gave them cannabis to smoke in his apartment. As time went on, he would convince the boys to undress and sit on his knee when they were drunk or high. Suggestions were made by him about taking photographs of them as they were undressed. The boy and his friends were being groomed for sexual abuse and exploitation. Luckily their parents learned about what was happening and stopped them from having anything to do with this man.

The mother of this boy, together with other parents involved, made formal complaints but no prosecution was ever brought. The woman believed that this man was financially supported by someone else who paid for him to live in the brand new apartment. His role was to act as a kind of a paedophilic Pied Piper.

Meanwhile, the effects on her son were devastating. He started to abuse alcohol and to get involved with others who had serious social problems and were constantly coming to garda attention. The mother also learned from her son that another child had been heavily involved with this man. That child was Robert.

In March 2005, Judge Ní Chonduin agreed to grant bail to Robert under strict terms and adjourned the case until April. Robert agreed to reside with a relative outside Dublin and not to have contact with any of the suspect people he had been caught up with before his case came to court.

Counsel for the HSE told the court that while it could not be compelled to attend the court case, social workers would make a referral to have Robert assessed in a special centre that helps victims of sexual abuse. In April, the case was adjourned for three weeks, pending efforts to place him in a therapeutic unit. Robert was remanded on continuing bail.

At first, the plan to put him into hiding with relatives outside Dublin seemed to have worked but, over the following weeks, he was tracked down. Having been kidnapped and taken away in a car by an unknown person, Robert became the object of a garda search.

The suspect who had taken him away in the car escaped capture as Robert got out of the car before it had reached a garda checkpoint. The checkpoint had been alerted to watch out for a car with a man and a boy matching Robert's description in it. Meanwhile, the HSE had investigated a placement in a therapeutic centre, but it was found to be unsuitable.

On 28 April, Robert's solicitor told the court that the HSE had earlier said it would arrange for a social worker to be appointed to Robert, but that that had not yet occurred. The officials in the health service were 'distancing themselves more and more,' she said. Judge Ní Chonduin directed that a care plan be put in place for Robert and adjourned the case. 'This child is only 15. It will not be long until he is 18 and his life will have been absolutely ruined,' she said.

Over the following months, as a result of the kidnapping, Robert was moved again, to live with other relatives, and he started in a new school where he began to show some significant progress. On 29 September 2005, now aged 16, he was praised in court for these efforts.

'I can see that this is a sign of you putting in efforts to behave properly,' Judge Murphy said. 'You are suddenly starting to see things in your life change and become more beneficial. . . . We can see that you are making efforts and we can see today that you now have a lot of self-respect. If you keep that up, things will go well for you.'

At his next court appearance, in early 2006, there were signs of continued progress and good reports from his school. A mobile phone that had been seized from him when he was put into custody for his own protection was also returned to him. However, it was given back to him only after gardaí were satisfied that a number of telephone numbers he had stored in it were deleted. These were mobile numbers whose owners could not be traced. They were believed to be the numbers of the people he had been involved with when he was embroiled in the web of child vice. For years, these shadowy figures had exerted control over him; his family was powerless in breaking their grip and they had gone to great efforts to ensure that he would never reveal their identities to the gardaí—and he never did.

II. FAMILIES

06 | THREE BROTHERS

From September 1999 until early 2002, Dan waged his own campaign of criminality which culminated in a violent robbery that would yield him and his accomplice €47,625 in cash. He was aged only 16 years old but built like a tank and, during the armed robbery, acted as the muscle for a 20-year-old man. His case, as well as that of his next younger brother, was a damning reflection on the juvenile justice system and the lack of social service intervention when it was needed most.

The elder boy already had seventy-six convictions by the time he was returned for trial over the armed robbery. The case was deemed too serious to be heard in the Children's Court where he had become something of a fixture. Until he was detained for the robbery, he had never served a significant sentence.

Dan was one of four children from a dysfunctional family in a deprived part of inner-city Dublin. His father died when he was very young. A relative stepped in to act as a father figure but this man had amassed a massive criminal record for serious, violent crimes, including rape. Although now having reached the later stages of his life, he was still feared by gardaí as a serious character to contend with. He often brought Dan to court and when he was not available, an aunt who lived in west Dublin would take on the task.

Dan's mother suffered from severe ill health, and was rarely seen out of doors. Later years would see her health improve, allowing her to come to her children's court cases.

From a very early age, Dan started having confrontations with the Garda Síochána. Initially he was arrested for throwing stones at them and for generally being disorderly in public places. On turning 13, he became involved in petty crime, larceny and handling stolen goods. His first prosecution came before the Children's Court in September 1999; he was just shy of his fourteenth birthday. That day, he was convicted of three larceny offences together with skipping court. A one-month detention term was handed down to Dan. After his court appearance, he was put in a car, escorted to the detention centre where gardaí were told that there was no place available to take him. Consequently he was brought back to the city and released.

His first impressions of the court system could only have taught him that he could take part in unlawful acts with impunity. By the following May, he faced ten charges, mostly for public order violations where he had failed to leave an area when cautioned to by gardaí. He had also been involved in breaches of the peace, theft and attempted stealing of cars. There were two charges which he picked up after he had failed to turn up in court. He was bound over to the peace to be of good behaviour for two years.

His offending escalated; just over two months after his last court appearance, he was facing more than twenty charges which included a number of charges of assault, including some attacks on gardaí, as well as stealing cars. He was sentenced to two years' detention in Trinity House. In a re-run of his previous sentence hearing, he was put in a car, and escorted to the detention centre where gardaí were told that there was no place available to take him. That afternoon, he was returned to the Children's Court, put on probation for twelve months and released.

Over the following eleven months, he accumulated seven charges: five for larceny, another for criminal damage and once again he was charged with a car theft, for which he was sentenced to two years in Trinity House. Once again, he was put in a car, escorted to the centre and when gardaí were told that there was no place available to take him, he was released.

Later that month, when he faced four charges of similar types, he received two months' detention in Trinity House. He was again put in a car, escorted to the centre, and when gardaí were told that there was no place available to take him, he was released back on to the streets. Any attempt to continue to hold him in custody further would have been illegal and would have been a case of *habeas corpus*. The committal warrant that ordered his detention specifically stated that he was to be detained in Trinity House from that date. Having being turned away by that centre, the gardaí or the courts had no power to hold him, or even activate the sentence at a later date.

A few weeks later, Dan was in court again on seven charges, mostly for breaches of the peace. The judge did not attempt to sentence him to a period in the detention centre, but put him on probation for twelve months. By now, just short of his sixteenth birthday, he had a criminal record of fifty-seven convictions and had not spent a day in any of the custodial institutions that would have been best equipped to try to rehabilitate him. He was again released on condition that he took up a place in a centre in Ballyjamesduff, in Co. Cavan, which helps give guidance and training to young offenders.

On 22 October 2001, a security guard parked his van at the front of the AIB bank on Lower Drumcondra Road at 4.20 p.m. and went inside to do a cash pick-up. Meanwhile, both Dan, who was supposed to be in the centre in Ballyjamesduff, and his accomplice, who was four years older than him, were standing at a bus stop not far away, trying to look inconspicuous. The fact that they did not get on any of the buses that came to the stop aroused the suspicions of a passing off-duty garda who was now observing them intently.

The security guard came out of the bank, at which point Dan and his friend suddenly broke positions and lunged at him. The security box he had been carrying contained £37,500. He was viciously kicked and punched as the two youths tried to free the money box from his grip. Having done that, both ran off but the off-duty garda saw them make their escape. He tried to stop them as they ran towards him but they managed to get away and fled on to Botanic Avenue where they jumped into a van and took off from the scene. The security box was later found slung into a garden nearby; it had been opened and emptied of its contents within a matter of seconds.

Dan immediately became a chief suspect. He was arrested a week later and charged. Gardaí objected to bail but were unsuccessful and the Children's Court granted bail with six strict conditions. These included that he stay in the centre for youths in Ballyjamesduff, five days a week. On his return to Dublin at weekends, he was to avoid the city centre and stay with his aunt in the west of the city. He was warned that breach of the bail conditions would lead to bail being rescinded. But within weeks he was picked up by gardaí in the city centre. A patrolling garda noticed Dan walking around a part of the city from which he had been barred and went over to caution him. Dan was laden down with shopping bags which contained thousands of pounds worth of designer clothes. Gardaí suspected that the clothes had been bought with the proceeds of the robbery. Having breached his bail conditions, he was remanded in custody to St Patrick's Institution.

Gardaí believed he was now a seriously dangerous criminal. Physically, he was quite overpowering and he had a talent for boxing; during many of his arrests it often took up to seven gardaí to restrain him. But he was also able to present himself in a favourable way when he wanted to. A probation report was compiled on Dan after he was first put into custody. It described him as feeling 'embattled' by his past experiences with gardaí. The report also said that Dan was under peer pressure. In the four weeks he had spent in the Cavan centre, prior to the robbery, he had posed no problems. The report expressed the hope that this would provide 'something solid' for him.

Because of the seriousness of the crime Dan and his accomplice had committed, it was deemed that the case should be sent forward from the Children's Court to a higher one, the Dublin Circuit Criminal Court, in the Four Courts. Dan was duly returned for trial and later arraigned on 23 July 2002. The case was adjourned until 18 October 2002, when he pleaded guilty to carrying out the robbery and also admitted viciously assaulting the security guard.

In evidence, Detective Garda Kevin Stratford said that in addition to the observations of the off-duty garda at the scene, CCTV cameras outside the bank had captured two culprits arrive at the scene and then make their escape. Following their arrest, Dan's accomplice had arranged to have his girlfriend call to the garda station and hand over £1,000, claiming that was all that was left of the stolen money. However, gardaí believed that the money had been split between the driver of the van and three others who were inside, with Dan and his main accomplice getting the lion's share.

Dan, now aged 17, was detained for three years in St Patrick's Institution. His accomplice, now aged 21, had suffered at the hands of his violent father for years and dabbled in cocaine use, the court was told. He was detained for four years. Judge Yvonne Murphy suspended the last year of their respective sentences in light of their early guilty pleas and because of their difficult family backgrounds. But she said that the attack on the security officer had been extremely vicious and also noted that only a small amount of the £37,500 had been recovered.

Four years on and shortly after his release, Dan was jailed for drug dealing.

On the same day that Dan made his first appearance at Dublin Circuit Criminal Court to enter a plea for the robbery, just a few hundred metres away, on the steps of the Children's Courthouse in Smithfield, his younger brother, aged 14, floored a garda who had tried to arrest him having spotted him rolling a cannabis joint. It was his second time to attack a garda at the courthouse. Dan's days in the Children's Court were over, but his younger brother would take over where he left off. Although he never became involved in anything remotely as serious as Dan's security van robbery, he nevertheless represented as much of a policing problem as his older brother. Sean had been blazing a trail of his own and, by the time he was 14, he was coming to garda attention on a regular basis.

On 9 April 2002, he was in court to face sentencing for a criminal damage offence to which he had admitted. But new charges were also pending and the case was put back to later in the day until the paper work had been completed and the charge sheets lodged in court. During that short interval, he managed to get arrested again at the courthouse. When Sean was later brought back from the Bridewell Station, the arresting garda said that the boy had engaged in 'threatening and abusive' behaviour as he was leaving the court. Sean had given a false name when he was arrested.

Giving evidence on the other new charges, a garda from Store Street station told how Sean had broken his nose when he had tried to arrest him on 26 March 2002. This incident had also taken place outside the courthouse, minutes after the boy's previous appearance there. Sean had been cautioned over an incident in which a car window was broken. He had run before he could be arrested and had fled into the courthouse but was pursued by gardaí. He had then become threatening and abusive towards them and tried to resist arrest. He had been put into a headlock to restrain him but he had clenched his fist and thrown a punch at the arresting garda, breaking his nose. The court heard that it had taken fifteen minutes for Sean to calm down.

Judge Catherine Murphy warned the boy that he should respect the Garda Síochána and said that maintaining his present attitude would make life very difficult for him.

Sean told the judge that he could not control his temper. 'They provoke me and say things for me to react to,' he claimed. Judge Murphy adjourned the case until 10 June and advised the boy to learn to control his temper and walk away if someone said something that angered him.

In June, staff from a residential care unit said that Sean had been in their care since the previous March and his progress had been excellent. They said that he had got on very well with the care workers but his relationship with the Garda needed to be improved. At the time he was attending counselling for personal development and drug addiction. A care worker said that a custodial sentence would only criminalise him.

Sean's aunt told the court that her nephew was at home on the night when the window was smashed. Evidence had already been given that the boy had been seen smashing the window with his elbow. Judge Connellan said that he had known the boy's aunt and mother from numerous other court appearances involving members of their family. He said that the boy's mother needed to take more responsibility or else her children would be in and out of jail all of their lives.

At this stage, Sean had two previous convictions for breach of public order and larceny and was also facing other charges. Sean was remanded on bail for nearly two weeks.

The judge did not know it then but he would be seeing more of Sean just two days later. On the morning of 12 June, the teenager was brought into court to have other charges that had been pending dealt with. These were adjourned and Sean was released on bail to allow him to take legal advice. After the lunch break, he once again faced Judge Connellan.

This time, Sean was charged with having created a disturbance and then bragged about stealing a car the night before, adding that he had been in a 'good chase'. The court heard that he had tried to incite the other youths to resist arrest and had told a garda to 'f**k off' or he would 'kick his head in'. During his arrest, he put up a struggle and repeatedly tried to punch the arresting garda. Judge Connellan convicted Sean. He said that this was his third time to see the boy in the court that week alone and he was 'fed up seeing him'. Sean was described as a 'little thug' and the judge added that he and his mother were in and out of the court 'like a yo-yo'. He fined Sean €50 and remanded him on bail for six weeks. Adjourning the case, Judge Connellan quipped: 'I've seen him, his mother and family in court so often I'm beginning to think I'm related to them.'[1]

At Sean's next appearance, on 23 July 2002, the day his older brother was arraigned in the Circuit Court, he got into a row with a garda outside the courthouse a short time before his case was called. A Ballyfermot garda had spotted Sean with what was believed to be cannabis resin right outside the courthouse and tried to seize it from him. When the garda was trying to take the substance, the boy lashed out and resisted. He hit the garda 'very forcibly' and to such an extent that he could not carry out the arrest. Apart from the ongoing prosecutions relating to the other attack on a garda at the court and the breach of the peace and criminal damage offences, there was another older charge for attempted car theft. Judge Bryan Smyth remanded Sean on bail to the community-based residential home where he was living, until the following September. Sean was warned that this was 'no laughing matter' and was told, 'You have to be of good behaviour when you are outside the courthouse.'

Over the next twelve months, the number of offences snowballed. On 17 July 2003, now aged 16, he was facing a total of thirty-three charges. He had been involved in a joyriding incident where he was the rear-seat passenger on a stolen moped which led gardaí on a dangerous high-speed chase throughout the north inner city. While he and the driver were pursued, Sean stood up on the motorbike to wave to people in a block of flats, until they eventually crashed. He had also been charged over repeated car thefts, attempted car thefts and for taking part in handbag and phone snatches, as well as several breaches of the peace. A care worker from the home in which Sean had been living told Judge Bryan Smyth that Sean had made significant progress and recently there had been fewer arrests.

Gardaí applied to have very strict conditions imposed on the boy, forbidding him to enter numerous areas in the city centre and north inner-city flat complexes in which they said he had been repeatedly getting into trouble, and requiring him to comply with a curfew from 9 p.m. to 9 a.m. However, acceding to a submission from the boy's solicitor that these conditions were too restrictive, Judge Smyth refused to impose the curfew and ban from these areas.

Releasing the boy on the charges, he imposed a twelve-month probation bond and ordered him to sign on three times weekly at Store Street Garda Station. Later that month, Sean was arrested for travelling in a stolen car. In September of that year, he was again released on probation for being involved in violent behaviour in a garda station.

He now had fifteen convictions for public order violations, seventeen for joyriding-related offences, three for assaults, six for possession of drugs, three for theft and four for skipping court – forty-eight in total.

However, over the next twelve months, there was a definite tapering in his pattern of offending. He was still residing in the care facility and progressing well there; he had also managed to complete the Junior Certificate through FÁS. The rate at which he had been picking up charges dropped significantly. He was to pick up just five charges over that period. But gardaí were concerned that he was now using cocaine.

In May 2004, now aged 17, Sean was at the centre of a fracas in which two gardaí were attacked while on late-night patrol. The gardaí came across Sean and two other teenagers at the bottom of a dingy stairwell, a known haunt for drug addicts and users. The trio were cautioned on suspicion of possessing illegal drugs. When the gardaí attempted to bring them to the garda station to be searched, 'all hell broke loose.' Sean resisted heavily and violently lashed out as his friends tried to free him. While one garda was trying to arrest Sean, another teenager jumped on his back and he was knocked to the ground. The third boy attacked the second garda and then jumped off a high balcony and escaped.

That month, Sean was also arrested for possession of a stolen bicycle and being drunk and disorderly. It was these two offences which would see him get his first detention sentence. He pleaded guilty to the offences and, in October, was detained for six months. At the hearing, the teenager had admitted using the stolen bicycle and also being intoxicated but, when questioned by the judge, he refused to name the person who he claimed had lent him the stolen bicycle.

This conviction was followed in December by another detention order on foot of the attack on the two gardaí attempting to arrest Sean and his friends for possession of drugs. On 17

December, Judge Peter Smithwick said that a probation report had highlighted the teenager's cocaine and alcohol problem. The court heard that when released from the existing sentence, the teenager would return to the care home where he had progressed. According to his solicitor, the environment had been good for him and he had recently started to tackle his drink and drug problem.

Detaining him, Judge Smithwick said: 'Your record is appalling, you have a chance to get your act together. If you don't you will end up with 24-month sentences one after another, it is up to you.' Sean was detained for four months and had notched up two more convictions.

Social service intervention, although it did not come at an early stage, did have an impact on this second brother's behaviour. He had been a policing nightmare for about two years. But in his last two years as a juvenile, his offending had peaked and, in the following months, it went into a stark decline while he was living in the more stable environment of a care unit. In contrast, his brother Dan had not been given the same level of attention and, as a juvenile, had not been able to break the cycle of sustained criminality.

It is interesting to note that the third and youngest of the brothers, Barry, did not come before the courts until he reached the age of 15. At a hearing in late 2004, a garda told the Children's Court that the schoolboy had driven at speed after attempts were made to have him pull over and stop a 650cc motorcycle. The teenager sped along several streets, repeatedly ignoring gardaí who were trying to get him to stop. He broke a red light and turned a corner on the wrong side of the road; then he steered the motorcycle to get in front of the garda car, resulting in a collision. The boy came off the motorcycle and tried to escape on foot.

The garda was punched on her throat as she tried to arrest Barry. He managed to escape for a brief period but was apprehended shortly after. He denied that he had been the driver. The judge found the boy guilty and remanded him on bail for sentence, also ordering a probation report on him.

But the background mitigation tendered to the court was much different from what had been used in the cases of the elder brothers. Barry's solicitor said that the teenager had no previous convictions, unlike his older siblings, and prior to the incident had never come to garda attention. She added that the boy had not been in trouble with the law since. She also said that he came from an area in the city where there was a huge temptation for young people to become involved in crime but, notwithstanding that, he was still at school and doing quite well. In July 2006, a welfare report detailed how co-operative he had been. The report made favourable recommendations to the court which had also been told that in the two years since the incident he had not been arrested at all; he had not come to negative garda attention and crucially he was still in school. During the sentence hearing, in which Barry was supported by his mother who sat anxiously on a bench near her son, the Probation Act was applied, leaving him without a criminal record.

Early intervention from social services had been a big factor in why this boy turned out different from his older brothers. His mother too had been given more assistance and support. She had also benefited from being allowed take part in personal development courses. In contrast to Dan and Sean, her youngest boy had a more stable home environment, received more positive parental guidance and was still in the mainstream education system. At an age when his older brothers had over forty convictions, Barry had been found guilty of only one criminal act. While his brothers had appeared at the Children's Court on a weekly and sometimes daily basis, the youngest boy walked out of the courthouse that July day and he never had to come back.

07 | A PUBLIC ORDER DISASTER

22 JULY 2002: A 16-year-old north inner city Dublin boy was released on a three-month suspended sentence for a series of public order offences, even though his mother did not want to take him home. His first conviction had come on 19 March 2000 when he was aged just 14; over the following years he had become a public order disaster, demanding constant garda attention and actually straining their resources. Once when a garda managed to co-ordinate a prosecution which led to the boy being given his first substantial sentence, the officer in question was called into the office of a garda superintendent to be congratulated and commended personally. The superintendent told the officer that the prosecution and resulting sentence had freed up garda manpower significantly.

On arriving at the Children's Court on 22 July 2002, the youth already had fifty-four previous convictions for offences including larceny, assault and possession of an offensive weapon. A constant law-breaker, he was an alcoholic whose family wanted him to be put in custody.

The boy, who had become a regular at the Children's Court, had pleaded guilty to being intoxicated to such an extent that he was a danger to himself and others, engaging in threatening and abusive behaviour and failing to appear in court. He had failed to avail of numerous chances to get help from the Probation and

Welfare Services, and now it was believed that if he were not given a custodial sentence, he would continue to re-offend.

On 30 June, he had been found drunk on Bachelor's Walk, in Dublin's city centre, and had refused to move away from the area. In one of his earlier appearances, his parents had refused to come to court with him and had had to be served with a witness summons to force them to attend his subsequent hearing. Although the boy's solicitor said that his client planned to go for rehab for his alcoholism and was taking part in youth training projects, the boy's mother stood up and emphatically told the judge that there would be no point in her son going back home. By now, she was fed up with the situation. Wringing her hands, she said: 'I have stopped coming here for the past two years; he was getting out all the time because there was no room for him.'

In December 2001, her son had been sentenced to six months' detention in St Patrick's Institution. He had been convicted of seventeen public order offences including seven charges of being intoxicated to such an extent that he represented a danger to himself and others. There were also eight charges of engaging in threatening and abusive behaviour, two charges of failing to comply with the directions of a garda, and three assault charges.

The litany of charges against the boy on that occasion also included failing to appear in court to answer to charges of interfering with the mechanism of a vehicle, ten larceny offences and also three further charges for causing criminal damage. Earlier, in November 2001, he had been convicted of four larceny offences, one criminal damage charge, and for interfering with the mechanism of a vehicle, failing to appear in court and a breach of public order.

In July 2000, when aged 14, he had been convicted of possession of a piece of timber as an offensive weapon, engaging in threatening and abusive behaviour, and failing to come to court on three occasions. For the bulk of his charges he had been dealt with in a non-custodial way.

Judge Malone ordered the boy to enter into a bond of good behaviour and said that a three-month suspended sentence would be hanging over him. The boy walked out of court. As early as that night, he was arrested for being drunk and disorderly and for brawling with his girlfriend on O'Connell Street. He was brought back to court two days later, charged with being drunk and disorderly and causing a breach of the peace.

After that appearance, the boy was remanded on bail to appear again the following September. Over the following months, he continued to pick up more charges.

17 OCTOBER 2002: Having been arrested 106 times over a period of only two years, the youth was in court facing his seventy-fifth conviction.

The teenager, who now had over four convictions for every year of his life, claimed in court that he had been out of his family home for four-and-a-half years and in that time had become addicted to ecstasy, cocaine and heroin, and lately he had become an alcoholic. His circumstances and living on the streets were the reasons he gave for having broken the law so many times. Pleading for leniency, with arms outstretched, he said that his girlfriend was expecting his child and he needed 'something to look forward to'.

The bulk of the youth's convictions had been committed while he was on two separate one-year probation bonds. He had skipped court thirty-four times over the previous two years, five times since he had been given the suspended sentence the previous July. The majority of the thirteen new charges had also been committed since then.

These new charges included public order offences and being drunk and abusive to the public. A garda told how, on 8 August, after he had been given the suspended sentence, the youth had been arrested after he started a fight with staff in a shop on O'Connell Street and again became 'threatening and abusive' to members of the public. He had been caught as a passenger in a stolen car in the early hours of 9 August, and less than twenty-four hours later had been spotted by gardaí walking along Ormond Quay, 'trying the handles' on parked cars before stealing two bicycles from the back of a camper van. The next day, while heavily drunk, he had gone into a restaurant on Parnell Street, sat down and proceeded to take a handbag belonging to a woman at the next table, before leaving. Shortly afterwards, he had returned and tried to sell her mobile phone back to her.

On 23 August, at 3.30 a.m., the boy had been seen on Marlborough Street, carrying a wheel brace for use in a burglary; he had been drunk and abusive. Later that morning, he had again been arrested for being dangerously drunk and aggressive to members of the public.

Finally, Judge Coughlan heard how the now 17-year-old had been found on 3 October, on O'Connell Street, drunk and arguing with a night club's doormen. Judge Coughlan remanded the boy in custody to St Patrick's Institution for two weeks for a Probation and Welfare Service report prior to sentencing. Bail was opposed by the Garda Síochána who also applied to have the boy's suspended sentence activated.

On that date, Judge William Early activated the three-month suspended sentence that had been handed down in July. He also ordered the furnishing of a Probation and Welfare Service report on 28 November to assess the boy's suitability to go to the Coolmine residential treatment centre, a non-secure unit for people with addiction problems. This sanction had been recommended by the Probation and Welfare Services on his latest convictions.

When that date came, the boy was brought before Judge Geoffrey Browne who was told that the Probation and Welfare Services had recommended putting him on probation for one year, on condition that he attend drug-abuse counselling, live with his family, obey an 11 p.m. to 7 a.m. curfew, stay sober and not commit further crimes.

10 JANUARY 2003: The teenager was back in court following his arrest at 2.30 a.m. that day for being drunk and disorderly on Dorset Street during the hours of his curfew. Objecting to bail, a garda from Fitzgibbon Street said that previously thirty bench warrants had been issued for the boy's arrest because he had skipped court. He told the court that during the latest incident a motorist parked on Dorset Street had witnessed an incident in which the teenager attacked a man and a woman. This man had contacted the authorities because he felt worried for his own safety. Judge Browne remanded the youth to St Patrick's Institution for a week

A week later, he was further remanded in custody until his sentencing. He now had seventy-seven convictions.

4 FEBRUARY 2003: A Probation and Welfare Service report furnished to the court showed that the youth had made reasonably good progress since being put into custody. Judge Browne told the youth that he was prepared to give him one more chance. However, he warned him that should he 'so much as cross a red light' while on bail, he would be 'sent away'.

The teenager was released on strict bail conditions requiring him to obey an 8 p.m. to 8 a.m. curfew, to reside with his family and not to drink. He was also ordered to attend counselling for his alcohol problem. The case was adjourned for the furnishing of updated welfare reports on his progress.

25 JULY 2003: The boy was remanded in custody again after he turned up to court for his case review drunk and facing allegations of further petty crimes committed during his release on the probation bond. Judge Sean McBride was told that probation officers had recommended an adjournment with bail until the following October, for another report on his behaviour. However, gardaí objected to bail on the grounds that the boy had previously broken several bail conditions imposed on him and was now facing new charges including throwing a bottle at a garda outside the courthouse. The bottle had been aimed at the garda's head. In addition to coming to court under the influence of alcohol, which was in breach of the bail condition that he was to remain sober, the youth had taunted foreign nationals outside the courthouse and had made racist comments to them. He had broken his curfew and had also accumulated eleven further charges since his previous release.

Explaining the teenager's behaviour, his solicitor said that the boy had received some tragic news relating to the ill health of a member of his family and that this had upset him greatly. However, refusing bail, Judge McBride said 'that was no excuse for breaking curfew, his behaviour outside the courthouse or throwing the bottle.' He rescinded bail and remanded the teenager in custody to St Patrick's Institution and directed an urgent probation report on him.

7 AUGUST 2003: At his sentencing hearing, he was detained for eight months in St Patrick's Institution, on his eighty-fifth conviction. At this hearing, all the charges that had been dealt with by the probation bond had been re-entered, as well as further charges he had picked up in the meantime.

Judge Leo Malone heard that the boy had taken part in a city-centre mobile phone snatch from a young woman on O'Connell Street, on 13 June. The boy had grabbed the phone, worth €510, from the woman's hand and then had hidden in a nearby block of flats. The phone had never been recovered.

Judge Malone invited the teenager's mother, who was present in court, to speak on her son's behalf. She stood up slowly and gathered her breath before replying: 'He has no home to come to, I've had enough of him. He was let out on bail and told not to drink but he has been drinking, taking tablets—the lot.'

An eight-month term of detention in St Patrick's Institution was imposed. In mitigation, the teenager's solicitor said that the boy had pleaded guilty to the offences and that he had been struggling with his alcoholism at the time they were committed.

That day's sentence hearing ended the youth's affairs in the Children's Court. Adulthood, however, has continued much in the same way as his wild juvenile years. Repeatedly arrested for new petty offences, he is now a cog in the wheel of the criminal justice system and a regular face at the adult District Courts.

In the wings, watching the constant fighting and discord between the boy and his parents, a younger sister had been growing up and she too, perhaps inevitably, would eventually find herself before the Children's Court.

27 APRIL 2004: Aged 16, the younger sister appeared before Judge Sean McBride charged with involvement in a breach of the peace twelve days previously. Following her arrest and first court appearance, she had been remanded in custody to Oberstown Girls' Centre. She was now before the court seeking to be released on bail.

Having completed the Junior Certificate, the girl had quit school and now hoped to enrol on a FÁS training course. Prior to her arrest, she had lived at home with her parents and had no previous convictions. Although it was the girl's first arrest, she had been remanded in custody because her father did not want her to be released. On hearing this, Judge McBride reminded the girl's father of his parental duties and warned, 'You cannot expect the State to do your duties.'

The girl's father was adamant that in his opinion his daughter needed to be locked up. 'She's been running the streets for the last year,' he said. 'She said if I did anything about it she would press charges against me.' Judge McBride suggested that the father seek help from the social services, adding, 'It's a very crude solution to be sending her away to a place of detention, particularly in the context of it being her first appearance here.' He applied the probation act, allowing the girl to return home immediately.

6 JANUARY 2005: The girl's situation had worsened drastically over the six-month period since her release. She had taken to the streets in preference to staying at home with her family. In December 2004, she had been remanded in custody to Oberstown Girls' Centre, having picked up new charges. Now she was back in court and Judge David Maughan heard that she had run away from home, was living on the streets and had started taking drugs. Her mother said that after years of trying to cope with her son, she could not go through the same ordeal with her daughter. 'She chose this herself at 15,' the mother said, adding resignedly, 'I gave up, I did it with her brother for five years, I'm tired now, I'm getting too old for this.'

The girl was facing petty theft and public order charges and had started taking heroin through people she had met on the streets; this was causing great concerns for her health and welfare. Some of the people she had opted to live with were on the margins, chronic heroin addicts who had been on the streets for years.

Judge Maughan was also told that since the girl had been held in custody over Christmas, she had been given minute doses of methadone, to help wean her off heroin. The judge expressed reservations over young people being given methadone, saying that they often ended up addicted to it instead.

One of the people with whom the girl was associating was a homeless traveller boy who had become a chronic heroin addict after running away from home at the age of 12. In the ensuing years, he had become wild and had committed thefts and burglaries to feed the addiction that was consuming him.

The girl's solicitor told the court that her client wanted to quit drugs and start an addiction treatment course. The judge was also told how the girl had previously refused to comply with efforts to place her on a treatment course but had since changed her mind and was anxious to address her drug problem. Judge Maughan refused to grant bail and remanded the teenager in custody for a further three weeks, pending efforts to place her on a treatment course. He told the girl, who was in tears during the proceedings: 'If you use your time properly you can make something of your life. If you continue on drugs you are going to spend the rest of your life in and out of prison.'

7 JULY 2005: Having later been released on conditional bail compelling her to reside with her parents, the girl had repeatedly skipped court, which had resulted in bench warrants being issued for her arrest. This led to her being before the court again, looking dishevelled and malnourished. At the time of her latest arrest, her mother had been away on holiday and her father, an alcoholic, had barred the girl from the family's home.

The girl's solicitor explained to Judge Mary Collins that her client's social worker had been told that a place would be available for the girl in a hostel and that she could receive methadone there. The garda who had arrested the girl said that she had concerns that the defendant would end up back on the streets if released by the court. Judge Collins remanded the girl in custody to Mountjoy

Prison for a week and ordered medical attention to be provided to her.

11 JULY 2005: The girl's next court appearance was extremely heated and a physical clash between mother and daughter was narrowly averted.

Judge Angela Ní Chonduin heard that the trespassing offence, in which the girl had been found drinking and abusing drugs, stemmed from her having nowhere to go. Her parents were present during the proceedings as the issue of bail was raised. If released, the girl would be assessed to take part in a drug rehabilitation programme, which would also lead to her being provided with hostel accommodation.

Her mother then stood up and addressed the court. 'I have been in this court umpteen times asking for her to be put away. She has been living on the streets since she was 13. She's been on drugs and smoking heroin. I don't think for a minute she should be let out.' The mother said that she had been looking for help for the girl for five years and added that she would never again come to one of her daughter's court appearances. The distraught girl also spoke up, at which point the mother suddenly charged at her and had to be stopped by a garda.

Judge Ní Chonduin ordered the mother out of the courtroom and the girl suddenly pointed accusingly at her parents and, with her voice shaking, said: 'It's her. That's why I am not living at home. Her and him [her father], they threw me out.' She added that she would prefer to be placed in hostel accommodation than to go home.

Judge Ní Chonduin remanded the girl in custody for another night, saying that bail would be granted then to allow the teenager to be assessed for the drug rehabilitation course. That day, she was released from custody to allow her to access a drug rehabilitation programme, to start a project for troubled young people and to be monitored in hostel accommodation. Stringent bail conditions were imposed and she was warned that if she breached a nightly curfew at the hostel, abused drugs or re-offended, she would be put back in custody. 'Why would I want to take drugs? I'll be on methadone,' the girl chirped jovially in reply.

Judge Ní Chonduin ordered a short remand, until the following week, to see how the girl coped. She said that the mother's attendance would not be required as it had upset the girl and caused chaos in the courtroom.

Over the following months, the girl's ability to deal with her addiction started to improve steadily. Eventually the mother took her home, realising that her daughter needed extra help, especially now that she was pregnant and due to give birth in early 2006. Over the following year and at time of writing, her efforts to beat her addiction continue. Meet the baby's father in the next chapter.

08 | MEET THE FATHER

On 8 November 2001, a wiry looking 14-year-old boy from north inner city Dublin was convicted of his first offence, larceny. It would be the first of forty convictions he would amass over the following four-and-a-half years, dominated by a slide into chronic drug abuse and a need to fund his addiction through petty crime.

On 22 April 2002, on being described as 'out of control', he was sent to Oberstown Boys' Centre at the request of his mother. She explained that she was calling for her boy to be detained because he had become embroiled with a group of older petty criminals, was keeping late hours and causing trouble for her. The boy was before the court for breaching the peace and breaking a curfew previously imposed on him, but he had been arrested for breaking bail imposed on him just a few weeks before.

The mother told Judge Miriam Malone that she was worried for her son as she never knew where he was. She believed that he could get into more trouble because he was hanging around with an older crowd of troublemakers and she was becoming increasingly concerned for his safety. Judge Malone said that she would remand the boy on bail to Oberstown House for one week because his mother was 'at her wits' end' with worry. She said that the boy was a risk to himself and the public.

Over the next year, the boy made regular appearances in court. His demeanour in the courthouse changed significantly from that of a reserved boy to that of a cocky street-savvy youth who would openly brag about the muggings in which he had been involved. In the public seating area outside the courtroom, he often sat surrounded by other teenagers as he regaled them with stories of how he 'worked' packed pubs from which he claimed that he could walk in and come out minutes later with his pockets laden down with stolen mobile phones, wallets and purses.

Inevitably he continued on a path which led to his detention. On Monday, 30 June 2003, he was sentenced by Judge John Coughlan to two years in Trinity House. In total, he had pleaded guilty to twenty-two charges of joyriding, burglary and mobile-phone thefts which had taken place from May 2001 until May 2003. In one of the incidents, he and another teenager had stolen €6,000 worth of Playstation video games from a HMV store in the city centre.

Judge Coughlan heard that the boy's family had been extremely supportive of the teenager since his first court appearance and had arranged for him to start a job if he were released. They also wanted him to attend the Ballyjamesduff centre in Cavan, for troubled youths, in the hope that it would break the cycle of crime. However, care workers had recommended that the boy be held in a secure facility where his educational needs and offending behaviour could be addressed. Many of the teenager's offences had been committed after he had repeatedly absconded from the National Remand and Assessment Centre, a non-secure unit where he had previously been held on remand for psychological and educational assessments to be undertaken. Judge Coughlan concurred with the care workers' recommendations. In sentencing, he said: 'He is re-offending and needs a secure unit.'

On Thursday, 1 July 2004, now aged 16, the boy was back in court where it was explained that part of the reason he had spiralled out of his parents' control was a lack of help for his learning disorder as a result of which he had turned to drug addiction. Since his release from the detention centre, the boy had been found drunk and stumbling around a Dublin street at 9.20 in the morning of 15 June 2004. This had led to his arrest for being drunk and disorderly. He was described as having learning as well as hyperactive behavioural problems which had first manifested themselves in his early childhood. Despite having been sent to a treatment centre, his condition had not improved.

In his early teens, and following the separation of his parents, he had started using cocaine and an assortment of other drugs. This had led to his arrest for a string of offences over the previous two years.

Judge Anne Watkin also heard that the boy had been arrested one month previously for driving a stolen car in Summerhill, Dublin. He had been signalled to stop by a garda and had fled the scene. By this stage, he had a significant criminal record for his age which featured numerous convictions for theft and motoring offences, most of which had been committed after his release from Trinity House. Because he had turned 16, these convictions meant that he could be detained in St Patrick's Institution where he had spent a year.

Judge Watkin imposed a six-month term in St Patrick's Institution and placed him on a probation bond for two years, so that his personal development could be supervised after his release.

That, however, did not conclude matters. More charges were dealt with on Wednesday, 14 July 2004. The boy was in court for stealing a mobile phone four months previously, a charge he had admitted.

Defence solicitor Sarah Molloy explained to Judge Connellan that when the boy reached the age of 13, he 'went off the deep end and became involved in crime'. 'His mother has tried her utmost but this is where he finds himself now,' Ms Molloy said.

Detaining the teenager for a nine-month term concurrent to the existing sentence, Judge Michael Connellan noted the mitigating factor of the boy's educational problems but also took into consideration the boy's criminal record of twenty convictions.

Over the following two years, a litany of drug-fuelled offences would follow: on 18 July 2004, he was given probation for another earlier theft; on 26 July 2004, he was detained for a month for another theft; on 10 September 2004, he was detained for three months for theft; ten days later, he was put on probation for handling stolen goods; on 20 December 2004, he was given three months in St Patrick's Institution for a robbery.

The following year passed in pretty much the same vein. On 8 February, he was detained for theft; on 23 August, he got a further three months for theft; at Dublin Circuit Criminal Court, on 10 October, he was given a one-year suspended sentence for robbery; on 17 November, he was given a four-month suspended sentence back in the Children's Court.

At the start of 2006, now aged 18, he was given two months' detention from the Children's Court for theft. On 8 February, at Dublin District Court, for the first set of charges since he had reached adulthood, he was put on probation for twelve months for attempted robbery.

Throughout his dealings in the court, his mother continued to support him and to hope that he would change. However, that did not happen. She answered the door one day and was told by gardaí that her son had been identified from CCTV footage of a violent robbery at a take-away the previous night. On hearing the time of the offence, the mother told the officers adamantly, 'Listen, I know he's been involved in a lot but I can tell you this time for certain that it could not have been him. He was at home with me all night, watching TV.' The gardaí were quite perplexed as they had a good relationship with the mother who had never tried to shield her son from the consequences of his crimes. They returned later that day and showed the woman print-outs from the CCTV footage, which made her gasp. She agreed that there was no doubt that it was her son. Exasperated, she sat down and wondered aloud how her son could have done it. Then she remembered that she had gone to take a bath for half an hour. In that time, he had sneaked out a window, gone into the city centre, attacked the chip-shop worker, stolen the till's takings and made it back to his home. By the time she had finished her bath, he was sitting on the couch, watching TV.

By March 2006, the youth was a father of one and battling a heroin addiction. He was before the Children's Court that month to plead guilty to the last offence he had committed while still a juvenile. He claimed that he wanted to change his life. He now had forty criminal convictions, most of which were drug-fuelled thefts in which he had stolen mobile phones, wallets and handbags to fund his heroin addiction. He had been associating with a boy who was semi-literate and a girl who had a history of self-mutilation and would later become involved in organised prostitution.

Judge Catherine Murphy was told that on the previous 7 May, he had approached a woman sitting on the Liffey boardwalk and had stolen her purse. As he was fleeing across the Ha'penny Bridge, he had been spotted by a plain-clothes detective who was able to identify him.

At the time of this court appearance, he was fresh out of serving a two-month sentence for thefts. He was already beginning to face charges in the adult courts, for similar offences, and had been arrested for joyriding. Now the judge was recommending that he would be a suitable candidate to be dealt with by the Drugs Court, given his chronic addiction problems.

The court heard that during his latest sentence, he had used his time in custody to 'detox' and had left the detention centre clean of drugs. He hoped, with the support of his mother, to secure a placement on a rigorous three-month drug addiction treatment programme. During this case, he appeared under the influence of some intoxicant, which the judge commented on, but which the teenager vehemently denied. The judge told him that his type of offending left a mark on his victims, who were mostly women. She told him how his actions could have left people terrified, insecure and vulnerable every time they went out in public. 'I'm going to treatment,' the boy replied. 'I'm on a waiting list, for proper treatment and counselling on what led me to where I am today. I don't realise what I'm doing when I'm strung out of my head. That's why I'm willing to go to treatment.'

The case was adjourned to allow him to commence his placement on the course.

The early days of his adulthood have seen this young man continue with a pattern of being held in custody then released on bail and then locked up again, as the cycle of drug-fuelled petty offending continues.

09 | TWO BROTHERS

In mid-2005, social services in north inner-city Dublin decided to offer a troubled mother the chance to take part in a parental skills course. This offer came after her two young sons had gone completely out of control and ended up in detention centres. Earlier, concerned gardaí had approached social services, asking them to help the mother who was clearly unable to cope with her children who were about to embark on a sustained spree of petty offences.

The mother, a single parent, appeared to have been blind to her children's actions, and numerous times in court she levelled blame at gardaí for targeting her children, even though the teenagers had freely admitted responsiblity for what they had been charged with. It was clear that her two sons were extremely bright, but from the age of 13, the eldest had been involved in petty offences in his locality. His younger brother followed suit and by the age of nine was becoming a thorn in the side of gardaí. The pair had been living a lifestyle that was influenced by peer groups of older troublemakers, giving them a 'street smarts' age far above their actual one.

On 9 July 2002, the younger boy, Ed, then aged 11, appeared at the Children's Court for attempted car theft. With cherubic features, barely over four feet tall and with the demeanour of a shy child, the image he presented in court was quite at variance with how he behaved on the streets. The court was told that the boy

The Children's Courthouse in Smithfield, Dublin. (© *Irish Times*)

Another day at court. A common scene outside the Children's Court as a young offender is escorted in to face the judge. (*Courtesy of Independent Newspapers*)

Graffiti on the wall outside the Children's Court. (© *Derek Speirs*)

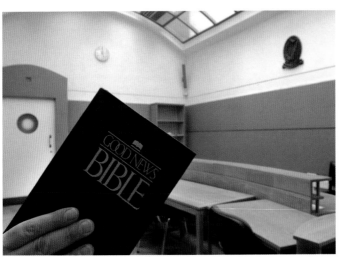

The Children's Court. Officially titled District Court 55, it is dubbed 'Juvy Court' by gardaí. The judge sits at the centre of the bench. The white door leads to the courthouse's holding cells. (© *Maura Hickey*)

Brain-damaged teenager 'Paul' (centre) is led from the Children's Court to await transfer to Cloverhill Prison; while he was on remand and often suicidal, efforts were made to find a suitable therapeutic placement for him. (© *Collins Photos*)

Michael Padden. On 14 April 2002, Garda Michael Padden and Garda Anthony Tighe became the fortieth and forty-first members of the force to die in the line of duty, when a 16-year-old joyrider smashed a stolen sports car into their squad car on the Stillorgan dual carriageway. (© *Collins Photos*)

The scene captured in the aftermath of the crash. The force of the impact propelled the Garda Ford Mondeo car about 9 ft off the ground and into a somersault through the air—at 40 mph —before it came to a stop on a grassy mound. (*Courtesy of Independent Newspapers*)

Gone but not forgotten. A memorial to Garda Padden and Garda Tighe, unveiled by their families and gardaí from Donnybrook Garda Station, lies at the spot where they were tragically killed. (© *Collins Photos*)

Alan Higgins: 'a cameo for an ideal young man', the teenager was brutally killed by three boys for his mobile phone. (© *Collins Photos*)

Three-year-old Daniel McGowan with his grandmother, Rita McGowan. His father, Robert, was killed horrifically by a teenage joyrider in the early hours of Saturday, 11 January 2003. (© *Collins Photos*)

had been previously arrested for car theft, breach of public order and for failing to appear in court. Before those charges were brought, the boy had also been dealt with through the Juvenile Liaison Office for other misdemeanours.

At that time, he had been living at a residential care home because his mother could not control him. The care home was not secure but it was planned that Ed would stay there until he ceased his criminal activities. Ed had been charged with joyriding in a stolen car and was brought before the court for a *doli incapax* hearing to determine whether he was fit to plead to the offence, in light of his young age. Gardaí from Finglas Garda Station, on patrol in an unmarked garda car, had entered a flat complex through a lane way and had found a Mitsubishi Lancer car which had been reported stolen earlier that day. The door on the driver's side of the car was open and Ed was crouching down into the car but, when he saw the gardaí coming, he made a dash into the stairwell of one of the blocks of flats. The engine of the car was running and the ignition mechanism had been tampered with. The gardaí also found various implements, including a screw-driver, for use in the hot-wiring of the car. The driver's seat had been pushed up as far as it could go, to bring the small boy closer to the steering wheel and pedals.

Prophetically, Judge Michael Connellan told the boy's mother that unless her son were controlled, he would inevitably be locked up in a detention centre. He adjourned the case.

Four months later, the court was told that Ed, still aged only 11, was facing eighteen charges for offences committed over the previous eighteen months, some going back as far as when he was under ten years of age. A Juvenile Liaison Officer from Fitzgibbon Street station explained that after Ed had been assessed in the National Remand and Assessment Centre, he had actually got worse.

When a curfew was imposed on him, the boy said he believed that it should start at 10 p.m. each night. When the judge then said, 'I think that is too late for a boy your age to be out,' the boy replied with a shrug: 'That's you, not me.'

A garda appealed to the court to have all cases against the boy dealt with on one date, instead of having separated hearings. This, he believed, would give the full picture of where Ed was in his life. 'At 11 years of age he is ruling the roost; if something is not done then we will have lost him.' The court ruled that all charges involving the boy would be dealt with on 27 January 2003. An entire afternoon's sitting of the court was dedicated to the hearing of his cases.

A little while before his special court appearance, Ed turned 12. He was now facing twenty-five charges, for breaches of the peace, so-called joyriding, hot-wiring cars, larcenies and attacking gardaí. The facts on seven new charges, including five of skipping court, would have to be heard at a later date. He was still living in the residential care unit because he was too troublesome for his family and out of their control. He had continued to re-offend having been granted bail on each individual charge, the court heard.

Garda Sergeant Barry Moore explained to Judge Bryan Smyth that he had co-ordinated the prosecution of the boy which involved several gardaí. He said that he had been dealing with the pre-teenage boy since summer 2000 and it was obvious that his behaviour had become 'steadily worse.' Garda Sergeant Moore also said that he knew the boy's family was deeply concerned and he recognised the family's need for help.

One by one, uniformed gardaí, who had packed the court-room, sat in the witness box to give evidence of Ed's offending. The boy had been arrested for shouting obscenities and throwing missiles at gardaí at a Halloween bonfire. On another occasion, he had smacked a garda on the mouth. On 4 January 2002, the boy had been arrested at a flat complex in the north inner city. He had been caught in possession of a wrench while interfering with property there. When approached, he had confronted the gardaí. As the garda was dealing with a crowd that had gathered around, Ed had smacked him on his mouth, Judge Smyth was told.

In other incidents, little Ed had been caught trespassing on property, trying to steal a car; had damaged another car; had been caught handling a bag of stolen tools; and had brazenly hit a garda on the leg while she was arresting another youth. The last attack had created a diversion which had allowed the other youth to escape arrest. Late one night, Ed had been picked up for creating a disturbance and screaming 'scumbags' at gardaí. He was also charged with trying to sell a stolen mobile phone in St Stephen's Green and with travelling as a passenger in a stolen car. He had been arrested along with a number of other intruders when they were caught trespassing on a premises on the North Circular Road, and he had taken part in a number of mobile-phone thefts, mostly from women. On the evenings of 13 April, 3 March, and 5 February 2002, he had snatched mobile phones from three women as they were using them. He had also stolen two mobile phones, valued at €150 and €120, on 10 April 2002. A week later, in Summerhill, he had stolen a mobile phone worth €130 from another woman.

After all the officers had completed their evidence, the boy's mother told the court that her son 'had brains to burn' but refused to go to school and would go out at night without her knowing where he was.

A care worker from the non-secure unit where Ed had been residing said that they were willing to work with him when he 'settled down', but advised that in the meantime he should be sent to a more secure environment.

The boy's solicitor said that the boy needed intervention in his life and a long-term placement in a juvenile institution, which could provide him with education, help and specialised guidance. However, it was not known when one would become available.

That day's sitting of the Children's Court typified the crisis that existed in the juvenile justice system in relation to shortage of spaces in the state's detention facilities for under 15s. Before Ed's case was called, his older brother, Gary, then aged 14, had been in court where a remand bed had also been sought for him. There was only one place available, however, putting the brothers in a bizarre position where they were in competition to take up the last available detention space in the country. Gary was given the place.

As the day ended, Judge Smyth learned that a temporary remand bed had become available in the Oberstown Boys' Centre, and he remanded Ed in custody, pending efforts to find a long-term suitable placement. He also directed the attendance of the health board at Ed's next court appearance, to help determine when a long-term placement could be found for the troubled boy. Oberstown was regarded as inappropriate as a long-term solution for Ed as he would be there with older children, some more criminalised than he, prompting fears that their influence would rub off on him.

The older boy, Gary, had been blazing a trail of his own. He too was intelligent, regarded as quite friendly and witty, but shortly after making his confirmation in primary school he had started to go wild through lack of control at home and the negative influence of older teenagers in his neighbourhood.

On 25 February 2002, aged 13, he had stolen a mobile phone from a student garda, who had been inputting a message when a group of youths came up to her and Gary swiped the phone from her grasp and ran away. On being spotted later by gardaí, the youths had fled. The following day, Gary went to Store Street Garda Station. The student garda told him that she just wanted her phone back but the boy replied, 'I can't get it.' The judge took this to mean that he knew it had been wrong to take the phone.

At a fitness-to-plea hearing the following July, Judge Mary Collins said that the boy's actions on the day had shown that he knew that what he was doing was 'seriously wrong' and that the onus on the state to show that the boy had understood the charges against him had been proved. Gary was remanded on bail.

Three days later, he was back for another hearing for offences that had taken place two months previously. Gary had been caught after security guards spotted him ripping the security tag off a jersey in Marathon Sports in the Ilac Centre. The incident took place at 4.32 p.m. and the boy was charged at Store Street Garda Station before he was released. Less than four hours later, he became involved in a high-speed chase with a stolen Mazda MX5 in the Summerhill area. After the chase, Gary, who had been a passenger in the car, got out and fled into his family's flat, where he locked himself onto the balcony. A garda had to climb over from the balcony of a neighbouring flat to arrest him.

The boy's mother told Judge Michael Connellan that she had been trying her best to control her son and had done everything she could for him. However, Judge Connellan said that the boy was out of control, had been 'knocking around' with the wrong kind of company and suggested perhaps his mother had done too much for him and should have let him do more things for himself. He remanded the boy on bail until the following 9 September. Over the following months, Gary's cases were adjourned, pending welfare reports.

Once, after a period of breaking all of his bail conditions, he appeared in court facing a certain spell in custody. He had been unaccompanied to court as his mother had gone away for a holiday, leaving him with his grandmother, and as the number of charges against Gary grew steadily, the judge indicated that she wanted to remand him in custody pending an educational assessment. However, before doing so, she wanted a member of his family to be present as the order was made. Gary piped up and said that an aunt lived near the courthouse and that he would go and fetch her, and come straight back. The judge let him out to get the aunt. However, Gary had tricked the judge and did not come back; a bench warrant was issued by the embarrassed judge.

Meanwhile, Ed, who had been remanded in custody to Oberstown Boys' Centre in January 2003, was still waiting for an appropriate care environment to be provided for him. Most of his court appearances over the next four months had a 'Groundhog day' quality, with the court being told the same thing: the state had no suitable facility for him. In the meantime, he was to stay in Oberstown with older offenders.

His mother was disheartened about the situation and wanted him released on bail from Oberstown. Ed had become frustrated in the institution where he was kept separated from the older juveniles detained there, and his mother wanted him home while further efforts were made to find a suitable placement. The Juvenile Liaison Officer described the boy's needs as 'exceptional' and added that nothing had been done to help him.

'There are no votes involved in this type of situation; that is why they are ignored,' said Judge Fitzpatrick. 'I have been sitting in this court for fifteen years and same situation applied then. It has not changed.' The Government, he added, had failed in its duty to provide placements for young offenders such as the boy and it was not the courts', health board agencies' or the institutions' fault. He released the boy on bail for two weeks to see what further efforts could be made to secure a placement

The case dragged on until 9 May 2003, when it was indicated in court that judicial review proceedings were being contemplated to vindicate the constitutional rights of Ed, a minor, to care and protection. The court heard that since his release on bail, Ed had been arrested for being drunk and disorderly at five o'clock in the evening and had also been arrested for theft of a mobile phone. Judge William Hamill heard that a placement in the Crannóg Nua facility in north Co. Dublin, a health board unit for troubled children such as Ed, would not become available. Ed's solicitor had been instructed by the boy's mother to take the case to the High Court to vindicate his rights to care and protection and to compel the Northern Area Health Board to find a suitable placement. Judge Hamill remanded Ed back into custody, this time to the National Remand and Assessment Centre. A place in this more suitable detention facility had just become available. Meanwhile, he had been approved by the Crannóg Nua unit, which was the first step that had to be taken in getting him placed there. However, there was still no place available.

Finally, on 14 May 2003, Ed, who now had thirty criminal convictions, was detained for a year in a secure wing of the Finglas Child and Adolescent Centre, where it was hoped he would receive educational help.

With much of the focus on efforts to find help for Ed, Gary's behaviour became more problematic. On Thursday, 20 November 2003, Judge Mary Collins gave him an ultimatum: he had six months to turn his life around and stop committing crimes or face a lengthy custodial sentence. Gary was facing forty-three charges in total. His litany of petty crimes had involved over twenty gardaí from Fitzgibbon Street, Pearse Street, Bridewell, Store Street, Mountjoy and Ronanstown stations.

However, Gary had recently started a training course and the court heard that he was prepared to put crime behind him. Now more optimistic, his mother said that her son had at last begun to settle down and was now ready to accept whatever guidance was offered to him. Evidence was also given that Gary had attacked a man on a city-centre street and left him with a black eye. Judge Collins described him as acting like a 'bully boy' but said that she was prepared to give him a final opportunity to change his life. He had also been involved in a number of car thefts, joyriding and phone snatches throughout the north of the city. Judge Collins ordered him to continue with his educational and training course and to co-operate with the probation and welfare services who had been working hard to divert him from an offending lifestyle.

The judge adjourned the case for sentence until May 2004. She made it clear to Gary that this would be his 'last chance', and failure to co-operate with probation workers or any new crimes would result in his automatic detention.

On 12 February 2004, at the Children's Court, Judge Bridget Reilly heard that on Christmas Day 2003, Gary had been caught riding a moped and was charged with not having a licence or insurance. He had also been caught for a similar offence in a car, a few weeks later. And he had committed two Public Order offences, in one of which he had threatened to shoot a garda and, using hand gestures, had simulated the pointing of a gun at the officer before he ran away. He had also caused a disturbance outside a primary school where he had shouted profanities at a garda in front of young children who were going to class.

A bench warrant for his and his mother's arrest had been issued by the court earlier that week when they failed to turn up at the Children's Court to pay €500 compensation to the owner of a moped, which the boy had stolen and wrecked. The mother apologised for not coming to court, claiming that she had her dates mixed up. She also appealed for more time to come up with the money. However, Judge Reilly heard that over the previous months the woman had been repeatedly cautioned over paying the compensation to the victim, who had been left out of pocket since his moped was damaged. A garda said that the mother had told him in colourful language that she had no intention of paying for her son's damage. In mitigation, the boy's solicitor told the court that the boy now wanted to return to school and get an education.

The judge ordered a further probation report to be furnished to the court on 29 April and he granted bail. A strict curfew from 8 p.m. to 8 a.m. was imposed and Gary was warned that he had to co-operate with probation officers, accept whatever guidance they gave and attend all appointments and assessments.

On 14 June 2004, then aged 15, Gary was detained for two years on his sixty-fourth conviction, for the litany of petty crimes committed over the previous two-and-a-half years. However, there had been an eight-month period from March to December 2003 in which he had not been arrested at all. This was the period after he began his placement and pledged that he would turn his life around. But he had found it difficult to stay away from trouble. By December 2003, the placement in the training centre had broken down and inevitably the offending pattern had begun to reassert itself and he had started coming to garda attention.

The bundle of charge sheets before the court on that date resembled a telephone book in thickness, and Gary's mother wept as she was told that her son would be detained for the next two years in Trinity House. One of the boy's latest misdemeanours was abusing gardaí patrolling his neighbourhood while he was intoxicated. He had been asked to cease his breach of the peace at which he had run to his doorway and exposed his penis to the gardaí, in the presence of his grandmother and passers-by, including some children. His grandmother had scolded him and ordered him to stop this behaviour, at which he had knocked her to the ground and run at the gardaí. During the arrest, he had tried to bite two officers. He had also been caught trying to steal a jumper from a shop on Dublin's Liffey Street. Having removed the security tag, he had stuffed the jumper under his jacket and attempted to leave the store but was stopped by shop staff.

Judge Mary Collins, who had taken a special interest in the case, told Gary, 'I had hoped that it would not come to this.' Having heard that the boy had been involved in more offences as recently as the previous month, she said: 'I have to make a two-year detention order.' She also reminded Gary that he had once admitted that he would be better off in custody rather than released. Gary's solicitor explained that her client understood that he was facing a sentence. But she added that the boy, while not wanting to 'chance his arm', was asking for a final chance to show that his offending could be stopped. 'I want to start on a FÁS course,' Gary chirped. But having been told that he would not be released from the court, he inquired if he was facing any more charges. 'I've no more charges?' he asked, and then added, 'I'm off to Trinity House; that's fine.'

At that stage, his mother broke down and wept. 'I'm sorry it has come to this, I really hope things work out for you,' Judge Collins said. Gary nodded, and with a hint of gallows humour, replied: 'As long as them muppets [the gardaí] stay off my back, I'll be all right.'

A few months later, Ed reappeared at the Children's Court. Now aged 13, he was facing a litany of charges for offences committed after his release from custody in May 2004. These included possession of knuckle dusters, an offensive weapon; possession of an implement for use in a theft; skipping court; and interfering with and causing €350 worth of damage to a car he had been trying to steal a few weeks after his release.

Ed, who was remanded in custody on these charges, also admitted trespassing on the grounds of Croke Park with intent to commit an offence and theft of bottles of beer from a shop on Westmoreland Street. He had other charges for car thefts, burglary and vandalising cars.

It was almost a re-run of the events a year-and-a-half before. In November 2004, Judge Angela Ní Chonduin asked for the Northern Area Health Board to attend the case to outline what intervention it planned for the welfare of the out-of-control boy. On the next court date, 18 November, the health board did not appear in court which infuriated the judge.

Ed's mother again said that she had tried her best to control the boy but needed help from social services. She reiterated her long-held fear that he would either become a drug addict or end up 'dead on the streets'.

Regarding the absence of a representative of the Northern Area Health Board, the judge told a garda, 'Contact them again and seriously consider a witness summons.' She said that she was angered by the health board's stance. 'I am having to keep a child in detention; that is what is making me very cross, they do not care,' she said and added that the health board must be pressurised into intervening.

Ed was remanded in custody to Oberstown Boys' Centre until the following week. The Northern Area Health Board attended that day's proceedings and resolutely rejected Judge Ní Chonduin's earlier criticism. A solicitor for the health board said that it had been working with the boy and his family for a number of years, had put in place several programmes to help the boy, and that all had failed. A representative of the Special Residential Services Board recommended that a referral be made to the special detention school, St Joseph's, in Clonmel, Co. Tipperary. She said that the school would give an answer in a week on whether it would take the problem child. Ed's mother told Judge Ní Chonduin that her son was prepared to go to the school if the place became available. Ed was remanded in custody to Oberstown Boys' Centre, pending a progress report on the proposed placement.

On 13 January 2005, Ed was sent to St Joseph's special residential school in a bid to rehabilitate him and restart his education. The court had opted to pursue a welfare route by sending him to the school rather than holding him in a detention centre, in an attempt to steer him away from a life of crime. It was hoped that in the school he would be able to start working towards completing his Junior Certificate. The court also heard that a parental skills course was to be made available to his mother who had difficulties controlling him and also had to rear another young child as well.

Judge Ní Chonduin warned that if the teenager failed to take the help offered to him, he would be brought back to court and could be put in a detention centre. His progress was to be monitored by the court and reviews were to take place every two months to ascertain whether the placement had a positive impact on the teenager. At time of writing, the placement was shown to have had some benefits. Ed had opted to stay at St Joseph's beyond one year. Staff there reported that he was doing well but seldom received visits from his mother.

Gary was released from Trinity House, after a year. It seemed to have had a real positive impact on him. He went home and began taking part in a training course, and in his spare time he even did some voluntary work in his community. However, he has also been arrested once, for drug dealing.

10 | LOST COUSINS

She often sauntered into the courtroom with a jaunty manner, sometimes grinning, but her smile masked a life of turmoil, violence and drug abuse. She had been damaged by years of neglect and later self-abuse. In March 2005, the then 17-year-old girl was back in court again. She had previously made several appearances, sometimes obviously under the influence of drugs. Life for her was care home, hostels, custody, being arrested, going to court, being held in custody, being released. Then the cycle would repeat itself.

Erica was a member of the travelling community. But her community and her family in particular rejected her because she had spent a number of years in care among settled people and had become 'too settled' for their liking. It was an acutely dysfunctional family background which had led to her being put into care in the first place. Two of her siblings had suffered drug-related deaths. Erica had been made subject of several care placements including foster homes but she had refused to co-operate and they had been unsuccessful. Her situation was compounded by her biological family's rejection of her.

Erica had started to take drugs and had also begun to hurt herself through self-mutilation. This she often did in front of her 14-year-old cousin. Judge Angela Ní Chonduin heard that the girl, who had no family support in court, actually wanted to be detained and had developed a 'fatalistic' attitude.

A seven-month detention term was imposed by the court, but Judge Ní Chonduin added that this was not the solution for the girl who she said had become 'institutionalised'. Erica had pleaded guilty to a litany of offences, mostly assaults when she was in care homes or while she was held in the secure Ballydowd Special Care Unit, in west Dublin. She had been put into the high-support facility for her own care and welfare. However, in early 2005, she had been remanded in custody after she had absconded from another residential care home. 'Mostly, she has been in trouble because of what happened in the institutions; that is a sad reflection on the institutions. She will be sentenced by me for the wrong reasons,' Judge Ní Chonduin said.

The offences had taken place over the previous two years and she had committed six assaults while she was in care. When the teenager was not in care homes, she had been involved in four incidents, one relating to a mugging, another for handling stolen goods, and two other incidents where she had attacked gardaí. 'She got into less trouble when she was out with no one to look after her. That suggests that she needs help and has not got it,' the judge said. Erica remained silent during most of the hearing but, as the case concluded, she spoke once, simply saying 'Thanks' to the judge for detaining her in Mountjoy Prison.

Gardaí had found that the girl had been hardened by her tough life and she had become prone to sudden violent behaviour. While in Mountjoy, she started to pick on a 17-year-old recovering heroin addict whom she attacked and repeatedly threatened that she would 'cut up'. Her victim was already extremely traumatised; she was facing allegations of being involved in prostitution, with gardaí believing that she was pimped by her own mother.[1]

However, Erica's time in Mountjoy was not as long as the court had wished because appeal bail was lodged and she was released. She returned to her chaotic lifestyle. On 22 May 2005, she stole €500 from a friend whom she had originally met in the Ballydowd Special Care Unit. She also took the other girl's jewellery and watch and refused to give them back. In another theft incident, on 31 May, outside a hostel in Dublin, she stole €22 from a homeless girl.

Efforts were made to have her placed in a special-care home in Cork, but that arrangement broke down miserably, with her repeatedly absconding and spending her time on the streets, although she had made repeated pleas to be allowed to take up the placement to change her life. During an incident in Cork city, she was found on a street, intoxicated from sniffing an aerosol can. She also intervened in a garda's attempt to arrest a second person at the same time. Predictably, bail was revoked and she was returned to Mountjoy.

When she appeared in court again, on 12 September 2005, Erica was homeless and efforts were under way to get the health services to provide her with accommodation. She pleaded guilty to a number of public order and theft charges.

Judge Ní Chonduin was told that there was an indication of a ray of hope: the girl now had a last chance to change her life and was adamant that she would not end up like her dead siblings. Since going into custody, she had taken part in training courses and was anxious to continue these in the community, if released, in the hope that it would lead to employment. Judge Ní Chonduin further remanded Erica in custody to Mountjoy Prison for another three days, after which an interim plan for her was outlined. She was granted bail to take up hostel-style accommodation, pending efforts to have her allocated her own flat.

However, the case did not end there. Erica was later the subject of a number of bench warrants, with rumours that she was working as a prostitute in a brothel, near the Irish Financial Services Centre, in Dublin.

Even at this stage, Erica was the one of the few links her younger cousin had to his family. She was his role model and exerted the most influence over him. Sometimes this was done cruelly, in that when he refused to do what she asked, she would harm herself gruesomely in front of him. He too had gone through the care system starting when he was an infant. As a babe in his mother's arms, he had spent time on the streets with his homeless parents, both of whom had addiction problems.

At the age of 14, he had been put into the secure Ballydowd Special Care Unit, but that placement had failed, with allegations that he had attacked a staff member. As a result and in the absence of any other accommodation, he was remanded in custody to Oberstown Boys' Centre in the presence of older more criminalised boys.

On Thursday, 13 January 2005, the Children's Court heard that a complaint had been made to the Social Services Inspectorate over the boy's treatment. He was facing charges for assaulting a staff member in the unit and for an act of criminal damage there. However, his solicitor said that although he had been in health board care since infanthood, no care plan had been put in place. She said that the boy had witnessed another person (Erica) in the unit who was involved in episodes of self-mutilation, which distressed him. As a result of witnessing these gruesome scenes, he had asked to be moved to another part of the facility, but he had not been not moved and later he too had attempted to harm himself. The alleged assault and criminal damage incidents had occurred on an evening when the boy had tried to harm himself with a cigarette lighter. 'He was supposed to receive help in a secure therapeutic unit. He was in court on charges relating to when he was in care, in an institution set up to deal with children with behavioural difficulties. The alleged incident of criminal damage occurred on an evening when he tried to set fire to himself,' said his solicitor.

Judge Ní Chonduin adjourned the case for a week pending the outcome of High Court proceedings in which the South Western Area Health Board would be asked to outline its care plan for the troubled teenager. The boy was held on remand in the Oberstown Boys' Centre detention unit. Judge Ní Chonduin also ordered the attendance of the health board at the Children's Court the following week. On that date, the health board did not show up.

The boy's solicitor invited the court to issue an order of contempt in relation to the Health Service Executive (HSE) over its failure to attend the case. Judge Ní Chonduin approved and went further, saying that she was holding the HSE's chief officer in contempt of court. She also agreed that the health board should be notified to allow it the opportunity to purge the contempt. In relation to the criminal charges against the boy, he had entered a not-guilty plea and was to face trial in the coming weeks.

The case featured heavily in the media and not surprisingly the HSE was present on the next date. Counsel for the HSE argued that a health board is not a parent or guardian and therefore cannot be compelled to attend the proceedings. He said that since the initial order directing the health board's attendance was unsound, the arising order of contempt made by the judge was also unsound.

He also said that the boy's case was an exceptionally difficult one and outlined that every possible effort was being made by the health board to provide him with the care and welfare that he needed. Documentation was presented to the court outlining the health board's care strategy for the troubled boy. The judge vacated the contempt of court order. Meanwhile, other issues about the allegations made against the teen were simmering.

On 1 March 2005, the judge accused the HSE of obstructing the court case by withholding evidence from gardaí and the now 15-year-old who was charged with assaulting the care worker in the Ballydowd Special Care Unit. Solicitors for the HSE were told that they had been 'monkeying around' with the Children's Court for failing to comply with court orders and witness summonses.

The boy's solicitor said that the HSE had been ordered by the court to furnish her with the documents relating to the incident in which her client had been restrained while in the Ballydowd Special Care Unit. It was practice that after a restraint took place, the details were recorded on a document and then signed by the person who had been restrained, as well as by the person who had conducted the restraint. She said that the boy was entitled to access to this material as he was a co-signatory.

Gardaí had sought a witness summons to compel the authorities in charge of the Ballydowd Special Care Unit to furnish them with any available evidence relating to the incident, including the documents detailing the restraint incident. However, according to the prosecuting garda, the HSE had not complied with the summons.

Solicitors for the HSE disputed that a court order had been made to compel the HSE to disclose the documentation which recorded the details of the incident. Judge Ní Chonduin dismissed the charge and accused the HSE of obstructing the boy's right to mount a defence in the face of the assault allegations. 'I feel the health service is really acting the monkey with me. I feel that in view of my experience of thirty years of practice; in my dealings with the health boards, I have not met an obstacle like this. If you are not provided with information you cannot defend yourself,' she said. Afterwards the boy's case was brought to the High Court which detained him in Oberstown Boys' Centre, for his own welfare, not because of any criminal acts.

On 25 February 2006, the Orange Order held its 'Love Ulster' rally in Dublin. The Orangemen's presence sparked a wave of violence and rioting. The young boy was there. Now aged 16, he followed the crowd. Gardaí later linked him to the looting of a shop on O'Connell Street that had been ransacked during the rioting. The teenager was arrested on the morning of 4 March 2006, at Kildare Place, in south Dublin city, where he had been sleeping rough. The boy was taken to Pearse Street Garda Station where he was held for questioning. He was then released and charged in the presence of an 18-year-old woman, another cousin who was now also his acting guardian. In court a few days later, Judge Catherine Murphy granted legal aid to the boy whose parents were not present during the proceedings.

The boy had been accompanied to court by a staff member from the Focus Ireland agency for the homeless, his cousin and a traveller care assistant. He had spent the night before his court appearance on the streets, having made a home with two other vagrants behind a building near Leinster House.

On 22 May, he pleaded guilty to the charge. Following his arrest, he had been shown CCTV footage from the scene and a photograph taken from a newspaper's coverage of the riots. He had immediately identified himself in the photo and on the video footage and admitted that he had taken a hooded top from the shop. The top, priced €70, had not been recovered.

'He was not part of the core group involved in the riot,' said the prosecuting garda, who also agreed that the teenager had come on the scene and acted in an 'opportunistic way'. In mitigation, the boy's solicitor, Catherine Ghent, said that her client, who had no criminal convictions, had one of the most difficult backgrounds she had come across. 'He was homeless from a very young age with his parents, who had alcohol problems. His mother died on the streets.' She continued, 'He was then in and out of health board care for the last number of years.' She added that High Court proceedings were under way to secure accommodation for him.

Judge Catherine Murphy was satisfied that the boy had acted in an opportunistic way, like a 'child in a sweet shop'. She released the teenager without a criminal conviction. The boy was released to resume his life on the streets, at constant risk of becoming a drug addict. Months later, protracted efforts were still under way to compel the state to provide him with appropriate accommodation and care.

11 | BALLYHAUNIS TO BLACKROCK:
A CRIME WAVE

In 2003, a small but fierce-looking 13-year-old boy started coming before the Children's Court in Dublin. It was not his first time to be in a court: just his first appearance in one in Dublin. He first came to garda attention when he was just 11 years old. By that stage, Sean, who was a member of the travelling community, had attained notoriety in the west of Ireland, for a spree of burglaries, which resulted in his being detained in the Finglas Children's Centre, in north Co. Dublin. In 2003, his family moved to a halting site in west Dublin.

By then, Sean's track record was shocking. He was serving a two-year detention order imposed by a court in Leitrim, on 22 May 2003, for a litany of assault and theft offences as well as twenty-two burglaries, in Counties Mayo, Tipperary and Clare, bringing his number of convictions to thirty-eight. On 11 December 2003, he was convicted at Clare District Court on four counts of escaping from lawful custody, theft, two counts of burglary, criminal damage, and one charge of skipping court. On 21 February 2003, at Ballinrobe District Court, in Mayo, he was convicted of ten counts of burglary and one count of larceny of property from an unattended vehicle. He had been given the Probation Act on one of the burglary charges with all other charges taken into consideration. On 12 December 2002, when he was 12, he was detained for two years at the Finglas Children's Centre, by Ballinrobe District Court, for five charges of escaping from lawful custody, trespassing, theft, and criminal damage to property. On 22 May 2002, at Carrick-on-Shannon District Court, he was convicted of stealing €6,350, two larceny charges and eleven burglary charges.

However, on 11 July 2003, he was rushed from the detention centre into the Children's Court following an incident at the centre. The deputy director of the institution told Judge Michael Connellan that young Sean was at risk to himself and others; he had absconded sixteen times and had found it impossible to settle down there. During his latest escape attempt, care workers had approached him and tried to persuade him to stay in the non-secure centre. With that, Sean had smashed a window and held a shard of glass to his own throat in a bid to stop their efforts.

Sean, who was described in court as having the IQ of a seven-year-old, was unhappy and had been involved in several incidents of self-mutilation. During that week alone, he had used a cigarette lighter to set his own hair alight after he had wrecked fittings in the unit. Staff in the detention centre were afraid for the boy's safety—as well as their own.

Sean needed medical and psychiatric attention and the only option available to the court was a remand in Oberstown Boys' Centre. Sean could be better supervised and put under stricter observation there than in the non-secure Finglas Children's Centre. Judge Connellan remanded Sean to Oberstown for one week. It was Sean's first court appearance in Dublin and by no means his last.

That November, Sean was back in court for a fitness-to-plead hearing, given his young age, in connection with an offence committed while he had been at large from the detention centre in Lusk. On 22 June 2003, the young boy had snatched a walkie-talkie earpiece from a security guard in the Square Shopping Centre in Tallaght and damaged it in the process. Sean had run from the scene but was later arrested sitting on a wall nearby. When taken to Tallaght Garda Station, he had struggled with officers and tried to bite one of them. He had also given a wrong name and date of birth.

The prosecution submitted that because he had run from the scene, given a false identity, and later had told gardaí that he could

have avoided arrest by jumping over a wall, Sean had demonstrated knowledge that he had committed a criminal offence.
However, Sean's counsel said that the facts described bore more
resemblance to 'messing' than to intent to commit a crime.

When Sean had been convicted previously, the question of his
fitness to plead had never been raised, which counsel described as
'surprising'. The defence also submitted that this had rendered the
teenager's earlier convictions invalid. Two reports, one from a
social worker and one from a care worker in the National Remand
and Assessment Centre, had found that the boy had a 'vague
knowledge' of what was right and wrong, the lawyer said. The
reports also showed that his understanding of the consequences of
his actions was extremely limited.

Judge O'Neill ruled that the teenager was fit to plead and
understood the difference between an act of mischief and a crime.
On 27 November 2003, Judge Angela Ní Chonduin, having noted
that Sean was already serving two years in detention, concluded
the case with a one-month sentence for his failure to appear in
court, as well as a €250 fine for his conduct in the garda station.

In mid-2004, Sean's brother, Peter, who was just under a year
younger, and then aged 13, came through the courts. The evidence
used in his case revealed that gardaí held him to be a veteran
burglar behind a massive wave of house raids. On Tuesday, 11 May
2004, Judge Ní Chonduin was told that Peter was on the
educational level of a child in Senior Infants class and, according
to a computerised trend analysis of crimes, had been responsible
for 60 per cent of burglaries in the Rathfarnham and Tallaght
areas, over a three-month period. Whenever Peter was remanded
in custody, burglaries in these areas dropped by exactly that
percentage.

A detective sergeant attached to Rathfarnham Garda Station
told Judge Ní Chonduin that Peter had been involved in a wave of
crimes 'from Ballyhaunis to Blackrock' which had begun in July
2002, when he was 11 years old.

The details emerged during a preliminary hearing to determine
whether, given his young age, he was fit to enter a plea and

understood the difference between a crime and a prank or act of childish mischief. Peter, who the court was told had learning difficulties and behavioural problems, had been arrested and brought into garda custody for questioning thirty-seven times between October 2003 and March 2004, mostly for burglaries, which were under investigation by gardaí from thirteen stations.

In total, Peter had been questioned in connection with eighty crimes. That was apart from his history of earlier convictions. On 5 May 2003, he had been given a two-year suspended sentence, by a court in Co. Roscommon, for eight offences: two burglaries, an attempted burglary, assault, criminal damage and breach of the peace. The sentence was suspended on condition that he be of good behaviour.

The type of offence committed by Peter had evolved from breach of the peace into large-scale burglary. 'Elderly people have suffered and have lost a lot of property. He has been given so many chances in court and has demonstrated contempt for court orders and the probation services that have been working tirelessly to help him,' the detective said.

Ten gardaí gave evidence of his alleged crimes which included stealing a handbag from the staff area of a McDonald's takeaway in Tallaght; travelling as a passenger in a stolen car; and burgling a house on St Patrick's Road, south Dublin, by forcing a window and stealing a gold engagement ring, a gold eternity ring and a Nokia digital camera, which were never recovered. Fingerprint analysis had placed the boy at the scene.

Peter had also burgled a house in Dún Laoghaire and allegedly stolen a laptop computer; three days later, he had sneaked into the staff area of Dunnes Stores in Nutgrove Shopping Centre, in Rathfarnham, and stolen some loose change and cigarettes from a locker; and he had burgled St Mark's Junior School, in Tallaght, and stolen a small amount of money.

On 12 March, he had burgled a house in Rathfarnham but was captured after the homeowner chased him and held him until gardaí arrived; three days later, while being escorted into the Children's Courthouse, he had refused to be searched before he was put in a cell. He had repeatedly lashed out at gardaí and spat at them. On 31 March, he had sneaked into an elderly woman's home in Rathfarnham, while she was on her front lawn, gardening. However, neighbours had spotted him entering the house through the front door, and called gardaí.

The boy's solicitor submitted that the prosecution had given evidence of crimes but no evidence to show that Peter had understood that he was committing a criminal act. She said that there was no evidence to show that the boy had been questioned in a direct and understandable way suitable to his education level. A recent assessment, she said, had found that he was on the level of a child in 'junior or senior infants'.

However, Judge Ní Chonduin was satisfied with the prosecution's evidence, which, she said, rebutted the presumption that he did not understand what a crime was. The court was then told that Peter was pleading not guilty to the charges and that a further hearing would be required. Judge Ní Chonduin remanded Peter in custody to Oberstown Boys' Centre until 16 June 2004, to await the hearing.

On that date, however, he owned up to the bulk of the charges which, in addition to many of those outlined above, included breaking into a house in Knocklyon Grove in Templeogue, in the early hours of 12 January 2004, and stealing a wedding ring and some bracelets, worth €800, which had never been recovered.

However, he denied the burglary which had taken place in Dún Laoghaire on 10 February 2004, in which it had been alleged that he broke into a home and made off with a laptop computer. He was convicted after the court heard that he had been identified by the homeowner who had spotted him leaving her home with her laptop.

He also denied trespassing in the staff area of Dunnes Stores in Nutgrove Shopping Centre and taking a small amount of cash. He was convicted after the judge heard that he had been identified by the store manager as having been in an area restricted to staff only. The manager also said that the boy had emptied his pockets of the stolen items in her presence.

He denied the break-in at St Mark's Junior School in Tallaght, but the school cleaner told Judge Collins that she had seen the boy with her purse in his hand. She admitted that she had thought the culprit had freckles and longer hair, which Peter did not have, but she was adamant that he was the intruder who had stolen her property.

When questioned about the missing handbag, Peter had told the gardaí: 'I hope whoever took it got five million inside, best of luck to them.'

Judge Collins said that an identity parade would have been a preferable setting in which to identify the accused as opposed to the prejudicial setting of the witness pointing the boy out in the dock. However, she was satisfied with the prosecution evidence and convicted him. At that point, Peter looked at her and said: 'Judge, there'll be no school there when I get out; I'll burn it down.'

Peter was remanded in custody and the case adjourned to allow time for the preparation of a pre-sentence probation and welfare service report.

On 26 August 2004, the case finished with the court ordering his committal to St Joseph's special detention school, in Clonmel, Co. Tipperary. Peter, whose father was present, had come to court with his 'bags packed', and was apparently willing to stay in the school.

Judge Thomas Fitzpatrick ordered a term of two years in the detention school.

However, that was far from the end of matters for the brothers. In September, Sean was back in court over more offences which had taken place after he had escaped custody in February 2004. At this time, he was aged 14 and charged with taking part in three burglaries within the space of an hour. He pleaded guilty to the charges.

At approximately 5 p.m. on 6 February 2004, Sean, who was acting in cahoots with two other youths, had broken into a house in Terenure. Having smashed his way in through a window, he had stolen five gold chains and a diamond ring. A half an hour later, Sean had broken into another house nearby, and stolen a Playstation console, as well as ten Playstation games, coins to the value of €100, a pair of trousers and a jumper. At 6 p.m. that day, reports having been received of another burglary on Melvin Road, in nearby Harold's Cross, Sean and two accomplices were arrested. Initially, Sean gave a false name to the gardaí but subsequent enquiries revealed his true identity.

The diamond ring, taken in the first burglary, was the only item of stolen property, and also the most valuable one, not to be recovered. Sean's father had been contacted to come to the garda station, which he did; however, he refused to sit in on the interview with his son. A peace commissioner was brought to the station and was present for the interview in which Sean admitted the burglaries.

Judge Ní Chonduin ordered the preparation of a probation report prior to sentencing Sean and adjourned the case to 19 October when he was sentenced to two years' detention. It was his fiftieth conviction.

Meanwhile, his younger brother's placement in the special detention school in Clonmel had broken down completely after he repeatedly absconded.

On 15 November 2004, 13-year-old Peter was back at the Dublin Children's Court for theft and criminal damage charges. He ended up getting a further conviction for contempt of court for a series of profane outbursts in which he swore at the judge and threatened to break a garda's nose during the proceedings.

The small boy had told Judge Angela Ní Chonduin to f**k off seconds after he had approached a garda in the Children's Court and told him he would attack him. Just minutes previously, his father had been ordered out of the heated proceedings in the courtroom for encouraging his son's abusive behaviour.

Peter had been before the Children's Court for another *doli incapax* hearing to determine whether he was criminally responsible, given his young age.

He had been charged with four offences, including theft and criminal damage, but gardaí explained that they would be unable to proceed with the prosecution of two of the cases due to the future unavailability of witnesses. Judge Ní Chonduin struck the charges out accordingly, and, in relation to another charge involving Peter, she was told that a material witness was unavailable. She adjourned that hearing until early February when the witness would be present.

At that point, the boy's father stood up, waving a rolled-up newspaper, and said that the witness, a garda, was supposed to be present and that the case should not proceed against his son. 'The guard is supposed to be in court—they have been given plenty of notice,' he said.

Having warned the man about his repeated interruptions, Judge Ní Chonduin ordered him out of the courtroom, saying that his conduct was encouraging his son to act likewise. After the father had been escorted from the court, the judge proceeded to adjourn the case. Peter then screamed abuse in the courtroom and approached one of the gardaí shouting, 'I'll break his f*****g nose.'

The judge sternly warned him to stop his outbursts and aggressive behaviour immediately, at which he told her to 'f**k herself'.

When she then said that she was detaining him for seven days for contempt of court, he responded angrily, 'Give me f*****g seven days.'

The judge warned him that he was at risk of having that period in custody doubled if he did not change his attitude. But Peter carried on using foul language and shouted at her to do 'what the f**k' she wanted.

She immediately imposed two weeks' detention in the Trinity House Detention Centre for contempt and he was taken from the courtroom while his father waited outside.

On 1 June 2005, aged 14, Peter was given a concurrent one-month detention term after he pleaded guilty to charges of assault and criminal damage. The court heard that he had criminally damaged a car that was parked at the Square Shopping Centre in Tallaght on 10 January 2005 and, nine days later, had attacked a security guard at the same shopping centre.

The boy's solicitor said that her client had 'an appalling litany of convictions' but that anger management had been identified as one of his key problems and this was being addressed at the detention centre.

Judge Ní Chonduin ordered a one-month term in Oberstown Boys' Centre, not pro-longing his time in custody, so the court order would not interfere with the educational and welfare programmes already in place for him. She also said that previously in court the teenager had been aggressive but this had been the result of his father's presence. At this case, the teenager's father was not present as he was serving a prison sentence of his own.

More cases involving his older brother, Sean, were still coming through the system. On 25 January 2005, Sean was back in court again to plead guilty to two remaining charges for a burglary at an elderly woman's home in Ballinteer, as well as another charge of trespassing at the home of an elderly man, also in the same area. Both offences had taken place on 9 August 2004 and no property had been taken. The woman had been in her home, when the teenager had forced entry by smashing a rear window with a rock.

Judge Cormac Dunne was told how Sean had been detained the previous October in Trinity House. Having read a probation report, Judge Dunne ordered a further two-year detention term, prolonging Sean's time in custody by three months.

The father, now out of jail, was sitting in court and pleaded with the judge to backdate the sentence, saying that he wanted to move out of Dublin and return to the west of Ireland, where he and his family had previously lived.

'If you read the report you would have another approach. What is happening is a good thing; I am guided by the report,' Judge Dunne told the father.

Sean had remained silent during most of the hearing. However, at one point, he had been slumped forward on the defendant's bench and had been warned that his manner was disrespectful to the court. Judge Dunne told him that the courtroom was 'not a dormitory' to which Sean replied sarcastically: 'I thought it was; I'm a bit tired.' Judge Dunne closed the case, ordering that the teenager should stay in Trinity House on a two-year term commencing from that day.

Later that year, however, Sean managed to escape custody. He had been brought from the detention centre for a day trip but managed to slip out of the car he had been travelling in. He remained at large for a number of weeks with gardaí believing he was sheltered by his extended family.

During his time at large, he managed to get involved in an opportunistic theft at a shop in the Square Shopping Centre in Tallaght, which yielded him €3,500. Because of the seriousness of the offence, the case was heard at the Dublin Circuit Criminal Court where, in March 2006, he was given another two-year detention order, bringing his number of criminal convictions to fifty-three. He also received twenty months from the Children's Court in August 2006, for a vicious mugging in which he and a teenage gang, who had been roaming wild like a pack of wolves, had threatened to stab a terrified man with a syringe as they pinned him against the railings of the Liffey Boardwalk in Dublin City Centre.

Together the brothers represented a massive failing by the state to intervene for their welfare. They had reached their mid-teens barely literate yet they had become fearless and skilful criminals who gardaí were convinced had been working at the behest and under the direction of someone else.

Sean was regarded as volatile and with a massive propensity to commit crime. The younger boy, Peter, had been the subject of a special garda task force where a team of investigators had been set up specifically to monitor him. Before the pair and their family had moved to Dublin, they had been the subject of a similar garda operation, in the west of Ireland. That probe had reached the same conclusion: they were behind the bulk of burglaries wherever they were at any particular time.

Despite their educational limitations, they had an acute understanding of how the courts worked and how to act when questioned by gardaí. Although they were barely able to read or write, they could accurately estimate, off the top of their heads, the black market price of stolen goods such as laptop computers, digital cameras, camcorders, and—with particular expertise—gold and jewellery.

Gardaí also believed that when they were aged around 12 and 11 respectively and living in the west of the country, they had employed an ingenious technique to aid them as they burgled houses and then mysteriously disappeared into the night: they used the sewers.

Under the tutelage of a Fagin-like figure, they had been guided in their venture into the world of criminality, and their father, for all his vocal participation in his sons' court cases, never once explained how his two young children had become so heavily immersed in crime or for whom they had been working.

In the course of their dealings with the two boys, the attention of gardaí soon turned to a third member of the family, the youngest, Brian, a then seven-year-old boy who was often heard boasting that he was the best burglar of them all. Tiny fingerprints that were found in houses which had been ransacked by Sean and Peter were strongly believed to belong to him.

On 15 March 2006, following his arrest in connection with a mugging, Brian appeared in the Children's Court, making him the youngest child to face a criminal prosecution in Ireland in a generation. The boy, who sported a shaved haircut, was dressed in jeans, a hooded top and runners, which were fastened by velcro strips, not laces. He cut a bizarre figure. Other young tracksuit-clad suspects towered over him as he hung around the courthouse, looking bewildered. In the courtroom itself, he was barely visible as he sat on the defendant's bench and remained silent throughout the proceedings during which Judge William Early said that intervention from the Health Service Executive was urgently needed. Brian, who was four foot tall, was charged with theft of a mobile phone and an MP3 player from two teenage boys, at the bus terminus at Belgard Square, in Tallaght, on 29 January 2006.

His arrest in the area where the alleged offence took place, which was several miles from his home, happened at 11.40 p.m., nearly three weeks later. The young boy was then taken to Tallaght Garda Station where he was charged, after which he made no reply.

Brian, who lived at a halting site with his family, was accompanied to court by his father, now a familiar face with most of the judges who presided in the Children's Court. On enquiring as to the child's age, Judge Early was told that the tiny boy sitting on the defendant's bench, with his legs swinging and not touching the floor, was nine years old. However, the youngster's father was 'unclear as to his son's exact date of birth'.

The judge continued, 'In principle, it is undesirable that a nine-year-old child should be before the criminal courts. If the child is so unruly and at risk, there seems there is a serious risk to his welfare, health and safety, section 16 of the Childcare Act 1991 requires that the Health Service Executive (HSE) intervene.'

He remanded Brian on bail to appear again in April, pending the DPP's directions. He then looked up from the bench and, directing himself at the boy's father, said: 'There is a heavy obligation on you to take care of your son.'

Ever ready with an answer, the father put the blame on another boy, telling the judge: 'He told this woman [the garda] that it was a 15-year-old who did it and not him. They should not be questioning a child of nine and banging him up in a cell.' The father then left with his child in tow. The boy pulled up his hood and smiled as he exited the courtroom.

On 5 April, the boy walked free from court after the robbery charge against him was withdrawn on the orders of the DPP. The victims had withdrawn their statements against him.

Brian remained silent during the case and, after the charge was withdrawn, sighed with relief and left the courthouse looking reassured. Before court started that morning, he had stood outside the building, smoking a cigarette. During the brief hearing, the court was told the boy was aged nine, at which Judge Patrick Clyne said in disbelief: 'He only looks about five.'

The victims, gardaí suspected, had withdrawn their complaints out of fear. The nine-year-old ran with a gang of violent teenagers who had been causing havoc in Tallaght. And he was regarded as the ringleader of the group. At the time, gardaí strongly suspected that he had been involved in six other similarly styled robberies in Tallaght, with victims mostly male and ranging in age from 15 to 20.

III. CRIMES

12 | CAR-CRIME ADDICTS

On 13 March 2003, a prolific and seemingly addictive car thief appeared in the Children's Court. He was 15 years old but the offences for which he had been arrested had happened when he was just 14. Functionally illiterate and out of school since he had turned 13 years old, he was one of west Dublin's most feared car-crime addicts. The court heard how a garda patrol car was written off when it was rammed head-on by him, after he performed a handbrake turn and drove straight at it. The Ballyfermot teenager had pleaded guilty to a litany of dangerous driving and criminal charges arising out of the incident. He had also admitted taking the car which was involved in the smash.

The teenager, from west Dublin, had used the stolen car like a battering ram and had written off both it and the garda car. The teenager walked away from the crash and luckily nobody else suffered any injuries. However, he was also facing a further, separate charge for criminally damaging a garda car and other offences. The case was put back so that all the charges could be dealt with together and the boy was released on strict bail terms which included a curfew keeping him at home from 8 p.m. to 9 a.m. every day.

Six days later, he was brought back to court for breaking the bail conditions. Bail was revoked and the boy was sent to the Trinity House Detention Centre to await sentence.

At the sentence hearing on 3 April 2003, a detailed account of the teenager's almost lethal driving was given. The boy, who was drunk, had attacked the car's owner outside his home prior to stealing his car. A squad car, which was alerted by the command and control desk at Ronanstown Garda Station, had taken up pursuit with sirens screaming and blue lights flashing, but the boy had responded by steering the stolen car onto a footpath where he collided with the garda car, hitting its front wing. He had then driven along a footpath where pedestrians had run desperately for cover.

The boy had then led the gardaí on a two-and-a-half-mile chase, reaching 50 miles per hour in residential areas. Twice the car had shot into the air having sped over the top of two humpback bridges. After the second bridge, the boy had lost control of the car and nearly collided with a row of trucks parked on the side of the road. On the Kylemore Road, a terrified cyclist had been forced to jump over a side wall to get out of the way. The stolen car had mounted a footpath in an area where many pedestrians were walking and had then dangerously swerved back onto the road in the path of other oncoming cars whose drivers had been forced to take sudden evasive action to avoid being hit. Finally, the boy had performed a 360-degree handbrake turn and driven straight at the garda car, which he had rammed head on. The boy had committed twenty-six offences from September 2002 until March 2003, and many while on bail.

In passing sentence, Judge Early described the evidence as 'quite shocking,' and also said: 'He put the lives of the gardaí and others at risk and is lucky not to be facing more serious charges.' He sentenced the boy, who had one previous conviction for travelling as a passenger in a stolen car, to twenty-one months in the Trinity House Detention Centre and banned him from driving for five years.

Two years later, the then 17-year-old was back in court for similar offences. In one of the incidents, which happened at night-time, he gunned the engine of a stolen car, turned off its headlights and stealthily drove at speed, directly at a patrol car. The unemployed teenager, who was now three years out of school and had been an alcoholic since he was 13, had pleaded guilty to a litany of charges, twenty-two in total, for car theft, dangerous driving, driving without a licence or insurance, failing to stop for a garda and public order offences where he was drunk and disorderly and in breach of the peace. All of the offences had taken place in the Ballyfermot area where he had attained notoriety among gardaí and respect from his peer group for his outrageous joyriding stunts.

The youth now had nine previous convictions on his criminal record, mostly for car thefts, and had been detained by the court in Trinity House detention centre where he had managed to complete the Junior Certificate.

The judge said that the slang term 'joyriding', which is often ascribed to such incidents, was a misnomer and added that conduct such as that of the youth on trial was nothing more than the 'driving of a lethal weapon, a potential killing machine.'

As he proceeded to detain the teenager, he told him: 'You will not realise it today but you should be grateful to the gardaí for stopping you on your tracks, from perhaps destroying your own life.'

The teenager, who was supported in court by his parents, received consecutive sentences totalling two years, and fines which came to €4,250, and he was banned from driving for twenty years. On foot of an appeal at the severity of his sentence, he was released temporarily from custody and became active in Ballyfermot again. On 5 August 2005, he was caught driving without insurance and a licence after gardaí received reports of a vehicle being driven recklessly. On 10 September 2005, he was caught breaking into a car and was charged with criminal damage.

He was also arrested for a brutal attack on a pensioner, in which it was alleged he brought a younger boy with him and terrorised an elderly couple with physical violence and threats to shoot them if they did not hand over their car keys.[1] When gardaí arrived at the scene, they found the teenager holding the elderly man in a headlock. Because of the severity of the case, trial in Dublin Circuit Criminal Court was ordered.

The youth was returned to custody; the appeal he had launched had some success and shortened his earlier term slightly and significantly reduced the fines on the basis that, given his circumstances and background, it would have been impossible for him to pay them.

On 13 March 2006, just turned 18 and now an adult, his last charges from the Children's Court were finalised. At this juncture in his life, the youth had spent the majority of his teenage years in juvenile detention centres and was described by his counsel as 'institutionalised'.

He was convicted for motoring-related offences, which had occurred when he was a juvenile, and was sentenced to a total of four months in St Patrick's Institution, which the judge directed, were to begin once his existing detention term ended, in January 2007.

In mitigation, the judge heard that the youth had left the education system when he was in sixth class, had gone back briefly for his confirmation but had no education beyond that until detained later. The youth's parents separated and for a time he had a difficult relationship with his father. According to the boy's defence, he was 'fascinated by cars, the theft and misuse of them'.

A two-year road ban was imposed on the youth who now had thirty-five previous convictions on his criminal record which was dominated by dangerous driving, car theft and assault offences.

It was the end of the road for him in the Children's Court but on the exact same day, his younger brother embarked on his journey through the juvenile justice system. The 13-year-old was remanded on bail pending a fitness-to-plea hearing, given his young age. His charge: dangerously driving a stolen car.

Judging by the cases that come through the juvenile justice system, 'joyriding' can be as much of an addiction as alcohol or drugs. Offenders who get arrested for car crimes go to great lengths to achieve their aims. Possession of everyday items such as hammers, screwdrivers or jemmies takes on an illegal quality and can lead to prosecutions for possession of implements for use in connection with motor thefts. And many go beyond using tools that can be bought over the counter in any hardware shop. The 'barrel popper' is one such example. Not satisfied with bringing a heavy bag of tools with them to help them break into vehicles, car thieves have invented their own crudely improvised device. The barrel popper is like a cross between a hammer, a crow bar and a screwdriver; it's all three in one handy tool. One end has a hammer head, with claws, used for leverage. This is attached, often welded, to a metal bar that extends about one foot in length. A sharp screw is fixed to the other end. The barrel popper gets rammed into the door lock of a car, screw-end first. The hammer head is then twisted. When enough force is used, the lock is wrecked, and the car door pops open. It can then be used to strip away the car's cowling and to hot-wire the car.

Some youths discovered that in older vehicles an ordinary car key that has been filed in a certain manner can work as well as one that was designed for the vehicle.

One of the most unusual tools, and the hardest to detect on a person, is ceramic. One teenager was arrested and brought to court after a garda spotted him acting suspiciously beside a number of cars. The 14-year-old boy had been spotted discarding a tiny white object which was recovered. When he was brought before the Children's Court in October 2003, the judge was told that a certain type of ceramic had diamond-like cutting properties, and was used by thieves in Dublin as a tool with which to break into cars. It was, said the prosecuting garda, 'unbelievably effective' when thrown against glass which shattered instantly on contact. It was easily concealed and many thieves hid the ceramics in their mouths to avoid suspicion. A small fingernail-sized piece of ceramic which the boy was spotted throwing away was handed into court as an exhibit, and a ballistic report outlining its capabilities as an implement for breaking into cars was also presented.

Fearless of danger, young joyriders frequently entice gardaí into chasing them, which creates an even bigger thrill. This is accomplished by audacious motoring stunts performed in the hope that the attention of a garda patrol car will be drawn. Often, when that does not work, a more direct approach is employed to spark off a chase. The driver of the stolen car goes in search of gardaí. Sometimes he might speed past a garda vehicle and 'clip' it by driving so close that both vehicles' wing mirrors make contact for a split second.

Another intriguing phenomenon is what is colloquially referred to as the 'company car'. These bangers, frequently death traps and not roadworthy, are old cars that have been bought and sold so many times that it is years since they have had a registered owner. Youngsters pool their money to buy them, often for as little as €80 and mostly from members of the travelling community. Then they drive them into the ground and, if they become bored, they simply abandon them.

CHILDREN'S COURT

The 15-year-old boy had been in the care of the health board after his family had 'washed their hands of him', the court heard. He was facing a total of twenty-two charges: nineteen for criminally damaging car tyres, which caused damages to the tune of €2,000, and three for burglaries. The batch of tyre-slashing incidents took place on 19 August 2002 in the same residential estate in Baldoyle, in Dublin. The burglaries happened around the same time in Dublin's Baldoyle, Sutton and Seafield suburbs. During the burglaries, the boy stole an expensive digital camera, car keys and a mobile phone. According to a health board care worker, the boy had been making good progress at a residential care home and was taking part in training courses. However, his drinking and staying out late had caused some concern for staff in the home.

Judge Connellan said that the care workers were doing their best with the boy and he was released on bail under strict terms whereby he was compelled to reside at the care home and to obey an 8 p.m. to 8 a.m. curfew.

On 4 July 2003, the 15-year-old pleaded guilty. When arrested, he had made a statement admitting his responsibility for the slashed tyres and had also come clean about the burglaries.

The court was told that the boy had suffered an 'incredibly difficult childhood'. However, the judge referred to him as 'a serial offender' and sentenced him to be detained for two years.

However, as frequently occurs in juvenile cases, the defendant was released early. From April 2004 until December that year, he would be charged sixty-five times, mostly for burglaries linked to car theft. With a penchant for bigger cars, he targeted prosperous areas of north Dublin and became an expert car thief. Faced with the challenge of vehicles with hi-tech security systems, he simply bypassed the problem by breaking into the owners' houses and stealing the car keys and alarm remotes.

He became something of a gentleman thief. Gardaí suspected that he went to the extent of intelligence gathering in these areas and employed slick techniques to learn which houses had the better cars. This he achieved by charming the local teenage girls and befriending them. Many of the girls were taken in by him and unwittingly provided him with the information he needed.

In one incident, he arrived at a house to find a high-powered car in the driveway. He was faced with two problems. He would have to steal the car keys from the house. While there, he would also have to find the keys for a smaller second car which was blocking the flashier one in the driveway. Having succeeded in finding both sets of keys in the house, he then sneaked out and reversed the smaller car out of the driveway onto the road fronting the house. With that obstacle out of his way, he then ran back to the car he wanted, disabled its alarm with the remote attached to the set of keys, jumped in and drove out of the drive. But he stopped just yards away from the front gates of the house. Cheekily he got out, went back to the smaller car, started the engine and kindly parked it back in the driveway of the house, before driving away in the high-powered car.

It was believed that he frequently and gladly stole cars to order. Criminals in need of high-powered vehicles would commission him to get what they needed. His payment was often as little as a few cans of beer or a carton of cigarettes.

After his release from Trinity House, the teenager went into a care home where initially he progressed very well. However, the placement soon broke down and he returned home to live with his mother.

On 18 May 2004, he was arrested for driving a stolen car on the Phibsboro Road. On 24 May 2004, he went to the Marine Hotel in

Sutton, Dublin, and stole a set of car keys from a coat. He walked to the car park and found the car to match the set of keys in his hand, and, once behind the steering wheel, he drove away unhindered. The car was recovered nearby undamaged. On 4 July 2004, he was driving a stolen BMW at speed, in the Sutton area. A garda patrol car gave chase, at which the teenager stopped the car and fled to a nearby housing estate.

After his hearing in the Children's Court on these charges, in September 2004, he was remanded on bail, pending sentence. 'If you blow this chance, you are facing custody,' the judge told him. Three months later, he was involved in another car theft and burglary. Because of the seriousness of the case it was decided that he should be dealt with in the Dublin Circuit Criminal Court instead.

In this escapade, he stole a high-powered 02 registration Mercedes in Sutton and proceeded to race it through Dublin city centre, reaching speeds of 80 mph. He broke red lights and stop signs, and drove on the wrong side of the road, forcing other road users to swerve out of his way.

When the teenager was arrested, he admitted having taken the car keys from the house in Sutton while the owners slept, blissfully unaware of what was going on. At this time there were two outstanding bench warrants issued for the boy in connection with missed court appearances. In fact, the boy has been charged sixty-five times since April that year. However, he said that if bailed he would not re-offend, and his mother assured the court that she would not let him commit offences.

On 4 February 2005, he received a one-year sentence for the earlier car thefts. In the meantime, gardaí had been working on other cases against him and, two months later, the boy, who at this point was 17 years old, was charged with thirty-one offences for a spate of house break-ins and connected car thefts in north Dublin over a four-month period in 2004.

Judge Angela Ní Chonduin refused jurisdiction to hear the case in the Children's Court and the teenager was remanded in custody to St Patrick's Institution until November 2005, when, at the Dublin Circuit Criminal Court, he received a seven-year sentence, with nearly half of the term suspended.

13 | IN THE LINE OF DUTY

The issue of young offenders hurtled to the forefront of national debate when a 16-year-old Dublin joyrider smashed a stolen sports car into two gardaí on the Stillorgan dual carriageway at 6.30 a.m. on 14 April 2002. Garda Michael Padden and Garda Anthony Tighe became the fortieth and forty-first members of the force to die in the line of duty. Driving the stolen car, a high-powered Mazda MX5, was a 16-year-old boy. That peaceful morning, Shane had become involved in a crime spree. He and a 15-year-old accomplice took part in a burglary in Dalkey and stole the keys of the black Mazda. They hit speeds of up to 130 mph as seven garda cars chased them through the Dalkey, Ballsbridge and Donnybrook areas of Dublin. They sped on, breaking red lights, with one witness claiming they raced past her car as if she were stationary, before they smashed into the garda car.

Witnesses claimed that there was no sound of any brakes and no skid marks were left in the road. The force of the impact propelled the garda Ford Mondeo car about nine feet off the ground and into a somersault through the air—at 40 mph—before it came to a stop on a grassy mound. Gardaí Tighe and Padden were killed instantly.

Garda Anthony Tighe, a 53-year-old father of four from Dublin, was behind the wheel of the patrol car as the gardaí attempted to divert traffic out of the way of the stolen sports car.

His colleague, Garda Michael Padden, was a 27-year-old single man from Belmullet in Co. Mayo who had joined the Garda Síochána in 1998. Both were stationed at Donnybrook Garda Station and had been on high alert following a series of robberies in the area earlier in the morning. Garda Tighe had joined the force in 1970 and for all of his career had been stationed in Donnybrook.

Shane broke his knees and stayed in hospital for two weeks. He would have to use a wheelchair for a while afterwards but otherwise he made a full recovery. The second boy in the sports car suffered a broken ankle and wrist injuries.

What horrified the public was not just that the driver was a child, but that he had a litany of convictions and had been released by the Children's Court about six weeks previously. Some editorial and leader writers penned vitriolic pieces about how the juvenile justice system had been dealing with repeat young offenders while others more soberly called for more attention to be given to the issue.

On 22 February 2002, just over seven weeks before the crash, Shane had been convicted of driving a stolen car without insurance, skipping court and a criminal damage offence for which he was also released by the Dublin Children's Court on a probation bond for one year. On 16 October 2001, he had also been released on a probation bond for one year for travelling in a stolen car. On 1 June 2001, he had been sentenced to two years in Oberstown Boys' Centre for a larceny offence, a sentence that was obviously not served in full. On 29 May 2001, he had been released on a probation bond for causing criminal damage and for breach of the peace. On 9 March 2001, he had been put on a probation bond for stealing a car. On 12 December 2000, he had been bound to the peace for a year for skipping court and larceny offences. Five days previously, he had been released on a probation bond for joyriding. On 30 November 2000, he had been released on a probation bond for two years for larceny, joyriding, driving without insurance or a licence, criminal damage and for failing to stop at the scene of an accident. On his first conviction earlier that same year, for interfering with the mechanism of a car, the court heard that he had been released on a probation bond for two years.

After a period recovering in hospital, Shane was charged with dangerous driving causing death and was remanded in custody to face Dublin Circuit Criminal Court in due course. In the meantime, a number of charges for other offences would be dealt with. On 16 December 2002, now aged 17, he was given probation for his part in a drunken prank during which he had sprayed fire extinguisher foam over a petrol-station forecourt. The boy's parents had paid €50 compensation to the petrol station's manager, on their son's behalf. He had been charged under Section 4 and 6 of the Public Order Act, for being intoxicated to such an extent that he was a danger to himself and others and for engaging in threatening, abusive and insulting behaviour, which he admitted.

In mitigation, his solicitor said that the incident was a drink-related prank that had got out of hand and Shane accepted that what he had done was wrong. The court heard that he had been held in Cloverhill Prison for some months and it was imagined that he would face a very 'lengthy sentence' arising from a separate Circuit Court case. Shane was given the benefit of the probation act, which meant that a criminal conviction did not result.

On 31 March 2003, the Children's Court heard that sixteen days before the crash Shane had been involved in a vicious attack on a garda during an arrest and had then tried to incite a riot by calling on youths to help him escape. In the middle of a crowded flat complex, the garda had been subjected to punches in the stomach and a headlock by the youth before other teenagers had joined in and attacked him, the court heard.

At this hearing, the teenager had pleaded not guilty to assaulting the garda 'causing harm'. He said that he had put up a struggle and got away. He said that he did not know who the other teenagers were, but admitted to having seen someone throwing a bicycle. A teenage friend gave evidence that he had seen the scuffle but denied having seen the headlock, the punches to the garda, the body check, the attempts to take the baton or the bicycle being thrown.

Judge Geoffrey Browne rejected a defence submission that the youth had not been cautioned before the arrest and was therefore using legal force to defend himself. He was satisfied from the evidence that there was a case to answer, and he convicted Shane. This conviction brought the number of Shane's convictions to thirty-seven, with Judge Browne detaining the teenager for six months.

Just over eight weeks later, on 28 May 2003, another case was to be dealt with, and again it related to an earlier offence. Judge Bryan Smyth was told at the Children's Court that the teenager had admitted and was sorry for attacking a man at New Street Junction in Dublin on 11 November 2001—just over five months before the crash. In an unprovoked attack, the man, who had had no communication with the accused before he was assaulted, was beaten in the face and some of his teeth were damaged from the blows. The court heard that the boy was 'extremely drunk at the time and had little recollection of the incident', but was sorry for what he did. Shane was then given a one-year detention sentence, bringing his number of convictions up again.

Two weeks later, on 11 June 2003, other charges for one of his pre-crash crimes were finalised at the Children's Court. Judge Gerard Furlong was told that the teenager had admitted driving his moped without proper documentation on 28 January 2001. Judge Furlong gave him six months' detention and banned him from driving for fifteen years. The serial offender told the court that the moped was his own. He had had it for only a week at the time and was using it to travel to and from work, he claimed. On hearing details of Shane's criminal record, Judge Furlong noted that the teenager had continued to re-offend after he had been let off by the court on probation. He said that in a number of Shane's previous convictions for joyriding and road traffic offences, there had been 'an odd litany of probation acts applied at all stages'.

Nearly six months later, on 3 December 2003, Shane faced the Dublin Circuit Criminal Court for sentencing over the deaths of the two gardaí. Courtroom eight in the Four Courts was packed for the hearing. Journalists filled the benches to one side of the courtroom. Family and close friends of the two gardaí sat in the rows behind the lawyers. At the back of the courtroom, a number of tracksuit-clad youths, many of them familiar faces at the Children's Court, came to support and to see what would happen to their friend. The emotionally charged setting saw many experienced gardaí reduced to tears as the details of the deaths of their fallen comrades were outlined to the court.

Shane pleaded guilty to reckless endangerment and dangerous driving causing the deaths of Garda Michael Padden and Garda Anthony Tighe on the Stillorgan Road on 14 April 2002. He now had forty-two previous convictions, eleven for road traffic offences.

Having listened to the evidence, Judge Desmond Hogan said:

The driving was deliberately criminal and it was an odyssey of endangerment to the public as well as to other drivers on the road and which regrettably culminated in the deaths of two fine people who were doing their duty and doing it in a way that included the safety of other people. This was nothing but an act of bravado that had terrible and far-reaching consequences. One of the gardaí was a young man cut off in the prime of his life and the other was a married man with children. Both of those families, and extended families, will have to live with the consequences of this for the rest of their lives.

Irene Tighe, the wife of Garda Tighe, broke down and tearfully told the court, 'My life and the lives of my children have been left ruined. I can't describe the loneliness without him. He was a great father, husband and the lives of everyone who came in contact with him has been ruined.'

Garda Padden's first cousin, Justine Reilly, told the court:

No words can describe what Michael's family have been through. He was a lovely person, the most courteous, the best of fun and only 27 at the time. He had a beautiful life ahead of him and a huge part of our lives have [has] been wiped away.

Every family celebration will now be tinged with sadness because he'll be the one we think of.

Detective Inspector Martin Cummins said that Garda Padden's long-term girlfriend, Lisa Mills, had returned to her home country, Canada, because her life was destroyed.

There was little Shane's counsel could say on behalf of his client, but he told the court that Shane had written a letter to the court and could only show his remorse and say he was sorry.

The judge concluded that the list of aggravating factors far outweighed the mitigating and said that it would come as no surprise to anyone to hear that a custodial sentence had to be imposed. Shane, now aged 18, was detained for eight years and also disqualified from driving for thirty.

Over a thousand mourners, including gardaí from all over the country, gathered in Mount Argus Church, Harold's Cross, for the funeral service of Garda Tighe. On the previous evening as the cortege carrying Garda Tighe's remains journeyed from St Vincent's Hospital through Donnybrook to the church, hundreds of people had stopped their cars or paused on the pavement in tribute.

Greeting the mourners in the packed church for the funeral service the next day, Garda Chaplain Fr Joe Kennedy said that the garda flag and tricolour which hung limp in the rain outside the church reflected the mood of all of those present. He extended his thanks on behalf of Garda Tighe's wife, Irene, and family to all in the congregation and said that the massive numbers present were a reflection of the esteem in which Tony and the garda force were held. Fr Kennedy gave praise to the father of four whom he described as a wonderful family man and a most kind and thoughtful neighbour. The priest recalled how Anthony Tighe was known by his neighbours in Belgard Road as 'Mr Fix-It' because he was so talented with his hands. 'How sad and tragic it was that he lost his life in such a fashion protecting the lives of others,' he said.[1] He said that both Garda Tighe and his colleague, Garda Padden, for whom prayers were offered, had been 'guardians of the peace who gave their lives for us'.

Fr Kennedy also recounted how he had gone to the scene of the awful crash and been especially struck by a message written on one of the many bouquets of flowers placed there. It said: 'With heartfelt sorrow and grateful thanks to two brave men who gave their lives for us.'

Tony gave thirty-two years of loyal and dedicated service at Donnybrook. We think of the many ways in which he protected the lives and homes of our citizens in this country. How sad and tragic it was that in the quiet hours, early on Sunday morning when the rest of us were asleep, he went to try and help other road-users from danger. How sad and tragic it was that he should have lost his life in such a fashion, protecting the lives of others. Tony was a family man with family values, a devoted husband, father and son, with Christian values who carried those values with him in his work and his job.

The chief mourners at the service were Garda Tighe's wife of twenty-four years, Irene, his children, Anthony, Colum, Paul and Fiona, his mother, Patricia, his brother and his sister.

President Mary McAleese attended the funeral and was accompanied by her husband Martin, Dublin's Lord Mayor Michael Mulcahy and the Minister for Justice, John O'Donoghue.

Mount Argus Church was filled row after row with gardaí who came to bid farewell to their fallen colleague. Garda Lorna Garland, who had worked with Tony at Donnybrook station, painted a vivid picture of the man who had been a father figure to so many young cadets during his career. 'He was the best friend I ever had,' she said.[2] Addressing Garda Tighe's wife and four children, Garda Garland said that Tony was 'so proud of you all' and spoke of them regularly to colleagues. 'Everyone who ever came in contact with him immediately knew how kind, generous and compassionate he was. I only hope Tony knew what we thought of him,' Garda Garland ended as a spontaneous applause erupted in the church. Garda Tighe's son Anthony read a poem which ended: 'Miss me but let me go,' before Fiona, his only daughter, spoke in his praise. Outside the church, rain poured down on Tony's colleagues who stood in a guard of honour as the tricolour-draped coffin was carried from the church. At Newlands Cemetery, the Garda Band played a final tribute as Irene and Fiona each cast a single rose onto the lowered casket.

Following Garda Tighe's funeral service, many left immediately to make the sad journey to Belmullet, Co. Mayo. A traditional wake was held that night. Garda Padden's remains were removed from his aunt's home near Belmullet, to Shanaghy Church on the Mullet peninsula. The parish priest of Kilmore Erris, Fr Kevin Hegarty received the remains at the Church of Our Lady of Dolours and led prayers for the popular young man who had grown up in the area. Garda Padden's mother, Marian, sat in the tiny 200-capacity chapel that was packed and unable to hold all of the massive number of mourners that had turned up. Many waited outside as the curate, Fr Michael Nallen, recalled Michael Padden as courteous and friendly. Although he had bought a house in Dublin, Michael hoped eventually to get a transfer within the Garda Síochána and move back to his native west of Ireland, the curate told the mourners.

The funeral mass took place at noon the following day. Mourners spilled out of the overflowing church and extra chairs were brought to the grounds allowing elderly mourners to listen to the ceremony through speakers outside. The Bishop of Killala, Dr John Fleming, presided while Fr Hegarty was the main celebrant. Among the mourners were the Minister for Justice, John O'Donoghue; the Deputy Garda Commissioner Noel Conroy; Chief Superintendent John Carey, head of the Mayo Garda Division; Judge Mary Devins of the district court and senior gardaí from all divisions around the state. Both the President and the Taoiseach were represented by their aides-de-camps.

Also present were Garda Padden's girlfriend Lisa Mills, and Garda Colm Tighe, son of the Garda Anthony Tighe. Fr Hegarty said that since that Sunday, a thick cloud of gloom had settled over the community where Michael Padden had spent most of his young life. 'He grew up in the shelter of Shanaghy, along our quiet roads he walked. In our small fields, he worked. Here he sported and played. By his granny and grandaunt's fireside he learned the religious values and civic responsibility that inspired his life. And so he became the man of whom we are proud, whom we loved and who loved us.'[3] He described him, as would all who knew him, as gentle, respectful, humorous and courteous. How he lost his life compelled us 'to look at the kind of society we are creating', Fr Hegarty said. 'We needed to ask ourselves if we have magnified social and economic growth at the expense of social cohesion. Unless we ask this deep, soul-searching question, Michael and Tony will have died in vain.'

Hundreds of gardaí from all over the nation marched in solemn and respectful silence behind the hearse for a time before boarding buses to finish the journey to the cemetery. The people filed in behind and filled the ground, row on row. As the funeral ended at Emlybeg Cemetery, the '*Last Post*' and '*Reveille*' were sounded by garda bandsmen. The Tricolour, which had been draping Garda Padden's coffin, was presented, along with his garda cap, to his aunt, Angela Padden.

In the aftermath, the younger boy who had been in the stolen car would also face court appearances for other offences which pre-dated the crash that killed the two gardaí. A few weeks before the tragedy, he had been sentenced to two years' detention in Trinity House but a place was not available for him there and he was released.

In the months that followed, cases which had been pending at the time of the crash were dealt with. On Friday, 14 June 2002, the Dublin Children's Court heard that the boy had been charged with public order violations and threatening and abusive behaviour to a garda on 10 April—just a few days before the crash. During the incident in south inner-city Dublin he had been cautioned twice for being in breach of the peace. He had turned more aggressive and abusive and was arrested.

Judge Sean McBride said that the boy needed a structured programme in a secure place of detention where he should get counselling. He would be 'a rudderless ship' if he were allowed home, the judge said. A social worker agreed. The boy's parents were recovering drug addicts and the boy had been in the care of the health board from a young age. Judge McBride said that the boy had an 'appalling' family background, needed psychological help and education and that he would be doing the boy a favour by detaining him. He also added that it was a great pity the boy had not got early intervention in his life. 'He would be a source of danger to himself and others if he is let out,' he said as he concluded this case.

Another charge relating to earlier offences was dealt with on 2 July, leading to another two-year detention order. The boy had pleaded guilty to two charges of larceny and assault. He had not co-operated with the Probation and Welfare Services as ordered when given bail earlier. The court was told that the boy had educational problems, suffered from dyslexia and had been abusing drugs. His social workers had also indicated that there was no option other than to send the boy into a place of detention. Details of earlier attempts to detain him with a view to helping him were outlined: before the crash, the boy had been remanded in custody to St Michael's Institution for a psychological and educational assessment to be carried out, but he had absconded soon afterwards. His mother did not want him home because she could not handle him and was afraid he would represent too much of a danger to others and to himself. Probation and Welfare Service reports also said that social workers had made every effort possible to engage the boy but he was not interested in their help.

In passing sentence, Judge McBride recommended that the boy should benefit from the help of a child psychologist, an educational psychologist for his dyslexia, an education programme and training, and drug and substance-abuse counselling. The boy did not show any emotion or speak during either of these sentence hearings.

On 31 January 2003, he became the first to be dealt with by the courts over the crash. Now aged 16, he came before the Dublin Circuit Criminal Court for sentencing. He pleaded guilty to three charges arising out of the incident which had started with the burglary of an apartment at Bullock Harbour, Dalkey. He admitted to having stolen from the apartment a mobile phone, a set of car keys, two sets of house keys, a cheque and a wallet containing cash and bank and credit cards. He also pleaded guilty to stealing the sports car and allowing himself to be carried in it on the same date. The resident of the apartment was asleep when the burglary took place, and became aware of it only through a telephone call from a neighbour.

The court heard that the boy had nine previous convictions. He was living with his father at the time of the crime spree but was also in the care of the South Western Area Health Board. The investigating officer agreed with the boy's counsel that he would not have been at large in the community at the time if there had been a suitable residential place available for him. The deputy director of Trinity House was quite optimistic about the youth's future 'given the correct supports are put in place'. Staff at Trinity House considered him to be one of the most easily managed detainees, and the structures and programmes there suited the youth who now liked attending school and would sit the Junior Cert the following June.

Because he had hitherto been on remand as well as serving detention sentences, he could not be granted home leave or temporary release. As a result, the detention centre had started him on a work programme with its gardener. 'He loves this and finds it very therapeutic,' the court was told. 'Though he may sometimes put on a hard exterior, he is quite soft-hearted and compassionate. He finds it difficult to express remorse but I'm in no doubt at all he is remorseful for what happened.'

The boy's social worker said that she had first come into contact with the youth in 1994. He was in residential care in the Los Angeles home in Blackrock from 1996 to 2000 and, following further assessment in 2002, it had been recommended that he again be placed as a resident in Lionsvilla Probation Hostel, Chapelizod. The place there had become available just three days before the crash. The social worker said that the boy's parents had by now stabilised their lives and also kept in contact with their son and were doing training programmes.

Judge Katherine Delahunt said that the boy had to face the consequences of his actions, which had resulted in the deaths of two serving members of the Garda Síochána who were trying to protect members of the public. She said that although he had been sentenced in March 2002 for similar offences, and would have been in a detention centre on the day of the 'joyride' had a place been available for him there, he had still engaged further in criminal activity. She said that in deciding an appropriate sentence for the youth, she had taken into consideration evidence given by his social worker, his dysfunctional family background and his early pleas of guilty.

She sentenced him to four years' detention in St Patrick's Institution, commencing on determination of the earlier two-year sentences handed down by the Children's Court in mid-2002.

The move from Trinity House to St Patrick's Institution came quicker than had been anticipated. In November 2003, the Court of Criminal Appeal granted an application by the DPP to direct the governor of St Patrick's Institution to detain him. A rehabilitation programme for the boy, devised at Trinity House, had failed. The Court of Criminal Appeal was told how when the boy was placed on an apprenticeship programme and granted home visits, he had on occasion returned to Trinity House under the influence of illegal substances. The evidence was that the boy was no longer suitable for Trinity House, and there was no evidence of any institution where he could be held other than St Patrick's.

14 | ANOTHER MOTORING OUTRAGE

Within a year of the crash that claimed the lives of Gardaí Padden and Tighe, another innocent man and a teenage boy would fall prey to a joyriding outrage. Father of one, Robert 'Bob' McGowan, a 30-year-old taxi driver from Drimnagh, died in the early hours of Saturday morning, 11 January 2003, after his car was hit by a stolen car. A teenage boy, aged 15, who had been travelling as a passenger in the stolen car, was also killed in the crash.

As the taxi driver was going about his business that morning, gardaí were frantically trying to intercept a stolen car. Sean, the driver, and his accomplices, Keith and the younger boy who was sitting in the back seat, were chased at high speed by gardaí through the north and south inner city of Dublin for almost an hour in the early hours of that morning.

The car had been stolen from a residential road in Killester by the three youths, shortly after 3 a.m., and they had headed to the city centre. When the car stopped on the East Link toll bridge, an alert operator noticed that there was no key in the car's ignition and that the steering column was broken. Suspicious at what he saw, he promptly contacted the Garda Síochána. The car was then chased by gardaí through the city before being hemmed in by three patrol cars near the Five Lamps in the North Strand area. The stolen car rammed the patrol cars before driving off at speed.

As the car sped off towards Ballybough Bridge, at times on the wrong side of the road, and with its lights off, it was going so fast that for a few seconds it became airborne. A short time later, it shot through a red light at the North Circular Road and Portland Row junction, hitting speeds close to 80 mph, just as Mr McGowan's taxi came on the scene.

The force of the impact lifted the taxi off the ground and threw it into railings at the side of the road. Emergency services arrived quickly and cut Mr McGowan from the vehicle. He was taken to Beaumont Hospital where he was later pronounced dead. The teenage back-seat passenger in the stolen car was taken to St James's Hospital where he died three days later. Sean and Keith received treatment for minor injuries.

Behind the wheel of that stolen car was a seasoned young offender, Sean, from north inner-city Dublin. Like the teenager who killed Gardaí Padden and Tighe, he had a massive criminal record with about forty-five convictions by the time of the crash.

On 7 October 1999, aged 13, Sean had been sentenced to twelve months in St Lawrence's Institution for an attempted car theft and two charges of failing to come to court. The following month, on conviction of car theft, he had been disqualified from driving for two years. On 29 December 2000, he had been sentenced to twelve months in St Lawrence's for a larceny offence and for failing to turn up for one of his court cases. On 31 July 2001, he had been given two years in Oberstown House for attempted robbery, larceny and criminal damage offences. On 6 December 2001, he had been handed down a two-year suspended sentence for five offences relating to motor thefts, attempted car theft, public order, criminal damage and larceny. On 5 May 2002, he had been given a one-month detention sentence for engaging in threatening, abusive and insulting behaviour and for one larceny charge.

The front-seat passenger, Keith, then aged 16, from Dublin 1, had about thirty convictions on his record prior to that fateful morning. His rap sheet was similar in content to Sean's. On 5 March 2001, he had been given twelve months' probation for two charges for motor thefts. On 3 June 2001, he had been bound to the peace for one year for attempted motor theft, criminal damage and larceny offences. The following month, he had again been bound to the peace for twelve months for a breach of the peace and an assault charge. A month later, he had been given a two-year probation bond for a larceny charge and, on 15 January 2002, he had been sent to Trinity House for two years for another motoring offence involving a stolen vehicle.

There were also several charges pending against the pair. On 15 October 2001, Sean and Keith had travelled from Dublin to Slane, Co. Meath, in a van. They had gone to the rear of an unoccupied house and thrown a brick through a glass sliding door. The house alarm had been activated and they had left the area but had been later arrested in Ashbourne. On 30 December 2002, just twelve days before the crash, Sean had been arrested after he was found trespassing on a private car park in Dublin city centre and failed to comply with the directions of a garda to move on.

Keith had also a charge pending from an incident on 18 April 2002, in which he had been caught travelling as a passenger in a stolen car which had been involved in a brief high-speed chase before it had crashed into two telephone boxes.

The day after the fatal drive, Sean and Keith were arrested and brought before the Children's Court. Sean was charged with the theft of the car that had been used in the crash. Keith was charged with being a passenger in the stolen car. When arrested, Sean said: 'I don't know what you are talking about.'

He had been injured in the crash and had bad bruising and a swollen face. He was denied bail but the judge ordered that he receive medical treatment while in custody in St Patrick's Institution.

In Keith's case also, bail was opposed on the grounds that a number of bench warrants were in existence for the boy's arrest for not attending court previously.

It was also believed that Keith had been in breach of a curfew previously imposed in relation to other charges. He too was remanded in custody to St Patrick's Institution. The judge warned the media to refrain from naming the pair, citing section 93 of the Children Act, which prohibits reports from identifying juveniles in the Children's Court. On the previous day, a Sunday newspaper, and that morning two newspapers had published names and photographs of the pair. The defence solicitor argued that such treatment by the media could jeopardise his clients' case.

During the fifteen-minute hearing, some extended family and acquaintances of the teenagers became upset after they looked through a port-hole window in the courtroom door to see the boys. On seeing the condition of Sean, one woman said, 'Poor young fellah.' Another was heard to say, 'My heart goes out to them', while a third woman said, 'I can't look any more.'

On their next court appearance, a week later, the boys were further remanded in custody. New charges were put to them arising from the incidents which had occurred before the fatal crash.

On 3 February, their earlier offences, which had been pending at the time of the crash, caught up with them. Both boys received consecutive sentences which totalled seventeen months. Meanwhile, in relation to the ongoing investigation over the collision, Inspector Gallagher told the court that some eighty statements had been taken and it was expected that a file would be sent to the DPP later that week. Significantly, he said it was expected that further charges would be put to Sean only.

By 14 March, the case against Sean had become more serious. In a mere eight minutes, he was charged with twelve new offences relating to the incident, including manslaughter, dangerous driving causing the death of the taxi driver, and dangerous driving causing the death of his teenage passenger. Other charges for criminal damage, dangerous driving and reckless endangerment relating to the same incident were also put to Sean.

When the first charge was put to him, his reply after caution was: 'I got done for E——'s death?' in disbelief at now being formally held responsible for the death of his teenage friend. To another charge relating to Mr McGowan's death, he replied, 'I can't remember, I am sorry about it.' His replies to each of the next charges were the same: 'I can't remember.' Sitting in the defendant's chair, Sean broke down and wept quietly as the details of the new charges were given to the court.

As Sean sobbed, Judge McBride was also informed that the DPP had directed trial on indictment in the Dublin Circuit Criminal

Court. He further remanded Sean in custody, 'due to the gravity of the charges', for the service of a book of evidence, which contained all of the prosecution's evidence in the case against him.

While the boys remained in custody in St Patrick's Institution, where they were serving sentences for the earlier offences, the state was building its case against them.

In the Dublin Circuit Criminal Court on 22 October 2003, Sean pleaded guilty to manslaughter and theft. He already had forty-eight criminal convictions—eight of them for stealing cars. Keith also pleaded guilty to the charges against him.

Normally children brought to the court for committing a crime are shielded from notoriety by legislation which bans the news media from identifying them. However, at the boys' sentence hearing, the judge ruled that the reporting restrictions set out in the Children's Act were specific to the Children's Court only. Making it a landmark case, he lifted the ban on naming Sean and Keith. This was in response to an application on behalf of Independent Newspapers, the *Irish Examiner* and RTÉ. (For further details on the identification of minors, see Appendix II.)

Inspector Anthony Gallagher told the court that the youths had said they had little memory of the crash and one of them had described the incident as 'a joyriding escapade that went wrong.' Both boys were on bail when the fatal collision on 11 January took place.

The defence counsel for both boys urged Judge Hogan to be lenient because they had pleaded guilty and had expressed sorrow at the deaths of the two people. They came from difficult backgrounds and Sean, who had spent various periods in custody since he was 12, recognised that he faced a substantial sentence and wished to get it out of the way.

Judge Hogan regarded Sean's offences as very serious ones which had and would continue to have long-term consequences not only for himself and his family but also for the families of Mr McGowan and the teenage passenger.

'He has pleaded guilty to manslaughter which carries a very severe penalty on one side of the balance sheet and there are aggravating factors concerning the driving of the car and I must have regard to the number and type of his previous convictions,' he continued. 'Eight of his previous convictions are for taking cars without the consent of the owners. It is from this type of offence that the more serious offences happened on that night. Under those circumstances I feel that the appropriate sentence would be one of ten years, however, I will take into account his guilty plea, his cooperation with gardaí and his young age and for that reason impose a period of seven years' detention.' 'The tragic events that occurred can not be laid at the door of his co-accused, who was being carried in the car and was not the driver but he also has previous convictions of similar type and nature,' Judge Hogan said in regard to Keith who was detained for three years.

In the aftermath of the teenagers' sentencing, Patrick McGowan, the deceased's father, said, 'We've been a broken family since this happened. We go to the graveyard every Sunday and break down every Sunday. My wife is a nervous wreck over it. Robert has left a three-year-old son who keeps asking for his father.'[1]

15 | SEX CRIMES

'The unfortunate victim was made to feel she was facing death and was given every reason to believe that. She is going to be haunted by this matter into the future, I would think indefinitely.'[1]

As those words were spoken, a 15-year-old boy sat in the highest criminal court in the land, awaiting sentence. The trail that had led him to this point in his life, where a Central Criminal Court judge was poised to pass sentence, was another example of a child being abandoned and bounced from his real family to foster care and back again from an extremely young age. He was first put into care just six weeks after he was born. Over the following years, a pattern was to emerge where he would be given back to his birth mother for a while and then returned to his foster parents. At the age of 13, he began to display behavioural, literacy and numeracy problems in school. At this time, he had gone back to live with his birth mother for nine months. This period, however, did little to benefit him and was characterised by incessant fighting. As a result of the continued rowing, he was sent back to his foster parents but more problems followed and he began to drink and smoke cannabis. 'Between the ages of 13 and 15, he was leading a rootless and aimless existence, bouncing between his natural mother and his foster parents before ending up in residential care,' his barrister was to tell the judge in the Central Criminal Court. The charge against the boy was one of the most serious—rape.

On Tuesday, 20 September 2005, as the Children's Court was about to finish its day's work, word came through from Dún Laoghaire Garda Station that a juvenile suspect was being brought in to be charged. The court had completed its day's business but awaited the teenager's arrival. Such situations usually relate to young people getting picked up on bench warrants for previously skipping court or for breach of bail conditions. However, this case was somewhat different and infinitely more serious.

The boy was charged with the rape and robbery of a woman in Dún Laoghaire, the previous day. The teenager had been arrested just after six o'clock on the evening of the attack. He had been brought to Dún Laoghaire Garda Station where he had remained overnight. At 1.35 that afternoon he had been charged with the two offences. Judge Angela Ní Chonduin was told that the teenager was in care and that social workers and care staff were in court. No application for bail was being made.

Judge Ní Chonduin remanded the boy in custody to Trinity House, to appear again on the following Tuesday, pending directions from the Director of Public Prosecutions (DPP). The following week, he was further remanded in custody to allow psychological, social and educational assessments to be completed.

Meanwhile, other charges against the youth started to surface. On 13 October 2005, he appeared again in the Children's Court to be charged over an unprovoked attack in which another youth had been beaten on the head with a dog chain outside a church in Killiney, the previous April. In what was described as a 'motiveless attack', the victim had been knocked to the ground by the defendant. Other youths who had been present had then started to kick the victim as he lay helpless on the ground. The teenager, who had been in foster care at the time of the attack, had instigated the attack and refused to name the other individuals who had kicked the victim.

The victim had received staple stitches to his head for injuries sustained from the blow from the chain. Judge William Hamill adjourned the case to allow for a report on the defendant's level of maturity to be furnished, prior to deciding on whether the case should be dealt with in the Children's Court or sent forward to a higher court.

On 24 October 2005, the youth was brought back to court over the rape charges but directions from the DPP were not ready and he was sent back to Trinity House. On 22 November, he was further remanded in custody for another week. Judge William Hamill heard that the DPP had directed trial on indictment which, due to the nature of the charge, meant the Central Criminal Court.

His assault case was also back before the court on that date. The teenager pleaded guilty to the charge, and he was remanded back into custody for another week pending sentencing. On 29 November 2005, he was detained by the court for one month in Trinity House for the unprovoked attack on the youth. Given his age, sentencing options were confined to either one month or two years. He was given the lesser because the judge knew that he faced the possibility of a more substantial sentence when his rape case went to the Central Criminal Court.

Four weeks later, the youth was formerly returned for trial to the Central Criminal Court. On 6 March 2006, he pleaded guilty to raping the woman and the grim evidence of his crime was outlined to Mr Justice Paul Carney.

On 29 September 2005, the 20-year-old woman left her house at 2.30 p.m. to bring her father's bike to be repaired. Unsuspecting, she wheeled the bike along, while listening to her portable music player. The youth, who was wearing a grey hoodie top, passed her by, and she thought nothing of it, but when she saw the same youth coming back in her direction a few minutes later, she thought it unusual. She was then grabbed roughly from behind and pulled backwards and downwards onto the ground. When the hooded youth asked her for her money, she thought she was being mugged. But he then put his hands down the front of her trousers and told her to shut up or he would stab her. He started to unbutton her jacket and her trousers and told her to put her hand over her eyes. At one stage, the woman attempted to run away but her attacker grabbed her and punched her. He then put his arm around her and began walking with her, saying: 'If anyone else asks, you're my bird.' The youth brought the terrified woman to an isolated area not visible from the roadway where there was a high brick wall and bushes to shield them from view.

He again told the woman to keep her eyes covered and commanded her to take off her clothing, before attempting to rape her. He also attempted anal rape and forced the woman to give him oral sex. The court heard that the youth told the woman, 'Meet me', which, it was explained, was a slang term for kissing.

The boy started to kiss the woman and then forced her to masturbate him before instructing her to lie down on the ground. He tried to force himself into her, saying: 'Isn't me riding you better than going into town?' He then asked her for her name. She gave him a false name and he threatened again to stab her if she didn't comply with his directions. Although she didn't see a knife, she believed he had one. She bit him on the hand at one point during her ordeal. The youth made the woman swear not to tell gardaí about what had happened and told her to keep on walking into the bushes. 'She was of the view he was going to kill her,' the court was told.

As the degrading attack ended and as he was about to leave, the youth asked the woman to kiss him. She stayed in the bushes for several minutes until she was sure the 15-year-old was gone and then got dressed and ran out onto the nearest road, where a local man spotted her in a distraught state.

The young woman, aged 21 by the time of the teenager's sentence hearing, told the court that she couldn't sleep in the dark any more because it reminded her of how she had been forced to keep her eyes covered during the rape. The trauma of the ordeal had left her with horrific and long-lasting mental scars. She did not like living in her home any more because every time she walked out her front door, she saw the route where the attack had taken place. She was no longer able to travel on the DART because she had heard the sound of it passing during the rape. Following her ordeal, she had been taking a drink before she went to bed because it was the only way she could relax, and had been drinking more when she went out. 'I feel he had pre-planned what he was going to do,' she said. The young woman looked at Judge Paul Carney and told him: 'I'm always being scared.'

In mitigation, the judge was told of the teenager's chaotic lifestyle and the educational and behavioural problems that had begun to manifest themselves when he was in his early teens. Assessment reports before the court addressed the question of why a 15-year-old had engaged in such savage behaviour in broad daylight. The court heard that the youth had pleaded guilty at an early stage and was a person who was capable of being rehabilitated if given the appropriate care. In imposing his sentence, Mr Justice Carney said that the facts of the case were truly appalling. He commented that a dysfunctional background, drugs and drink were factors that were sadly present in most of the people who came before the court, and he added that the only thing in the youth's favour was his plea of guilty at the first available opportunity.

He sentenced the boy to three-and-a-half years' detention at Trinity House for rape, three years' detention for attempted rape and two years' detention for the theft of €60 and the victim's mobile phone. All sentences would run concurrently and date from 20 September 2005, the day the teenager had been initially taken into custody.

The judge said that had it not been for the provision of the Children's Act which limited the maximum sentence he could impose to four years, he would have imposed a seven-year sentence. Outside the Four Courts, the victim, who had remained so composed in the witness box just minutes before, broke down in tears.

Finally, on Friday, 7 April 2006, the last of the teenager's prosecutions was finalised at Dublin Circuit Criminal Court. Again, a direction had been made that the incident was too serious for the case to be heard in the Children's Court. It related to the mugging of a man on East Essex Street, in Dublin's Temple Bar area, in September 2004. The then 14-year-old, together with his gang, had attacked a man who refused to hand over his car keys to them. They had knocked him to the ground where his keys were taken from his pocket. The gang had then repeatedly kicked him while demanding to know where his car was parked. Though beaten and bloody, he had refused to reveal where it was and the gang had run off. The Circuit Court judge imposed a four-year sentence in Trinity House to run concurrent with the three-and-a-half-year sentence imposed by the Central Criminal Court the previous month.

In recent years, children have been involved in some of the more serious sex offences that have come before the courts. One sickening example took place in a wood in Co. Clare and was perpetrated by a gang of Limerick teenage boys who were armed with a range of weapons including a golf club, a screwdriver, a wheel brace and a shovel. What happened at Cratloe Woods, Co. Clare, in the early hours of 23 January 2004, the barbarity displayed by the teenage aggressors and their disregard for the suffering of the victims, was extremely disturbing.

Three 16-year-olds, who were all on remand for other offences at the time of the brutal attacks, and another boy aged 14, launched the savage attack on the couple after they found them together in a car in the Cratloe Woods. The four ordered the couple out of their car and the woman was hit on the shoulder with a golf club when she refused to give one of them a kiss. The man was in possession of an extendable baton which he used in his job as a bouncer. On seeing this, the four presumed he was a garda which prompted them to shout, 'Do him.' The teenagers ordered the man to get into the boot of the car. A sustained gang rape then took place. The teenagers forced the woman onto the bonnet of the car and her shorts were pulled down. One of the youths grabbed her breasts and another tried to rape her anally. She was then dragged into the car where the four youths took turns raping her. They threatened to torch the car with her boyfriend trapped in the boot if she resisted them. Once they lifted the boot door open so that they could hit the imprisoned man repeatedly with the golf club. The ordeal lasted for over an hour and came to an end only after the man managed to escape from the boot and flag down a passing motorist who called for help. The youths were arrested nearby soon after. Luckily gardaí were in the area investigating break-ins at two schools.

The man subsequently underwent plastic surgery for a severe laceration to his arm. He also had cuts to his face and body, having been repeatedly jabbed with a screwdriver. The woman had severe bruising to her shoulder and marks around her vaginal area. The court heard that crime in the south Limerick area had been significantly reduced since the arrest of the four accused.

The teenagers, who looked deceivingly innocent as they sat in the courtroom, pleaded guilty to raping the 35-year-old woman. They also admitted falsely imprisoning the man, who was 36, and assaulting both victims.

In her impact statement, the woman told the court: 'My life and the lives of my family were devastated with what happened. A lot of pieces have to be picked up and a lot of pain has to be dealt with. I'm trying to get on and not let it destroy the rest of my life.' The man said that their lives had been totally destroyed and that they had gone from being ordinary people into a living nightmare.

The court heard that all four boys came from dysfunctional backgrounds and for a long time before the hideous attack had been out of control. Counsel for all four told Mr Justice Carney that little could be said in mitigation because of the appalling circumstances surrounding the case. However, the judge was asked to take into account their young ages and the fact that they had all pleaded guilty at the earliest opportunity.

The 16-year-old, who was referred to as the 'ringleader' and 'director of operations', had thirty-five previous convictions, for crimes including assault causing serious harm and aggravated burglary, as well as theft and road traffic offences. He was seriously disturbed and had come under the influence of a notorious Limerick crime gang. A ten-year sentence was handed down to him.

The second boy, also aged 16, had nine convictions, mostly for motoring offences, theft, criminal damage and failing to appear in court. The pre-sentence probation report said that he represented a continued danger to others. He received a nine-year sentence.

The third 16-year-old boy had no previous convictions at the time of the offence but had cases pending which later resulted in convictions for assault, criminal damage and theft. He had gone out of control after his baby sister died in an arson attack on their home. He was detained for eight years.

The youngest of the quartet, the 14-year-old, was given the maximum detention sentence for a person his age—four years. He was said to have been very easily led and under the influence of the others. Although he had no convictions at the time of the attacks, he would later be convicted of an earlier theft offence.

Mr Justice Carney suspended the final year of all of the older boys' sentences in view of their age and guilty pleas. Closing the case, he added:

> I am fully aware that I am dealing with children and they have to be rehabilitated. However, the protection of society is at the forefront of my mind and people cannot be exposed to danger by them in a short period of time. Because I am treating them as children does not mean I have to deal with them with short sentences and the community will have to be protected from their criminal propensities.

Another group of teenagers, this time in Dublin, was also involved in a brutal gang sex attack. The case was equally disturbing as two of the offenders were aged 14 and one was 13 at the time, and the victims were boys aged seven and eight. The abuse was discovered when the mother of one of the victims noticed her son behaving unusually and eventually persuaded him to confide in her and tell what had happened.

On 28 July 2003, the youngest of the three defendants was brought before the Children's Court, charged with two counts of sexual assault. He was 14, but had been 13, at the time of the attacks which had taken place inside an abandoned van that was parked in Dublin's north inner city, in mid-2002.

The Director of Public Prosecutions had recommended summary trial in the Children's Court on a plea of guilty only. Judge Michael Connellan heard that the small boys had been threatened and forced to perform hand manipulation and oral sex on the 13-year-old. Judge Connellan held that the case did not involve a 'minor offence' and therefore ought to be tried before a judge and jury in the Circuit Court. Earlier, a judge had made a similar direction in the cases of his two co-defendants, who were just a year older than him. They were facing charges of false imprisonment and multiple counts of sexual assault. One of them also had a charge of common assault.

The youngest of the teenagers came before the Dublin Circuit Criminal Court in November 2004 and, by then aged 15, was convicted by a jury. He claimed that he was not the main perpetrator of crime. The case was adjourned pending probation and welfare service reports to establish whether this boy was a 'a risk to other young boys or if this was a peer pressure activity'.[2] He was put back into custody in the Trinity House Detention Centre, where he had been on remand since late 2003. On 23 November 2004, Judge Michael White said that updated psychological and probation service reports showed that the boy had begun to recognise the seriousness of his offence and the impact it had had on his young victims and on their families. He said that it was evident the boy did not have a secure family background and would be 'at risk' if he were to leave Trinity House at that stage. Under no circumstances was the teenager to be allowed to return to the area where the attacks had occurred, the judge stressed.

Judge White ordered two years' detention in Trinity House, and recommended that the boy avail of a sex offenders' programme designed specifically for juveniles. An order was also made compelling the youth to stay under probation supervision for three years following his release from custody.

The two older boys also came before the Circuit Criminal Court and pleaded guilty to their parts in the attacks. Garda interviews with the pair showed that they and the 13-year-old had brought their young victims to the abandoned van, where one of the 14-year-olds had forced one of the victims to masturbate him.

The other 14-year-old boy's role had been more that of a bully. He was carrying a wheel-jack and threatened the two young boys with it, forcing them to comply with instructions to perform sexual acts. He would also continue to come to garda attention for theft offences while he was waiting for his case to be dealt with in the Circuit Court.

The indictment had originally included a false imprisonment charge as well as twelve sexual assault charges. But these were dropped by the DPP. The boy admitted the assault, thereby saving the two young boys from the ordeal of having to give evidence at a trial and face cross-examination. His counsel said that his client was just 14 years old age at the time of the offence and had since 'moved on, learned from his experiences, and now understands fully the consequences of his actions.'

The ringleader of the group, who had also been 14 years of age at the time of the offences, had also pleaded guilty at an early stage. This boy had gone to counselling since and had co-operated fully with the garda investigation. He was due to start a new job soon and was attempting to move his life in a better direction. Both boys' lawyers offered apologies to the victims on behalf of their clients.

Judge Desmond Hogan noted the age of the defendants and the victims and the case was adjourned several times. 'I am not giving any indication whatsoever yet as to how I am going to finalise the matter,' he said.[3]

His decision came on 12 May 2006, when he detained the ringleader, for eighteen months; a suspended eighteen-month sentence was handed down to his friend.

In 2002, the Children's Court in Dublin refused jurisdiction to hear the case of a 15-year-old boy. An order was made, given the seriousness of the allegations, that he would face trial on indictment in the Central Criminal Court. He was charged with the rape of a 50-year-old man.

On the evening of the incident, the 15-year-old and a 12-year-old girl bought drink from an off-licence and went to the girl's

grandmother's flat. The boy had a lot to drink. Later, the grandmother returned with a male friend who was also drunk. What
began as a trivial dispute erupted between the teenager and the
older man. Eventually, the older man left the flat to get a taxi
home. The boy went with him. As the man was trying to hail a
taxi, the boy pulled him into an area where rubbish containers
were parked. There he attacked and raped him.

The boy was not a habitual offender, but he had been in the
Children's Court on a few occasions. In July 2002, he pleaded guilty
to a robbery charge, for mugging a woman, who was in her forties.

The mugging took place at 9.30 p.m., at Kenilworth Square in
Harold's Cross. The boy had tailed the woman along Rathgar
Road then on to Grosvenor Road. She then turned onto
Kenilworth Square, not noticing the teenager steadily gaining on
her. Minutes later and with no one else around, his footsteps
quickened and he suddenly came behind the woman. He reached
around her and put his hand across her face. He then pulled her to
the ground and dragged her on her back. Her handbag's strap had
been wrapped around her neck and it tightened as the boy heaved
her along the ground. Eventually he managed to take her handbag.
Throughout the attack, the woman had been screaming. The boy
was arrested shortly afterwards.

Judge Leo J. Malone heard that the boy had pleaded guilty
which avoided the necessity of putting his victim through the
ordeal of giving evidence and having to be cross-examined.
However, he was told that on other occasions when this case had
come before the court, the boy had indicated that he would plead
not guilty which meant that the woman had had to come to court
on each occasion, which was very difficult for her.

The attack had had an enormous effect on her. A year later, she
was still frightened, traumatised, suffering from stress and afraid
to go out at night. She couldn't bring herself to be in the same
room as the boy and had sent her husband into the court on her
behalf.

The boy had previous convictions for trespassing, burglary and
larceny. He apologised in the court for what he had done. 'I am

sorry for causing trouble. I was confused and panicked and I did not mean to hurt her. I am really sorry,' he said. Judge Malone adjourned sentencing until 5 June 2003, when the youth was released on a twelve-month probation supervisory bond.

Meanwhile, another case was being prepared in relation to the rape.

On 27 January 2004, at the Central Criminal Court, the youth, now aged 17, pleaded guilty to buggering the 50-year-old victim at Dominick Street Flats on 12 November 2001.

Following the ordeal, the victim, who had been extremely drunk, had called 999 but had been unable to give gardaí details of the rape until the following morning. He also said that the teenager had taken a gold chain from around his neck.

The youngster was arrested shortly afterwards, having been found with the victim's gold chain on him. A medical examination confirmed that the victim had been raped.

Mr Justice Carney said that he could see exceptional factors in this case that warranted suspension of the sentence. The accused was genuinely remorseful about his offence and had pleaded guilty at the earliest opportunity. Mr Justice Carney noted that the boy had been at a difficult age at the time, and had been experiencing difficulties over his own sexual orientation. Mr Justice Carney also took into consideration the age gap between the boy and his victim: 'The victim was 35 years older than the defendant. The victim is of a stocky build while the defendant appears to be a reedy young man.'[4]

The probation officer's report said that the teenager would benefit greatly from the current treatment programmes he was on. By now he had accepted his own sexual orientation and was in a stable relationship. He was receiving the full support of his family, who had at first found his sexual orientation hard to accept. Mr Justice Carney said that a custodial sentence was not mandatory in rape offences, and imposed a three-year suspended sentence. The boy was certified as a sex offender and directed to remain under supervision of the Probation and Welfare Services for three years.

A decision was made by the DPP to appeal the sentence on the grounds that it was unduly lenient. However, on 22 June 2004, the Court of Criminal Appeal rejected the DPP's argument and said that it would not interfere with the sentence.

IV. HARDENED CRIMINALS

16 | AN ARMED ROBBER

The balaclava-clad 15-year-old stood in front of the shop's counter; he picked up the gun which had been placed in front of him by his accomplice and calmly pointed it at the owner, who was frozen with fear, telling him not to move and to hand over the money. John was a methodical young criminal who had learned the traditional way by starting small time, then building up to become the state's youngest armed robber of his generation. He would later be described by a judge as 'evil' and 'wicked', while another would say, more accurately perhaps, that through crime he had 'wasted five years of his life'.

John was behind a trail of disturbing crimes. The north inner-city Dublin boy started with run-of-the-mill offences, such as breach of the peace. He soon moved on to car crime and assaults but, as the years passed, his descent into serious crime escalated. Along the way, he learned how to deal with gardaí, how to resist arrest, how to intimidate witnesses, how to go on the run and how to take part in an armed robbery, which was quite an achievement for someone who, it was claimed, had an educational age several years below his chronological one.

John, like so many of the young people who come through the doors of the Children's Court, came from a disadvantaged part of Dublin. He lived with his mother; his father, who was on the long-term unemployment register, lived nearby. John had a history of learning disorders. He had quit school at the age of 11, unable to adapt to mainstream education. In the following five years, he ran wild, gaining notoriety among the gardaí in the north inner city and also acquiring a considerable criminal track record by the age of 16. Even at the age of 13, he had been involved in intimidation. During one of his first hearings, the court heard how John had threatened to burn down the house of a man who had previously testified against him for joyriding.

Evidence was given that John then had the educational age of a seven-year-old and his defence argued that he could not have understood that he was breaking the law by making such threats. The victim, a middle-aged man, explained the background to John's bitter animosity towards him. Two years prior to the threat, the man had heard a car screeching around on the street outside his business. John, then very small and aged only 11, was in the passenger seat. The stolen car crashed to a halt. Its driver got out and left. Fearing that John would start to drive the car and possibly get hurt, the man, acting as a concerned citizen, decided to intervene. He walked over and took John out of the stolen car and, not knowing where his parents lived, he brought him to a garda station. Charges were brought against John for travelling in the stolen car. The victim later testified against the boy in court when he was charged with joyriding. The court heard that the boy had been charged with a number of breaches of public order and for making a threat to cause criminal damage.

Because John was under 14, the onus was on the state to prove that the boy understood that what he had done was 'seriously wrong' and was a crime as distinct from an act of childish mischief.

Evidence was heard that John had been arrested outside a disco when he was caught lashing out his arms wildly in the middle of a crowd of young teenagers. On another occasion, he had called a garda a 'muppet' and told him to 'f**k off' when the garda said, 'I'm directing you to leave the area in a peaceful and orderly fashion under section eight of the public order act.' The boy's defence argued that although the boy was 13, he had the cognitive ability of a seven-year-old and did not understand these directions or that what he was doing was wrong.

The state argued that the boy had previously been convicted in the court, and, despite his educational standard, he did have the 'street smarts' to understand that he was breaking the law.

Judge Geoffrey Browne held that the boy's defence of not being fit to plead had been rebutted. John was remanded on bail for a later hearing after which he was released.

On 27 September 2002, John was arrested again for having a leading role in a vicious gang mugging of a young woman. The woman had come onto William Street and seen a group of youths on the path ahead of her. Nervous, she had reached for her mobile phone. However the phone's 'key lock' had been activated and as she tried to disable it, the 13-year-old John tried to pull the phone out of her hands. Bravely, the victim held on to her phone and a scuffle ensued. John shouted at the woman to let go, and sank his teeth into her hand. He bit her for two minutes until she kicked him off her. The phone then broke and the boy made off with its internal workings while she was left holding its plastic cover.

Later, the woman was given medical attention and received two tetanus injections. The skin on her hand had been penetrated and the bruises took over four weeks to heal.

The boy's defence told the court that the boy suffered from Attention-Deficit Hyperactivity Disorder (ADHD) and that he was due back before the court for a psychiatric report on other charges. Judge Hamill remarked that people suffering from ADHD 'do not necessarily do what he has admitted'. He remanded John on bail until the following March for a Probation and Welfare Service report and the psychiatric report.

Other charges followed. On 24 June 2003, John was again before the court for intimidation and threats. Judge Browne heard that, on 8 August 2002, John had caused a disturbance at a library, on the city's north side. A librarian had told John that he had to leave the building because he was barred. When he refused, she tried to call the gardaí but he grabbed her phone out of her hand and then threatened to burn down her home. The teenager was able to give accurate details of where she lived and directions to her house, which was a considerable distance away. A week previously, the boy had approached another staff member from the same library and had spat in his face. John pleaded guilty to the attacks on the librarians.

The adjourned charges for the mugging in which he had bitten the woman was also before the court for a probation and psychiatric report on the same day. Judge Browne heard that the boy had psychiatric and learning problems but that since these incidents, his mother had managed to find activities including a part-time job for him which had resulted in an improvement in his behaviour. Arrangements had been put in place to secure home tuition for him because he had been deemed unsuitable for regular schooling. Judge Browne said that John had 'frightened the living daylights' out of the librarian. When questioned in court, the teenager agreed that if similar threats had been made to his own mother, 'it would not be nice.' Refusing to finalise the case because the charges were too serious, the judge ordered a further report on the boy's behaviour. John was remanded on bail and the case adjourned until October.

As these cases were being dealt with, another prosecution was being prepared. In August 2002, John had verbally abused a female garda from Fitzgibbon Street Garda Station. It was alleged that when she went to caution him, he called her a 'dirty slapper' and went on to say: 'I bet half the station have been up on you.' As a result, a group of youths with him started to laugh and jeer at her. The crowd then became rowdy.

When the garda tried to arrest John for breach of the peace, he ran, but turned back when he saw her colleague approaching from another direction. He ran straight back at her and punched her hard in the stomach with both fists. The garda doubled over in agony and he then grabbed her shirt, dragged her onto her knees and pulled her along the ground. Her head and shoulders were banged against a kerb. Dazed and distressed, her knees bleeding and uniform torn, she dragged herself up onto her feet, by which time John had fled the scene.

Two days later, gardaí went to John's home to arrest him. However, John's mother said that her son was not at home as he had been away all night and had not come back. A search of the flat revealed John hiding behind a laundry basket at the rear of their flat. In the Children's Court in April 2003, John denied assaulting the female garda, causing her harm, and claimed that he had bumped into her by accident. He was convicted and released on bail, pending further reports. Judge Michael Connellan said that John acted the 'great man in front of a crowd' but hid like a 'coward' when the gardaí came to arrest him. He described the attack as 'vicious' and he said he was not impressed by the actions of his parents who had lied to gardaí when they called to their home. The case was adjourned until a date in May for sentencing.

The charges relating to the assault on the garda, as well as the mugging and the threats to the librarian, then went on a bizarre course and finalisation would come only in March 2005, nearly two years later. As Judge Geoffrey Browne had heard the bulk of cases against the teenager, it was agreed that he should deal with sentencing. Therefore the case was repeatedly adjourned until a date when he was sitting in the court coincided with a date when the boy was brought back there. Eventually the judge was appointed to a district court outside Dublin. This development delayed the cases even further.

On 27 September 2003, John was arrested for illegal driving. This case provided an insight into his family's attitudes to co-operation with the authorities. Gardaí had spotted the 14-year-old driving dangerously on a stolen moped, racing around a flat complex on the moped, and had then seen him run into his flat. The teenager had taken his helmet off as he was escaping and, as they had known the teenager for a number of years, the gardaí were '100 per cent certain' that they had identified the right culprit.

John flatly rejected the allegations. He claimed that he had been in his room listening to music and, having heard the noises of the moped, had walked out to see what was happening. His mother also gave sworn evidence that her son could not have been using the moped because he was in his bedroom all day. Having been told about John's mother's efforts to get him specialised tuition, Judge William Early replied: 'She does not help him by trying to protect him from the consequences of his actions.' He convicted the teenager who by now had seven criminal convictions for assaults, joyriding, larceny and public order offences. John was remanded on bail until 29 January 2004, for a pre-sentence probation report to be furnished.

On the next court date, the teenager was remanded on continuing bail. Later, he started to skip court, and gardaí found it impossible to trace him for a number of months, although they believed that he was being sheltered by his family.

However, on 11 May, he popped up on the radar again for a car theft in which he threatened to have the vehicle owner shot if he gave evidence. The following September, he was arrested for an incident in which he confronted gardaí with a metal bar and demanded a fight. He denied the allegations and was then remanded on continuing bail pending his trial in the Children's Court.

At this point, he was aged 15 and still out of school, unemployed, not involved in any course, and not taking his ADHD medication, although his family still maintained that he had the learning disorder. Gardaí often noted that despite the family's belief that the boy had the syndrome, he had never, in three years since the alleged diagnosis, taken his medication or been persuaded to do so by his parents.

On 20 December 2004, John took part in his most daring crime. Together with a seasoned criminal who was over twice his age and who had twenty-seven previous convictions for crimes such as larceny and assault, he entered an off-licence in Portmarnock, just as it was about to close. The owner, two employees and a customer heard a voice shout 'money' and turned to see the 32-year-old standing at the counter wearing a balaclava. He roared at them for money, pointed a gun at a male member of staff, and threatened to shoot him. His young accomplice, John, was in front of the counter, also wearing a balaclava. He picked up the gun which had been placed on the counter by his accomplice and pointed it at the owner, telling him not to move and to hand over the money.

The older raider continued to terrorise the off-licence staff with a vocal barrage, repeatedly shouting, 'shoot them, shoot them', as

John coolly kept the gun trained on his victims and ordered them to empty their pockets. The thieves became increasingly aggressive before finally leaving the shop with a total of €1,200 in cash and cigarettes. They escaped in a stolen car driven by John.

A garda patrol car was dispatched to track down the armed robbers. The patrol car pursued the getaway car at high speed through Malahide village. John drove through red lights and overtook other vehicles at speeds of over 100 mph before losing control at Darndale roundabout and smashing into another garda car. He abandoned his getaway car at Greenwood Lawns, leaving the gun, a claw hammer and the proceeds of the robbery in the vehicle.

When the teenager was brought into court the following day, the mood of his family seemed jocular and he entered the courtroom smiling. Judge Angela Ní Chonduin remanded John's partner in crime in custody to Cloverhill Prison. Because of the seriousness of the offences, she refused to grant bail to the teenager, saying that he had been in breach of bail conditions at the time of his arrest. 'He has been given breaks and he has broken them. When you break the rules you stay in custody,' she said, remanding him to the Trinity House Detention Centre until the following day.

The next day, Judge Ní Chonduin again refused to grant bail and remanded John in custody to Trinity House over the Christmas period until early January 2005.

In January, he was further remanded in custody. Now turned 16, he was eligible to be held in St Patrick's Institution instead. He was also given two months' detention for the earlier illegal driving incident in which his mother had falsely given alibi evidence for him.

He was to stay in custody on remand pending trial over the armed robbery. Because of the seriousness of the case it had been directed that it should be heard in the Dublin Circuit Criminal Court and not retained in the Children's Court. Meanwhile, pending the Circuit Court case, some of the older cases which had still been pending in the Children's Court were finalised.

On 15 March 2005, the now three-year-old prosecution against John for the attack on the female garda was finalised. Detaining the boy for nine months, Judge Michael Connellan said that John had been convicted for more offences since the attack on the garda and a probation report had highlighted that he was also re-offending and associating with older individuals who were negative influences. It was Judge Connellan's last day to sit in the Children's Court, as he was to retire from the judiciary the following month. It was John's first significant sentence.

On 30 May 2005, he was back to the court for a hearing over a suspected car theft in the previous May and also possession of an iron bar as a weapon the previous September. The boy, who now had twenty-nine criminal convictions, was found guilty. During the former of the incidents, he dangerously sped a stolen car, performed handbrake turns and later threatened the owner of the car that he would be shot if he gave evidence. In the latter incident, he brandished an iron bar and threatened gardaí.

John denied the ten charges for possession of an iron bar as an offensive weapon, breaches of the peace, car theft, dangerous driving and driving without a licence and insurance. The arresting garda told Judge Catherine Murphy that on 11 May 2004, at the North Strand Road area, in north Dublin, he came upon John, who was aged 15 at the time, driving a car at approximately 70 mph in a residential area which had a 30 mph speed limit. Over the course of five minutes, the teenager sped up and down a street and performed four 360-degree handbrake turns, a manoeuvre often described as 'doughnut', while a number of youths cheered him on.

John swerved across the roads and there was a fear for the safety of pedestrians, the court was told. The garda saw the teenager in the driver's seat each time it performed the handbrake turn and again when he abandoned the vehicle. John denied being the driver of the car, claiming that he was out walking in the area at the time.

The car had been stolen from a house in Clontarf the previous night. Its owner was called to give evidence that he had not given anyone permission to take it. The man also said in his testimony that after he collected his recovered car from Mountjoy Garda Station he proceeded to drive home. When he stopped at a red light on Clonliffe Road, John appeared, approached the car and shouted threats at him. 'I was approached by an individual who walked over to my car, saying, "I'm the person who stole your car; if you go to the gardaí I will get you." I was very rattled by that,' the witness said. He continued: 'I felt intimidated and insecure; that was compounded by the fact that when I drove on to the next set of lights at Richmond Road, the same person had followed my car. He was roaring at me. He said, "If you turn up in court, I will have you shot." That caused me to feel apprehensive for my safety and I felt intimidated.'

John was also convicted of possession of an iron bar as an offensive weapon, near his home on 5 September 2004. A garda had approached him over a bench warrant that had been issued over his failure to attend his court case earlier. John had needed to be restrained by his mother who held him back as he threatened the gardaí and demanded that they fight him 'without batons or badges'.

Refuting the allegations, John said that he had been out walking at the time of the joyriding and had not threatened the officers or brandished an iron bar. He also denied that he had needed to be restrained by his mother and said that he was in fear that he was going to be arrested over bench warrants, which he falsely claimed did not exist. Judge Catherine Murphy found him guilty of the charges and imposed a nine-month detention term in St Patrick's Institution.

Judge Murphy told him that she believed the prosecution evidence and said, 'The only person sending you to St Patrick's Institution is yourself. I believe you carried out these crimes and you have to take responsibility for the consequences.' She also urged him to utilise the detention centre's educational facilities and not to return to the same pattern of behaviour on his release. Gardaí, she also advised him, would soon lose interest in him if he stopped breaking the law.

On 28 July 2005, John pleaded guilty at the Dublin Circuit Criminal Court to his role in the armed robbery, where he was described to the judge as having the reading age of a seven-year-old and functioning at a 'low intellectual level'. He was detained for one year in St Patrick's Institution. Judge Yvonne Murphy jailed the adult accomplice for thirty months and said that the teenager lacked insight into his criminal behaviour. A Probation and Welfare Service report on him depicted, a 'grim picture' and suggested he was 'at high risk of re-offending'.[1]

Twelve days later, a number of charges, some of which had taken years to be fully dealt with, were finalised in the Children's Court. On hearing the details of the mugging in which he had bitten the woman, and the threats to the librarian, Judge Thomas Fitzpatrick described John as 'evil and wicked' and detained him for eleven months. He added: 'I can only try to imagine how the injured parties felt in these cases having been threatened in such a vicious way. I would hope that he would learn that crime does not pay. If he does not, he will be in and out of places of detention, and in years to come in and out of prison, for many years unless he realises that crime is not the way forward.'

Even at this point, justice had yet to be administered in relation to other offences committed by John, all while he was on bail. On Thursday, 13 October 2005, John pleaded guilty at the Children's Court to the theft of three U2 concert tickets, worth €255, from a woman at Summerhill Parade, the previous June.

His admission followed an earlier not-guilty plea which had required the victim to make a trip from Newry to give evidence. Some suspected that this was a cynical tactic. If the witness had not made the effort to make the lengthy journey to Dublin to give her evidence, the case would have been dismissed. Her decision to come to court, however, made the case against John stronger. He changed his plea to guilty in the hope that his admission would be to his credit when sentenced. 'If you do not change your ways, you will spend a substantial period of your life in prison,' said Judge Catherine Murphy as she sentenced him to three months' detention in St Patrick's Institution.

John's last case in the Children's Court was dealt with on 1 December 2005. The previous July, gardaí had seen him break the window of a car. They had chased him into a block of flats where he had dropped a screwdriver and grabbed onto railings. It had taken three gardaí to get him off the railings, with one using his baton to lever the boy away from the bars and loosen his grip. It was alleged that a group had gathered and John had incited them to attack the gardaí. Judge Murphy also heard evidence that John had spat at the gardaí and attempted to bite them as they tried to handcuff him.

John, who was supported in court by his parents, denied that he had broken the car window. He said that the gardaí set on him from behind and he had not let go of the railings because he did not know who was holding him. He denied inciting others to attack the gardaí and claimed that he had been assaulted with batons and pushed into the side of a garda van. He alleged that after his arrest he had fallen unconscious and was later taken to hospital. CCTV evidence which captured his arrest on video tape was introduced by the defence and viewed in court. It showed what could be described as a fairly normal arrest by officers faced with a violent suspect who was resisting. Although John had been taken to hospital and attended to by doctors, no medical evidence was introduced in court to shore up the claims that he had been rendered unconscious.

Judge Murphy ruled in favour of the prosecution and convicted John. The teenager, she said, had 'wasted five years of his life'. 'You have had about eight sentences in the last year for a number of serious matters, and you are getting another one today.' She imposed a further three-month term of detention which was to begin when the existing sentence expired. John apologised for his actions briefly saying, 'I am sorry for what I did.'

By mid-2006, John was out of custody after all his sentences had expired; the detention centre had granted remission leading to early release. Within weeks, he was arrested again, this time for an incident where it was alleged that he took part in a savage attack in which a man had half his ear bitten off and would require reconstructive plastic surgery. At time of writing, this case is still pending. A detective said in the Children's Court: 'This was an unprovoked attack on the man who could not defend himself; he was repeatedly kicked and his face stamped on.' Garda investigators also had evidence to show that the bottom of one of John's runners had been imprinted on the victim's body.

17 | OUT OF CONTROL

The wild-eyed 16-year-old stood defiantly with blood gushing from his arm. In a suicide bid that followed a frenzied attack on a contingent of gardaí, he had just slashed his wrist with a butcher's carving knife. After a terrifying stand-off with up to fifteen officers, he had made one last-ditch attempt to damage himself and cut the flow of blood in his veins. Some have compared his behaviour on that day to being symptomatic of an attempt at the phenomenon of 'suicide by cop'.[1] The teenager had beckoned armed detectives to shoot him following the showdown which shocked and seriously frightened several experienced officers. With blood spurting from his wrist and clutching on to his last knife, he made a final attempt to storm a cordon of gardaí before collapsing and finally being overpowered.

Michael's almost fatal last stand, on 9 May 2004, in a quiet housing estate in Lucan, Co. Dublin, was the culmination of what had been a life of sheer chaos and instability, stemming from early childhood. His parents first came to the attention of social workers in the mid-1980s following the birth of their first child. At this stage, there were grave concerns over his mother's ability to look after a child—as a result of her long history of broken relationships, exposure to and involvement in violence and her chronic alcoholism. His father also had a drink problem and would later end up homeless.

Over the following years, the welfare concerns grew, and it was during this period that Michael and two other brothers were born. One of the key fears the social services had related to the lack of supervision of Michael and his brothers. In the early 1990s, this problem worsened drastically following their parents' separation.

The children were moved from parent to parent until, in early 1992, Michael, his two brothers and a sister were taken into care on foot of a court order for their own safety. This intervention occurred after the discovery that the children were being looked after by a 13-year-old girl. Having been taken into care, the children had little further contact with their mother, aside from occasional telephone calls to their foster homes.

Their parents also reunited and had more children during this time, but given the history of neglect in their family, some of them too were taken into foster care. Michael's sense of unsettlement, it was believed, was rooted here, in his earliest and most formative years, when he had been moved from the care of one parent to another, into foster homes and care units and finally, when he reached his teens, to hostel accommodation. Eventually it would all lead to a detention centre.

As one of many children in his family, Michael felt that he had received little attention from his parents in his early years. His eldest sister, the first born, was the favourite. When the children spent time together in foster homes, their father would visit from time to time, bearing gifts for the girl only. Michael also found it difficult to comprehend how one of his older brothers had remained within the family home, while he had been put into a care home. By this stage it was believed that he felt he was unwanted by those who had brought him into the world.

Nevertheless, while in foster homes, he made a good start, and was noted to have settled in easily and was deemed to be a friendly boy. He also showed that he had ability and was able to work diligently; his sporting prowess, domestic skills and literacy levels started to improve.

However, deep problems remained, with Michael showing difficulties in understanding the concept of authority and being unable to take direction from others. His problems with rules and regulations became clear when school holidays came around; in the absence of school routine, he became more relaxed. It was also noticed that he had an insatiable need for attention and experienced fits of jealousy and became upset at witnessing other children in the home receiving attention.

His troubles continued throughout his school years. It was while he was in Junior Infants that he started to cause trouble, often running away from school, causing teachers to panic. When he did stay in school, he became aggressive, physically and verbally, to other classmates as well as to his teachers. Attempts by his teachers to reprimand him had no effect, and by the time he was 13, after years of moving to and from different care homes, he was out of the education system.

Despite his many difficulties with being in foster care, he stayed there for ten years. In his first placement, concerns mounted over his troubles. On one occasion, it was decided that he would benefit from a break and he was moved to another foster home. This respite worked well but on return to his original foster parents, his earlier pattern of disruptive behaviour and resentment of authority started to re-assert itself. He was moved and placed in a residential care home, but as a result of an attack on a female member of staff, he was put out of the care home. Having spent a night in emergency hostel accommodation for the homeless, he returned to his foster parents.

More problems followed, and within two months he had to leave; he had been stealing from his foster parents and starting fights with his foster brothers and sisters. At this time, he managed to reconnect with his extended biological family. But this proved to be a brief stay, and he then dropped off the radar and disappeared for nearly two months. He was now just 14 years old and homeless. It was during this period of instability that his behaviour took a further downward spiral, leading to the first of what would become many arrests.

Efforts were made to have Michael link in with social services again, and he was placed in various hostels for the homeless throughout the city. Attempts were made to give him some stability and to breathe life into his schooling, which by now had been defunct for over a year. He was placed on two courses, which were to occupy his time from mornings until 4 p.m., Mondays to Fridays. Social services also made extra efforts to help him to develop his social skills, by allowing him take part in activity-based programmes for troubled children, during the evenings and at weekends. This approach allowed specialists the chance to work with him on a one-to-one basis and to help him deal with his difficulties.

It was hoped that he would then be given the chance to move from hostel accommodation into a structured care environment. But his increasingly aggressive outbursts and involvement in crime thwarted the efforts that had been made on his behalf — leaving him deemed unsuitable for any of the facilities that had been on offer.

It was decided at this stage that he needed to be placed in a high-support secure care unit. But in October 2002, having been arrested for stealing a mobile phone, he was remanded in custody by the Children's Court to the Oberstown Boys' Centre. Throughout his period of detention, his inability to cope with rules again started to manifest itself. He bullied, harassed and attacked several members of staff in the unit—with one of them having to take sick leave because of his injuries.

Seven months later, in mid-2003, he was released from the detention centre. It was intended that he would again access the emergency hostel accommodation and also stay with extended family members in Dublin. However, this situation broke down quickly and he disappeared again. When questioned as to his whereabouts during his long absences, he would not elaborate on what he had been doing, but would just say that he had been 'okay', wherever he had been staying.

A team of care workers was assigned to his case but, following his release from custody, his behaviour showed increased violent tendencies and volatility. He attacked two staff members at one of the hostels he had been staying in and also assaulted a security man at another. This led to his being barred from the hostels— the only accommodation that could be offered to him at the time.

A special conference was then organised to formulate an action plan for him. During this meeting, which involved several care workers, probation officers, and also members of Michael's family, a long-term strategy was worked out. It was envisaged that he would move into the Ballydowd Special Care Unit, and, following a period of stabilisation, he would then be moved to a residential care home. But these plans fell apart at the seam following his arrest in August 2003 for an assault and a mugging.

He was remanded in custody to Trinity House where he was to stay for two months. In October, he was released after the criminal charges against him were struck out in the Children's Court because of legal technicalities. Released from custody, Michael then found a home with a member of his extended family. However, his placement with these relatives lacked stability and was as chaotic as his earlier home life.

In the meantime, efforts were under way to have him put into another residential care home. During the following two months, he was allocated a care worker who was tasked with working on his case full time. A transition plan for him to gain entry into the residential care home was worked out which would allow him to move in January 2004, after an integration stage where he would gradually be introduced into this environment by having overnight stays and day visits.

From the outset, however, this plan seemed doomed to failure. On a day visit, he stayed in the residential care home for just half an hour. Care workers made tireless efforts to persuade him to accept the placement but he refused point blank to have anything to do with their plans. Around this time, his involvement in serious and often violent crime, started to escalate.

On New Year's Day 2004, he was arrested for aggravated burglary and, on the following day, at the Children's Court, he was sentenced to two years in Trinity House for earlier offences. Now aged 15, and completely out of control, Michael was sent to Trinity House because the judge had been told that staff at Oberstown Boys' Centre were afraid of him. He had previously spent seven months on remand in Oberstown while waiting in vain for a place in a high-support unit. Having turned his back on the social workers' efforts to find him a suitable placement, he continued to commit offences.

The court heard that, having absconded from custody, he had taken part in phone snatches and once attacked a garda. It was said that these incidents were caused by his 'frustration' at the lack of progress in finding him a placement in a high-support unit.

The case had been adjourned for sentencing in July 2003, to allow time to monitor the teenager's behaviour. A condition of his bail had been that he stay at a hostel where anger management counselling and educational assistance would be provided. But on his sentencing date he had failed to appear in court and had avoided detention. Since then, he had been arrested for joyriding-associated offences. Detaining him, Judge Mary Collins said that the teenager had complied with none of the bail conditions set down by the court.

At the outset, it appeared that Michael was excelling in the Trinity House Detention Centre's educational programme, and it was hoped that he would study for the Junior Certificate. However, Trinity House had just thirty spaces, and its staff found it nearly impossible to cope with Michael's violence. Once, an entire wing of the centre had to be shut down—to give the care workers space to control him. The case was brought back to the Children's Court in April, where senior officials pleaded to have the boy moved. According to one official, Michael had attacked staff eight times, had been keeping weapons and was 'out of control'. The deputy director of Trinity House said that in the preceding three months there had been eight assaults on staff members and 'fifteen other issues. I can say that we are the only secure unit in Ireland but unfortunately we cannot look after him.' He added that if the boy was returned to Trinity House it would be necessary for them to close down an entire wing of the unit, including eight beds, so they could look after him. If he were returned to the centre, they would take steps to have the boy declared too unruly to be held in their custody and to have him moved. 'We have given him every chance; we have tried everything with him. If he comes back today it would require closing down a unit of eight beds to look after him.'

'We can't contain him, there is a history of assault and aggressive behaviour that we cannot manage,' he added.

The case was adjourned for two weeks, with an order letting Michael return to Trinity House. The fears expressed by the officials from the detention centre seemed well founded. In his short time there, Michael made no effort to engage in any of their behavioural assistance programmes. This period was marked by increased volatility with several incidents of aggressive and violent acts towards staff members.

Four days after returning to Trinity House, Michael threatened and attacked staff with a knife. He was eventually restrained and had to be moved into solitary confinement. The following day, he attacked a member of staff with a chair and also charged at him with a plastic knife. He then barricaded himself into a toilet and, when physically removed, had to be put into a special protection room for a lengthy period. During the attempts to move him to the room, Michael rammed his head into a care worker's stomach before proceeding to make frightening threats of violence to other members of staff.

Four days later, he refused to co-operate with the staff and became aggressive once again, requiring him to be restrained. This proved to be a difficult task and eight people were needed, working together, to control him. Because of his violence, handcuffs were necessary to restrain him. It was the first time in three years that it had been necessary to resort to the use of handcuffs in the detention centre.

The next day, he again tried to assault a staff member. Four days after that, having been taken to the Children's Court to face other pending charges, he tried to abscond from custody, and several gardaí were needed to return him to Trinity House.

A week later, back in Trinity House, in spite of warnings about his behaviour, he threw a tea pot against a wall, then threatened to stab a staff member and tried to punch him. Three days later, when he was challenged over his behaviour in the centre's gym, he attacked a staff member with a punch to his eye. Again, he had to be restrained and put into the protection room. Two days later, he broke the locking mechanism on a door. He had also taken to making improvised weapons. It was believed that these home-made weapons were designed specifically to damage one member of staff. Later that day, while again being challenged over his behaviour, he injured a staff member's shoulder. Four days later, he threw chairs around a room. He also broke a window frame to use as a weapon and with it threatened the staff.

On another occasion, he punched and head-butted a care worker. Later, while care workers tried to speak to him about his problems, he again lashed out with a punch and had to be put into the protection room. He then lit two fires, causing damage to the unit. Over the next six weeks, there were several more disturbing incidents. These ranged from the breaking of a stereo to serious attacks on the unit's beleaguered staff. Even the more minor incidents, such as the smashing up of the stereo, featured frightening factors, with Michael using the broken and sharpened stereo parts to make an improvised weapon.

In a desperate move to break the cycle of violence, the care workers decided to use an alternative approach to get through to the teenager. Arrangements were made for him to take part in an 'adventure therapy programme' which involved a tightly supervised outdoors hike. On the evening he was taken from the centre to take part in the hike, Michael leaped from the moving van in which he and a team of care workers had been travelling. The van was doing a speed of 60 mph when he made his jump for freedom which, in a feat that any veteran paratrooper would be proud of, remarkably left him unscathed. By now, he clearly had a total disregard for his own safety.

In his final month at Trinity House, Michael broke out of the unit and remained missing for three weeks. Having spent that time sleeping rough, he returned voluntarily to Trinity House and that night took part in a premeditated attack on a care worker. It was evident that the centre could no longer hold the increasingly violent and uncooperative teenager.

In April, the consequences of the burglary committed by Michael on New Year's Day 2004 caught up with him. At the Children's Court, it was heard that during a cocaine-fuelled burglary, he had broken into a house in Lucan through an upstairs bathroom window. On encountering the woman who lived in the house, he had produced a screwdriver. 'A number of threats were made to the woman that she would be stabbed,' the prosecuting garda said. Michael had made off with the woman's laptop, worth €1,500, together with her car. Michael pleaded guilty to the charges. His growing criminal record was outlined to the court; by now he already had twenty-three previous convictions for assaults, car thefts, criminal damage and public order offences.

Judge Angela Ní Chonduin read comprehensive reports on the boy's background and his conduct in Trinity House and remarked that she found elements of the report disturbing and frightening. 'That report is scary; I am inclined to give a long sentence,' she said. Noting pleas for leniency on the grounds of his cocaine addiction and troubled history, and taking into consideration Michael's guilty plea, Judge Ní Chonduin imposed a twenty-month sentence to be served in St Patrick's Institution. Now that he had passed his sixteenth birthday, he was eligible to be detained there.

After the case was concluded, Michael was sent down to the courthouse cells to await his transportation to St Patrick's Institution. While being transferred to the detention centre, he turned to the garda who had successfully prosecuted him for the burglary and chillingly told him: 'I'll have to get out some time and when I do, I'll get you.' The date was 28 April 2004.

Despite being detained by the court, Michael instructed his legal team to bring the case to the Circuit Court to launch an appeal against the severity of the sentence. Within days, he was released from custody pending the appeal, and within weeks he was again arrested, for attempting to make good the threat that he had made to the garda.

Michael was brought back before the Children's Court on 10 May and remanded in custody. Medical attention for him was also ordered. A week later, when the case was back before the judge, the court was told that he had been charged with a burglary in Lucan, Co. Dublin, where it was alleged he had also attempted to injure gardaí by throwing kitchen knives and swinging a shovel at them.

Noting the Garda Síochána's objections to bail, Judge Cormac Dunne remanded Michael in custody to St Patrick's Institution for two weeks, pending directions from the Director of Public Prosecutions. Two weeks later, the court heard further evidence that Michael had threatened to burn down gardaí's houses and would also interfere with civilian witnesses whom he had threatened.

Judge Ní Chonduin refused bail and further remanded the teenager in custody to St Patrick's Institution until 25 June. At a later appearance, the court was also told that some twenty prosecuting witnesses could be called, which suggested the gravity of the allegations.

In mid-July, Michael pleaded guilty to the range of offences and a full account of his actions on 9 May was outlined to the court. During the hearing, Judge Mary Collins heard how Michael had gone berserk and run amok in the incident which involved fifteen gardaí, including one in riot gear, the garda helicopter and armed detectives. During the incident, Michael, by now a cocaine addict, had repeatedly tried to stab four gardaí with an assortment of carving, steak and butcher's knives. He had then run from house to house, across rooftops, threatened civilians, tried to hijack a car to get away, and ultimately tried to slash his wrist, having made one last charge at a garda while wielding a knife. Several of the gardaí involved in the arrest said that they had been in fear of their lives while dealing with the dangerously out-of-control teenager.

The incident had begun when a garda had come across Michael in the Liffey Valley Park area of west Dublin. Michael had been in breach of bail conditions by being outdoors during court-imposed curfew hours. When spotted, he was drinking a bottle of Smirnoff Ice and was in an area from which the court had also barred him. On seeing the garda, Michael had run and entered the grounds of a house on Liffey Road, from which he had got into the back garden of a neighbouring house on Liffey Terrace. He had found a rake and threatened to hit the garda with it before picking up a shovel with which he smashed in the back door and window of the house, while making threats to kill gardaí.

Having entered this house, which was occupied at the time, and tried to escape through its front door, Michael had found his path blocked by other gardaí waiting outside. In the kitchen of the house, he had found the twelve knives which, minutes later, he would use as weapons against the officers who were trying to arrest him.

Michael had then run out of the house and thrown one of the knives at a garda while shouting: 'I'll kill you, I'll put a knife in you.' He had then re-entered the house and run out to the back garden. There he had been approached by another garda who had a 13-inch butcher's knife thrown at him, which hit him on his arm. Michael had repeated his threats: 'I will kill you, you f**king bastard.'

A 13-inch carving knife had narrowly missed another officer. Michael had then shouted at two others, reiterating his threats: 'I will f**king kill, I'll put a knife in you.'

Having been repeatedly threatened and had knives thrown at them, the gardaí had been forced to take cover. Michael had then climbed onto the gable end of a house on Liffey Place. He was now surrounded by up to fifteen gardaí who were desperately trying to seal off the area below him. As one officer was trying to clear civilians from the immediate area, to protect them from harm, he had had another knife thrown at him, which hit him on the arm.

As gardaí had then tried to talk Michael down off the roof, the teenager had tried to break into the house on which he was standing. Unable to gain entry, he had nimbly jumped off the gable end and landed on a garden side wall, and having threatened more gardaí who had approached him, he had then run along the rear walls of a number of houses and tried to climb on to the roof of one of the properties, while threatening to harm one of the residents. Finding himself surrounded by gardaí, he had charged at one officer with the knife. The court was told that this officer was in riot gear, which 'probably saved him from being stabbed'. Michael had then run at another garda and tried to escape along Liffey Drive where he had unsuccessfully attempted to hijack a car. When he was again surrounded by the gardaí, he had issued more threats to stab them, adding that he would also kill himself.

Armed detectives had been called to the scene, at which point Michael 'cut his own left forearm and ran at a garda with a knife'.

At this point, he had been captured and taken to hospital for his injuries to be treated.

The following day, when brought to court, the boy continued to make threats, saying that Ronanstown Garda Station would burn. 'I took these threats seriously as I feel he would be capable of doing so,' a garda told Judge Collins.

Concluding his evidence, the garda said: 'The incident on 9 May had fifteen garda at the scene, as well as the garda helicopter and armed detectives. This was also while the defendant was on bail on a curfew.'

The prosecuting garda said, 'It was an extremely serious incident where myself and other gardaí were in fear for our safety and that of civilians. There was a serious risk to life; he was totally out of control on the night in question. It was very dangerous for all concerned and a number of colleagues have said to me that they were totally in fear as he was out of control.'

Michael had pleaded guilty to the fifteen charges arising out of the incident on 9 May. This brought his record of convictions to forty-four. He remained silent and handcuffed throughout the hearing, in which courtroom security had to be heightened. He was flanked by two gardaí each side of the dock. Three more were in support nearby and another stood blocking the doorway. Judge Mary Collins imposed a term of detention totalling seventeen months. None of his family members were in court to support him.

At time of writing, Michael, now a father of one, is facing three separate trials, for incidents that occurred after his early release: one for stabbing a man in Stephen's Green; and another for going berserk and attacking his ex-girlfriend's family—over access rights to his young baby. There are further allegations of two car hijackings in which knives were used. He is also a suspect in a crime spree in north Dublin in which an elderly woman was bludgeoned, a child almost sexually assaulted and a garda very seriously injured from a beating.

18 DEVOTED TO CRIME

Many of the young people who are caught up in a cycle of crime are quite sharp witted, bright and innovative, and some have ingenious talents. A great many of them, having once had a taste of the system and the prospect of a criminal record, learn a lesson and there and then end their flirtation with criminal activity. One innovative teenager, a 16-year-old electronics buff from Finglas, in a once-off and misguided offence, used his remarkable talents to remove a CCTV system from a block of flats in Ballymun and install it around his own home. He cleverly managed to connect the stolen equipment to the family television set which picked up clear images from the four cameras he had positioned around the outside of the house. But the sight of the cameras around his home aroused suspicion and led gardaí to his doorstep. It was later revealed that over three nights the boy had completely dismantled four CCTV cameras, the property of a security company, from a lift shaft in a building in Ballymun.

In October 2002, in the Children's Court, Judge Anne Watkin was told that the boy's parents did not know that the equipment was stolen. They were 'horrified' when they found out what their son had done as they had believed that he had found the CCTV system discarded in a rubbish dump. To his credit, the teenager was extremely co-operative with gardaí and the property was returned and reinstalled shortly after. He had taken the equipment foolishly in pursuit of his interests in electronics. It had not been his intention to take the security system for resale, his solicitor said.

Judge Watkin said that despite the fact that the boy had not tried to profit from his crime, his conduct was 'inexcusable'. However, she gave him eight weeks to pay €400 to the St Vincent De Paul charity but stipulated that the money must come out of his own pocket. His parents told her that the boy would pay the fine himself by using money he had saved during the summer and his children's allowance. His mother had said that he could 'make do with the clothes he has' until the money was paid.

At a later date, the court was told that the boy had earned €200 through part-time work and that his parents had made up the balance. However, his father assured the judge that it would come out of the boy's children's allowance. The judge gave the boy the benefit of the Probation Act, which left him without a criminal conviction, and she told him that she hoped not to see him in court again. Never again did he come before the criminal justice system. He benefited from solid family support, a hardworking nature and an ability not to allow this brush with the law distract him from living an honest life.

Meanwhile, Mark, a similarly bright teenager, who was from the same area, had blazed a city-wide trail of petty crimes for two-and-a-half years. According to one judge, Mark, who had been entrenched in crime since his early teens, was 'a clever young man' who had dedicated his intelligence to crime. This 16-year-old boy's crime spree ended in November 2004 when he was detained for fifteen months. Gardaí strongly suspected that Mark had been involved in widespread robberies such as ram raiding of shops outside the capital. These antics had brought him across the country; he had once been arrested in Galway for stealing a substantial sum of money from a supermarket. He even had a brush with the law in Northern Ireland, where a magistrates' court had ordered six months' detention but put a stay on the warrant until that midnight with the proviso that he leave the jurisdiction in that time—and not return.

Mark, freckled and boyish looking, came into the criminal justice system when he was aged 13. Over the following two years, he was to make regular appearances at the Children's Court. On 10 February 2003, aged 14 and facing twenty-six charges, he was released on bail because there were no suitable places in the state's juvenile institutions to hold him. Mark had previously completed a three-week assessment in the non-secure St Michael's Institution, in Finglas,[1] and staff there recommended that he should be sent to a secure facility. It was believed that putting him in a secure institution would be a good step to improve his education and welfare. However, both Trinity House and Oberstown Boys' Centre were full up and could not take him.

Judge William Early was told that Mark was also facing numerous charges for offences such as larceny, skipping court, criminal damage, handling stolen goods, theft and joyriding. On 2 February 2003, he had been caught with two bottles of stolen perfume. On 10 August 2002, he had tried to steal a moped by breaking its lock using a bolt-cutter, but he was disturbed and fled. He had also criminally damaged an item of clothing in a sports shop on Mary Street when he was ripping off its security tag.

His family, the court was told, was anxious for him to be given bail and released from St Michael's Institution. However, a report from St Michael's said that Mark had continued to be involved in criminal pursuits and, in the interests of his education, he should be sent to a detention centre such as Trinity House or Oberstown Boys' Centre.

Judge Early let the case stand for two hours to see if there were any available detention places where Mark could be put. However, there was a waiting list for both facilities and it was unknown when he could get a placement. In light of these circumstances, Judge Early released Mark on bail for one week to see if a place could be secured by then. 'It is a matter of urgency that he does have a secure placement,' he said.

A week later, Mark made the journey to court and, a short time later, left smiling with his family, having heard that he could not be held because of the shortage of detention spaces. Judge Thomas Fitzpatrick said that in view of the lack of places, he could not sentence the boy and adjourned the case until 3 March 2003 with the hope that a placement would be available by then. It was almost as though Mark knew his detention was now possible, as on that date he skipped court and a warrant was issued for his arrest.

Ten days later, gardaí picked him up on the bench warrant and conveyed him to court. Judge Sean McBride refused pleas to release Mark into the custody of his father and remanded him in custody to St Michael's Institution for one week.

In the following months, he was in and out of custody on remand, with no permanent sentence beds becoming available for him. Throughout that time, he continued to come to garda attention with some of his activities becoming more daring. On 4 July 2003, he and his stepbrother stole €3,500 from a kiosk. He was arrested, charged with theft and remanded on bail.

On 6 November 2003, he pleaded guilty before Judge Leo Malone at the Children's Court. Evidence was given, detailing how his stepbrother had distracted a staff member while Mark, unnoticed, reached over the counter and snatched a bag of cash. Every cent of the stolen money had been frittered away by the pair, on tracksuits and games in amusement arcades.

The boys' solicitor told the court that Mark and his stepbrother were out of school and unemployed. She said that they wanted to compensate the injured party but, given their limited circumstances, it was unlikely that they could do so. Judge Malone said that the injured party was still at a loss of a considerable amount of money and that he was considering a custodial sentence. However, after pleas to adjourn the case pending intervention from probation officers, he remanded the boys on bail until 8 January 2004. Mark was back out on the streets again as these charges were added to the existing pile of prosecutions already running against him.

Months drifted by with remand after remand and further probation reports being sought. On 8 June 2004, he was back in court but the case got nowhere as he had come to court without a parent or guardian as required by the 2001 Children's Act. When he enquired as to the whereabouts of the boy's father, Judge

William Hamill was told that the man had not come to court and had opted to stay at home in bed instead. Mark, then aged 15, was facing about fifty charges, for offences committed over the previous two years.

That, said Judge Hamill, showed the extent of the man's interest in his son. He said that under the Children's Act 2001, a parent or guardian of a juvenile defendant must be present during the court proceedings. There had been no indication that the father had been sick but it appeared that he had simply stayed at home in bed when he was supposed to come to court with his son. The judge said: 'Section 91 of the Children's Act 2001 states: The parent or guardian of a child shall be required to attend at all stages of criminal proceedings.'[2] He issued a bench warrant for the father's arrest to compel him to accompany his son to court on the next date.

The case was adjourned and the teenager was granted bail until 28 June. The father was later brought to court by gardaí. Judge Michael Connellan presided in the court that day and did not hold back in his criticism of the father whom he blamed for Mark's having gone out of control. At that point, Judge Connellan was told that there had been a new development in Mark's life: he was going to become a father.

When Judge Connellan said that Mark's own father should have controlled him more, the man responded inarticulately and shrugged off the judge's comments with a smile. The case was adjourned to be brought back on a date when Judge William Early was presiding in the court, as he had dealt with most of the cases against Mark.

On 30 July 2004, Mark, still out of school and not in any type of training course or job, was given an ultimatum to change his life and to learn a trade or else face fifteen months' detention. Judge Early heard that Mark, now turned 16 had pleaded guilty to fifty charges of theft, assault, motoring and public order offences, which started in early 2002.

At this juncture, Mark was a father of one, had failed to meet with probation workers and had delayed the finalisation of his case, which pushed him into a new detention category: he could now be held in St Patrick's Institution. His solicitor said that Mark lived with both his parents and siblings but had dropped out of education after his second year in secondary school. He added that Mark was now out of work, but was taking steps to enrol on a FÁS training course.

Having inspected volumes of probation reports and assessment reports on Mark, Judge Early said: 'The reports indicate that you are a clever young man but it seems that your intelligence is devoted to the commission of crime.' 'Where do you see yourself in five years time?' he asked the boy. At first, Mark simply shrugged and, ill at ease, replied 'Dunno.' Then he spoke up and told the court that he would like to get a trade and become a carpenter. When further asked if he thought that he could do that, Mark volunteered that he had already been trying to find a placement on a FÁS training course which could lead to an apprenticeship.

The court also heard that in the weeks before that court appearance, Mark had not been getting into trouble as he had become a father. The youth was remanded on bail but received a warning that this would be the last chance he would get. 'Be under no illusion, you must co-operate in full. If you do not take yourself in hand you will be going to St Patrick's Institution for fifteen months,' the judge told him.

Adjourning sentencing until November, Judge Early indicated that if Mark had made efforts to start a course to learn a trade, he would suspend that sentence.

However, at the sentence hearing in the Children's Court, on 29 November 2004, Judge Early noted that Mark had missed all six of his scheduled appointments with his probation officer. Refusing to adjourn the case further, the judge ordered that Mark should be detained in St Patrick's Institution for the fifteen months he had previously indicated and he was also banned from driving for five years.

Mark stayed silent during most of the hearing but then started to shift awkwardly on his seat when it became clear that he was not going to be leaving court by its front door, as he had done so many times before. He looked around with a nervous smile and then his eyes filled with tears. He was taken from the courtroom through a second doorway which leads to the cells downstairs where he waited briefly and was then put in a van to be transferred to St Patrick's Institution.

The teenager had also been left alone to await his fate. There were no members of his family in court to support him. By not bothering to meet with probation workers and delaying the finalisation of his case, Mark had pushed himself into a new detention category, meaning he could now be held in St Patrick's Institution, with youths up to four years older than him, instead of either Oberstown Boys' Centre or Trinity House which have a greater focus on education and welfare.

In May 2005, a number of remaining charges were finalised which resulted in an extra month being added to his sentence. These included being drunk and disorderly and, when cautioned to leave an area, failing to comply with the direction; possession of a screwdriver for use during the course of a theft; and travelling in a stolen car. The teenager had admitted the offences which took place within the weeks prior to his previous sentence hearing. His solicitor said that since going into custody Mark had progressed well and was planning to study for the Junior Certificate. She said that although the boy's parents were not at the hearing, they did visit him regularly in St Patrick's Institution. However, Judge Mary Collins said, 'The reality is that these offences were committed as he was about to be sentenced on other matters.' She imposed two concurrent one-month terms, which she ordered must run consecutively to his existing term, giving him an extra four weeks in custody.

Since his release, and having now reached adulthood, Mark has gone on to become a regular defendant at the District Courts in Dublin.

19 | GIRL TROUBLE

As a child, Michelle was a normal girl who played with dolls and loved animals. Until she was nine years old, despite an unsettled family background, she did all the things that most little girls did. The next ten years would be a different story —though educationally she would remain at that age level. The ensuing decade would see her become one of Ireland's most troubled and troublesome girls. Of all the girls to come before the courts in recent years, she stood out on many levels; she was repeatedly involved in incidents of extreme violence, while her courtroom demeanour was that of a quiet and shy child. A key factor in her background was the lack of involvement of specialist help at an early age when she needed it most. Throughout her involvement with the criminal justice system, a paralysis set in in the court's efforts to deter her from the destructive path on which she had started out.

In August 2002, aged 15, Michelle was sentenced to two years in Oberstown Girls' Centre. Her father had personal problems stemming from alcoholism yet he was the one who stuck by Michelle's side most. Her mother had left the family. After her detention, her father gave his daughter 'one last chance' and posted appeal bail which saw her released after she had served eight months. By now, she already had ten previous convictions for assault, public order offences and possession of weapons.

Her father would later explain in court that when his daughter was aged 14, her social worker had left her job and in the following four years no replacement had been assigned. That would become a recurring theme in the case for the next three years. His firm belief was that his daughter had psychiatric problems which had never been addressed. He stated that he had been doing everything he could, as a lone parent, to look after his children. Amazingly, he estimated that he had come to court with his daughter over 200 times. This had resulted in him losing his job.

Michelle's father believed that his daughter had missed out on an opportunity to be helped through the Juvenile Liaison Scheme. Her first brush with the law had occurred when she was about 12. By then she had been missing school on a regular basis and had taken to hanging around with older youths. First, they loitered at a shopping centre. As time went by, and under the influence of the older teenagers, Michelle had become involved in violently confrontational situations. Not long after that, she started drinking heavily, and her conduct worsened drastically. The father claimed that his heavy working hours meant that he had not been aware of the change in his daughter's behaviour outside the family home and his wife had not alerted him to the signs.

In June 2003, Michelle was remanded back into custody after the court was told that she needed psychological and psychiatric help. Now aged 16, she was facing assault and breach of the peace charges arising out of an incident in which she had tried to attack a husband and wife, who were in their late sixties. This had happened in the couple's Tallaght home, on 23 May 2002, while Michelle's earlier offences were still being dealt with. Michelle had hurled herself at the couple's patio door and made death threats against them in the twenty-minute attack on their home.

In evidence, the elderly man told Judge Geoffrey Browne that he had heard a loud bang from their front porch. His wife had then seen Michelle's younger brother standing in front of their glass patio door, exposing himself to her. The worried man had brought his wife away from the door and kept guard himself. The little brother had backed off and started to wave a knife at the man, and then Michelle had appeared and threatened him. 'She told me she would cut my head off and dance on it,' the man recalled.

After this threat, Michelle had flung herself against the glass door, spat on it and kicked tiles off the front step. The man, afraid of Michelle and her brother, had pleaded with them to stop. His frightened wife, meanwhile, had sought sanctuary in another room and sobbed as he tried to hold the glass door shut while simultaneously dialling 999. 'She had evil in her face; there is something mentally wrong with a girl like that; she is dangerous. I was sure that she would force the door open,' the man told the court.

The man, who was still in shock months later, said that the events had been part of an ongoing campaign of harassment to which he and his wife had been subjected by these children for a number of years. His wife said that Michelle had made unrepeatable threats to her after her brother had exposed himself. When gardaí had arrived, Michelle was nearby with a can of lager in her hand. She had been arrested and taken to Tallaght Garda Station in handcuffs. Once there, she had lashed out and kicked a female garda. Judge Browne convicted Michelle and held that she needed treatment for her behavioural problems.

Michelle's father said that the incident had arisen out of a long-standing bad relationship between his family and the elderly couple. He claimed that the couple had verbally abused him and his children but agreed with Judge Browne that his daughter's actions towards the couple were unacceptable. The father told Judge Browne that he had known for some time that his daughter needed specialised help. He said that difficult family circumstances and his working hours meant that he had not been able to control her.

Judge Browne accepted the father's statement but said that Michelle needed treatment to prevent her from ending up 'on a slippery slope'. 'She is terrorising these people,' he said in relation to the elderly victims. 'They are entitled to enjoy to their lives.'

Seeing sense, the father then decided to rescind the appeal bail he had lodged for his daughter so that she could be sent back into

custody to serve out the rest of her term. Explaining that therapeutic intervention was Michelle's most important need, Judge
Browne remanded Michelle in custody to Oberstown Girls' Centre
for assessment and ordered a probation and medical report with
particular reference to her psychological and psychiatric needs.
The court was also told that Michelle's younger brother would be
cautioned by a garda from the Juvenile Liaison Office over his role
in the incident. The father agreed with Judge Browne that more
control needed to be exercised over his son too.

On 24 September 2003, Judge John Coughlan heard how
Michelle's offending partly stemmed from alcohol abuse. In
another incident, she had pulled a knife on a security guard in
Tallaght's Square Shopping Centre, telling him that she would 'slit
him up'. in addition to her attack on the neighbours she had
attacked a friend's mother with a half-empty whiskey bottle.
Having turned up at the friend's home, Michelle had been told by
the girl's mother that it was too late for her daughter to go out.
Michelle had then started a fight in the front garden of the house
and tried to hit the woman with the bottle.

She had also assaulted four gardaí when arrested for being
drunk and disorderly and had repeatedly bitten numerous gardaí
while resisting arrest. During the course of one arrest in which she
had needed to be restrained, she had managed to bite the same
garda twice. On another occasion, she had threatened to 'knee cap'
an unsuspecting woman she met at a bus stop.

Michelle's counsel said that much of her attitude and crimes
were rooted in her drinking problem, and that her father, a lone
parent, was also a recovering alcoholic.

Judge Coughlan held that the best place to detain Michelle was
Oberstown Girls' Centre where it was hoped she could receive
help for her educational and behavioural problems. Through
monosyllabic answers and nodding to the judge's questions,
Michelle told the court that she could not explain why she had
been constantly getting into trouble and she also agreed that it was
in everyone's interest that she be sent to Oberstown. In court, she
rarely came out of her shell. Instead she remained coyly
quiet, smiling. Concluding the case, Judge Coughlan imposed

consecutive one-month terms of detention on twenty of the
charges, with the rest of the offences taken into consideration. The
institution's sentencing regime could not accept a two-year term
for a girl of her age. In girls' cases, the Children's Court is limited
in its detention orders for under 17s and restricted to imposing
either one-month or two-year terms. However, Oberstown's policy
was not to take 16-year-old girls for longer than a month.

Despite the sentence, Michelle was released. This was against
the expressed wishes of her father, which left Michelle's lawyers
facing conflicting sets of instructions: her father was against the
appeal; Michelle wanted it. The case eventually ended up in the
High Court for a ruling on whose legal instructions, father's or
daughter's, should take precedence. The High Court held that
Michelle's lawyers had to take her instructions over those of her
father. The appeal was launched; Michelle was released on bail and
then ran completely wild.

That month, she took part in a serious attack on her elderly
neighbour. And on 10 October 2003, in Firhouse, she participated
in a vicious attack on a girl who was going out to celebrate her
eighteenth birthday. A week later, she was involved in another
cruel gang attack in which a woman was savagely beaten and set
on fire.

The 18-year-old victim was care free as she was making her way to
the city centre to celebrate her birthday with friends. She was
approached by Michelle and her 17-year-old accomplice who told
her she smelt like a 'whore' and 'would get pregnant dressed like
that'. They dragged her onto the ground by her hair and beat her.
They then stole her handbag which contained her passport and
some money which she had been given for her birthday. They also
stole her mobile phone and, to add insult to injury, they poured
beer over her head and left the scene jeering. Her passport was
recovered near the scene of the robbery but her mobile phone and
her money were never returned.

A week later, Michelle took part in the next, equally barbaric,
attack. A judge would later compare the behaviour of Michelle
and her accomplices in this attack to that of 'mad dogs'. The

victim, a young woman, left a disco with two male friends at about 3 a.m. They went into a Centra Shop at the junction of Parnell Street and O'Connell Street to buy some food. Outside the shop one of the men approached a 26-year-old woman who was there with Michelle and another young woman. This resulted in an altercation and Michelle and her two friends attacked. Michelle set the victim's hair on fire with a cigarette lighter; it was quickly extinguished but her two accomplices then pulled the woman by her hair and dragged her to the ground. It took two men to pull Michelle and her two female accomplices off the victim. The three fled but gardaí identified them from CCTV footage. A medical examination found that the victim had a patch of hair loss measuring 20 cm. She also had a large 10 cm bruise on her thigh and some bruising on her arm.

A garda, who had been given an adequate description of the perpetrators by the victim and her friends, subsequently saw the three women a short distance away and arrested them. These two attacks were deemed so serious that the case was heard not in the Children's Court but in Dublin Circuit Criminal Court instead.

On Tuesday, 28 October, Judge Michael Connellan, in the Children's Court, said that Michelle was 'running wild'; since being released pending her appeal, she had been constantly coming into the city centre and committing offences ranging from public order breaches, to thefts and assaults. The judge said that the girl was 'roaming the streets at night' and urgently needed some control in her life. Her father must take responsibility in curtailing her activities and come to court with her. 'I understand that he is working,' he said. 'But it is either that or his child.'

Judge Connellan adjourned the case and granted bail. Michelle was banned from going to the city centre and subject to a nightly curfew. He also directed that Michelle's father accompany her to court on the next occasion or a warrant would be issued for his arrest.

On 22 December 2003, Michelle was detained on her sixty-first criminal conviction. Before coming to court that morning she already had forty-one convictions. Thirty of the convictions had resulted in her detention that previous September; but her subsequent release had allowed her to commit a string of offences which brought her back before a judge again. Judge Bridget Reilly heard how Michelle had enormous personal problems which had developed after her parents' separation.

Her latest litany of offences did not include the attack on her neighbour or the fire attack on the woman on Parnell Street as these prosecutions were still in preparation stages. She had also been repeatedly arrested late at night in the city centre from which she had been barred.

On 22 March 2003, while at large, she had been found extremely drunk and barely able to stand. She became aggressive and abusive to a garda, telling him to 'f**k off'. She then tried to force herself into vomiting on to the squad car by sticking her fingers down her throat.

On 8 October 2003, she was arrested outside a children's disco for being drunk and disorderly. When arrested, she launched into a tirade in which she referred to a district court judge as 'a fat c**t' as well as calling gardaí 'queers'. She was then taken to Tallaght Garda Station but struggled en route. At the station, she attacked a female officer and pulled clumps of her hair out.

Six days later, she was found drunk, falling in front of cars travelling along Dublin's O'Connell Street. A member of the public had reported her to a garda for snatching a mobile phone, and when she saw that he was informing the officer, she called him a 'wanker' and threatened to smash his glasses. As in her other arrests, she resisted and violently struggled with gardaí.

In another incident, on 30 October, she walked into Tallaght Garda Station and created a disturbance and told gardaí to 'f**k off' before putting up another struggle. She was arrested on O'Connell Street on 19 November 2003, when she was caught screaming abuse at passers-by. She was repeatedly cautioned to leave the area, but was caught there an hour later, harassing members of the public.

A few days earlier, on 12 November, she had stolen a mobile phone from a woman at Bachelor's Walk. When caught, she

The late Robert McGowan's father, Patrick, and sister, Lorraine, outside the Dublin Circuit Criminal Court after a teenager was jailed for manslaughter. Robert was killed when his taxi was hit by a stolen car. (© *Collins Photos*)

Family man Thomas Farrell was murdered when he disturbed two people stealing his car. A teenager (aged 17) had been hot-wiring it. Thomas Farrell was stabbed by the boy's accomplice. (*Courtesy of Independent Newspapers*)

Darren Rogers (21) was found guilty at the Central Criminal Court of murdering Thomas Farrell and was sentenced to life. His 17-year-old accomplice was charged at the Children's Court with attempted car theft and given a suspended sentence. (© *Collins Photos*)

Oberstown Detention Centre, in Lusk, Co. Dublin. The centre—when it has places available—focuses on the education and welfare of the young people held there. (© *Collins Photos*)

The fate of a stolen car: this Nissan Micra at a breakers' yard was crashed by a joyrider in Swords, Co. Dublin, after gardaí had been led on a lengthy and dangerous high-speed pursuit. (© *Collins Photos*)

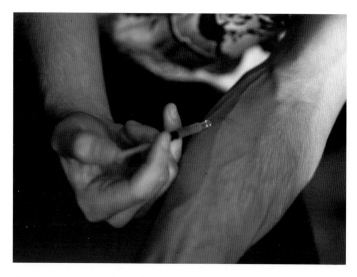

The scourge of heroin addiction affects many of the young people who come before the Children's Court, such as Peter in Chapter 2. (© *Collins Photos*)

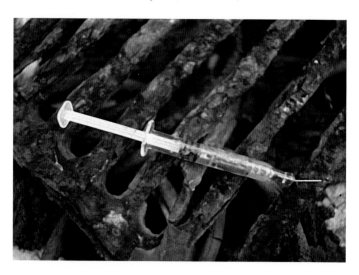

The nightmare of living on the streets is a reality for many troubled young people who have nowhere to go. (© *Collins Photos*)

A teenager is led from court in handcuffs to await transfer to St Patrick's Institution. (© *Derek Speirs*)

Two inmates in St Patrick's Institution pass the time. Here, young offenders find a hostile environment, with the free availability of drugs. Bullying is rife. (© *Derek Speirs*)

One of the recreation rooms in St Patrick's Institution. (© *Derek Speirs*)

Fearless, two young offenders break out onto the top of St Patrick's Institution, in Dublin; there they held a protest, which ended peacefully when they were lifted down by a hoist. (© *Collins Photos*)

A young offender in his cell in St Patrick's Institution where juveniles and adults, up to the age of 21, are held together. (© *Derek Speirs*)

threatened to 'slash' the garda's face. Later at Store Street Garda Station, she lashed out violently and had to be restrained. On 15 December, a week before her sentence hearing, she was arrested for an act of criminal damage at the Dublin Children's Courthouse. This was in connection with an act of graffiti in which 'Garda Scum' was engraved on the courthouse outside wall.

On 19 December, a garda on Dame Street had been dealing with a disorderly youth when Michelle attacked her, while screaming madly. The garda was kicked on her leg, resulting in a large and painful bruise below her knee. After the teenage girl was arrested, she became violent and struggled with the garda while she was being taken to Pearse Street Garda Station.

Michelle's father reiterated in court how he had been against his daughter's release to appeal her earlier convictions. He also said that the health board had done little to help Michelle at a young age when she needed it most.

Volumes of reports on Michelle's psychiatric and educational difficulties were handed into court for the judge's inspection. Having studied them, Judge Reilly referred to Michelle as a 'vulnerable young woman in need of a lot of help'. Referring to her problems, she said: 'It did not arise overnight; there had been difficulties in her family background going back a number of years.'

Michelle was given a series of one-month detention orders to run concurrently, detaining her in Oberstown Girls' Centre. She ended up serving only a couple of weeks. At the end of December, she turned 17 and appealed to the High Court that she was too old to be held in Oberstown. She was released by New Year's Day.

In March 2004, Michelle was back in court to face allegations for a second attack on her elderly neighbours. The couple were back in court for a second time. During the hearing, the man explained how he had been driven to sell his home and move 70 miles to get away from Michelle who had continued to terrorise, victimise and harass his wife and himself. His wife had suffered a nervous breakdown after the years of torment, he explained.

A garda from Tallaght gave evidence that on the previous 6 September he had taken a complaint from the victim who said that Michelle, then aged 17, had pelted his home with eggs. The man had gone outside to investigate what was happening and had found Michelle and her younger brother throwing the eggs and a variety of missiles at his windows. Michelle had left the scene as the victim pleaded with her brother to stop.

Michelle had then returned and 'grabbed the man from behind, ripped his shirt and tried to scrape his face'. When the man had tried to restrain her, she had lashed out, using her fingernails to scrape him on his chest and following up with a kick to his groin, leaving him in agonising pain. 'Later I cautioned her that a complaint had been made and she said she would never make a statement to the gardaí,' the Tallaght garda told the court.

Michelle had pleaded guilty to assaulting the pensioner at his home. He told the court that while Michelle was attacking him, 'Her gang was at the gate and she was screaming to them to get her older brother who is a big man. If he had come out to me, I would have ended up in hospital.'

Later that day, the man had met her and asked her: 'When are you going to grow up?' to which Michelle had replied that 'she would bomb my house.' He continued: 'That night she threw two blocks through my window. We have since moved and are the fourth family in the area to move out to get away from her.' Referring to the earlier attack, he said, 'She got her younger brother to masturbate in front of my wife, got him to say he would like to have sex and oral sex with her.'

Noticing the unapologetic girl's courtroom manner, the pensioner said: 'She is smiling there; we have had terror from the whole family, but mainly from this girl . . . she will kill someone.'

When Judge Ní Chonduin asked Michelle if she was prepared to say sorry. Michelle smiled and replied: 'I'm not apologising for anything.'

Michelle's solicitor applied for an adjournment, saying that psychiatric and probation reports had already been ordered in connection to other charges. He pleaded with Judge Ní Chonduin to let these charges link up with the other matters due back in court when a number of updated reports from psychiatrists and probation workers would be furnished. Michelle's father could not be present at that hearing, having suffered a relapse of his alcoholism, for which he was getting treatment.

Another prosecution in July 2004 served to illustrate how uncontrollable Michelle was. A garda from Pearse Street Garda Station had responded to a report of a massive public order disturbance at the Central Bank Plaza. There he found Michelle at the centre of the fracas and saw her and her friends intimidating passers-by. The garda said he was approached by a number of people who complained about Michelle's intimidating behaviour. Michelle was extremely drunk and told the garda to 'f**k off'. She and her friends were then arrested.

Two witnesses had come forward and offered to testify against Michelle, which is highly unusual as it is hard to get civilians to give of their time to come to court and give evidence in public order cases. One witness said that he and a friend had stopped in Crown Alley to watch a street performer's act. 'This girl was robbing him [the street performer] of his money. He kept asking her, "Why are you taking my money?" and she squared up to him and said, "because I can." . . . The man was doing nothing, and she and four others set on him like a pack of dogs. It was disgusting to watch.'

One of Michelle's friends started to expose himself and the gang then proceeded through Temple Bar accosting and intimidating others by throwing bottles, jumping on taxis and attempting to steal from passers-by. 'It was harassment for no reason,' the witness said.

The second witness, a taxi driver, described the scene at Dame Street, saying that he had seen frightened members of the public trying to get out of the way of Michelle and her gang. He had also seen Michelle throwing bottles and threatening people.

Michelle pleaded not guilty to the charges of being drunk and disorderly and in breach of the peace. However, Judge Geoffrey Browne convicted her and praised the two witnesses for coming forward to give their evidence.

Michelle's defence team submitted volumes of psychiatric and psychological reports on Michelle for the judge's inspection. Pleading for clemency, counsel said that Michelle's mother now planned to buy a home outside Dublin and intended to bring Michelle and the other younger children to live with her.

Michelle's father related how he had worked all his life 'like my father before me' until his marriage broke up and he was forced to leave his job to care for his troubled children on his own. The pressures of coming to court so often—250 times, he believed, for his two children—had also made it practically impossible for him to hold down a job. 'My kids came to the notice of the health board when she was 13. Recommendations have been made by judges and nothing has been done; the health board has a lot to answer for.'

The court was also told that in other court cases involving Michelle, judges had directed the health board to explain why no social worker had been appointed to Michelle. However, the health board had responded by saying that it did not have to come to court to explain what efforts had been made, despite the judge's direction.

Having noted the difficulties the father had gone through in recent years. Judge Browne said: 'Maybe the father has been let down by the health board but I have no choice but to give the maximum three-month sentence.' Michelle was detained in the women's unit in Mountjoy Prison because Ireland does not have a juvenile detention facility for girls over the age of 17.

After she had completed the sentence, Michelle was released into more chaos. Her parents had sold the family home and split the proceeds of the sale. The mother had bought a house outside Dublin and invited Michelle and her younger brother to live with her. When they arrived at the house, they found it uninhabitable. Michelle and her brother, who was then aged 15, returned to Dublin where they were effectively homeless.

Soon afterwards, Michelle was arrested for attempted robbery of a man at an ATM machine and for being drunk and disorderly. After her next court appearance, she was granted bail and ordered to obey a nightly curfew. On her following appearance, Monday, 15 November 2004, Judge Angela Ní Chonduin said that the South Western Health Board, in Dublin, had not intervened in Michelle's case despite having learnt that she was homeless and dependent on hostel accommodation. Michelle had to present herself at a garda station every night where she would find out which hostel had a bed for her.

'I am seriously concerned about her,' Judge Ní Chonduin said. 'I'm going to remand her in custody. This is going back years. I remember her father saying that at least three years ago he asked for assistance from the health board. Files were sent and nothing has happened.' As she remanded Michelle in custody to Mountjoy Prison for a week, the judge said, 'There are problems when she is on the loose.' She added that the problem also involved Michelle's younger brother, who had appeared before the court in the past also. He would later be arrested in connection with an arson offence and detained in Oberstown Boys' Centre by order of the High Court, for his own welfare.

On 30 November 2004, an important chapter in Michelle's life ended. All her Children's Court cases concluded and she was detained for five months—on her seventy-fifth criminal conviction. The court heard how while she was homeless she had attacked gardaí, tried to rob a drunken man of his money and taken part in petty thefts. Judge William Early was told that the girl had pleaded guilty to all the charges and was already in custody in Mountjoy Prison on remand.

In mitigation, the court heard that Michelle had nowhere to live and, as a result, High Court proceedings had been taken against the health board over her and her younger brother's welfare. However, these proceedings in relation to Michelle could become mute as she would turn 18 shortly, when she would be an adult and the health services could no longer be compelled to provide her with care and protection.

In Mountjoy, she had been getting on well and attended Alcohol Awareness meetings and planned to take part in a Christmas play and do other courses in the jail. Counsel said that

Michelle had now accepted that alcohol had a major role to play in most of her offences but she still denied being an alcoholic.

The father then spoke. 'I have been trying to get her help for three-and-a-half years,' he said. 'She is nearly 18 and it looks like they [the health board] will have reached the finishing post ahead of me . . . I'm afraid that she could end up as another statistic. But as long as I live I will do all I can. That is it, thank you.' And so he ended what would become his last address to the Children's Court over his troubled daughter.

Detaining Michelle for five months, Judge Early told her: 'It appears that the one common denominator to every offence before the court is the excess consumption of alcohol. That is the real problem you have to address and I hope you will have the opportunity to do so.'

Michelle remained silent during the hearing. Her latest offences in 2004 included being caught in possession of a stolen crate of alcopops; trespass at the Tesco Distribution Centre in Tallaght with intent to commit an offence or interfere with property there; skipping court; stealing four bottles of lemonade vodka worth €32 from a shop in Blessington; being drunk and disorderly and causing a breach of the peace; assaulting a garda in Naas, where she also was drunk and disorderly and caused another breach of the peace; stealing a bunch of flowers from a shop in Rathfarnham, and later being found to be drunk and disorderly; causing a breach of the peace at another shop in the same area; obstructing a garda in the execution of his duty and during her arrest, for another breach of the peace, at Spar on Westmoreland Street; giving the same officer a false name and address; theft of a small number of goods from the shop; being drunk and disorderly in Tallaght and refusing to comply with the directions of a garda to leave the area; failing to give a garda her name and address when questioned over a disturbance on Aston Quay; causing a breach of the peace on the same occasion and being drunk to the point that she was deemed to be a danger to herself and others; attempting to steal money from a man on Westmoreland Street, Dublin; causing a breach of the peace at O'Connell Bridge and being intoxicated to such an extent that she was a danger to herself and others and had obstructed a garda in the execution of his duty.

At the Dublin Criminal Court, in November 2005, the last of the charges that Michelle had amassed as a juvenile were finalised. These were in relation to the savage attacks on the two women which had occurred within a week of each other in October 2003. Judge Donagh McDonagh said: 'When I heard the evidence in this case I described all three as bullies and thugs and I cannot see any reason why I should change my view.' He continued to describe their actions as 'appalling behaviour of the worst kind' and he said he couldn't see 'any reason to distinguish between them.'[1]

Michelle's counsel said that his client was only 16 at the time of the offence and cited her difficult family background and history. He said that a favourable probation report indicated that she had a conduct disorder and had elements of 'Jekyll and Hyde' to her personality in that 'when she is being cared for, she can be a very pleasant person.' She was detained for two years in Mountjoy Prison.

On 26 June 2006, the Court of Criminal Appeal decided to increase Michelle's sentence to five years, with two suspended. She was then escorted out of the Four Courts complex to a prison service van for transfer to jail. Of course, it is impossible to say what the teenager really thought that day of her role in those incidents or to gauge her inner feelings about the resulting court case. Outwardly, however, she was quite communicative. Handcuffed, she passed by a number of news photographers, and as she did so, her broad smile was nearly obscured by the gesture she made, her middle finger raised.

20 | CHRISTINE

On 6 July 2005, at about midday, anyone standing on Dublin's Chancery Street could not have avoided being struck by the extraordinary sight of a radiant young woman whose face beamed with a broad smile. Closer inspection would reveal that Christine was handcuffed and the people either side of her were prison officers. It still would have been difficult to fathom that at that precise moment and with such an expression on her face, she was being escorted from a court to a van which would then take her to Mountjoy Prison to begin a sentence. Her happy smile was acutely beguiling in spite of what she had done.

On New Year's Eve, 2002, Christine and two friends broke into the home of an elderly woman who had taken care of her after her mother died. The 63-year-old woman had a grandmother-like role in Christine's life and had tried her best to look after her. Her altruistic efforts had been in vain, though, and Christine, who had no other family support, had gone out of control.

On the night of the horrific attack, the unsuspecting woman had two friends at her house to celebrate the New Year. The man had learning difficulties and the woman, a multiple sclerosis sufferer, was disabled. The hideous events that followed would later be described as an attack 'bordering on cruelly sadistic'.

Savagely, Christine and her accomplices doused the man and disabled woman in boiling water. They then set the disabled woman on fire, having drenched her with cigarette lighter fluid. The flames burning her skin were then put out—with more boiling water. The disabled woman was rushed to St James's Hospital, barely conscious, and spent nineteen days in a burns unit. The man suffered a broken nose, multiple stab wounds to his arms and legs and he needed twenty-six stitches to his head and face. Following the New Year's Eve ordeal, the gang mistakenly thought that the man was unconscious, which gave him an opening to escape and raise the alarm.

On 24 January, Christine and her two accomplices came to the Children's Court to be jointly charged over the attacks which had taken place in the Maryland area of south Dublin. Christine, then aged 17, and two boys—James, aged 16, and Robert who was just 14—were charged with assault causing harm to a man and woman. From the outset it was clear that the case was unusual and bore hallmarks of savagery.

The disabled woman was still in hospital and had received threats from the two boys. There was photographic evidence of the boys at St James's Hospital where they had intimidated the witness, first in the burns unit, then in intensive care.

The male victim had also been the target of intimidation; threats had been shouted through his letter box. A detective said that the man was in 'genuine fear' for his own safety, had been threatened twice and, as a result, had to wear a disguise. People had written to his house saying that if he went to court to give evidence, he would be burned out. The man was also too afraid to come to court to give details of the alleged threats, presiding Judge Bridget Reilly was told. Judge Reilly agreed to release the three on bail under extremely restrictive conditions.

James was given bail on condition that he reside at his home, keep away from St James's Hospital, the victims' homes and two flat complexes nearby, obey a curfew from 7 p.m. to 8 a.m. and sign on at his local garda station three times a week. The judge further warned him that as part of his bail conditions he must not have any contact with the victims, directly or indirectly, by voice, letter or telephone. He was also ordered not to have any contact with the two other teenage defendants.

Under oath, James's father gave an undertaking to make sure the boy abided by these conditions.

Robert, the 14-year-old, was remanded on bail until 31 January, with similar conditions, including a curfew and a ban from having contact with his co-defendants or the victims. His parents also undertook to ensure that their son abided by his bail conditions. Christine, who was responsible for bringing the two boys to that house, was released on bail with similar restrictions.

James and his younger brother, who was not connected with the Maryland attacks, had once been described by gardaí as 'walking crime waves'. Their story was another indictment of the juvenile justice system and of the lack of social supports for youths who repeatedly flouted the law with utter disregard. James, his brother and Robert had been friends for years and theirs were regular faces at the Children's Court.

Over the previous two years, the boys had run amok. They had repeatedly been arrested, then bailed, then arrested again for new offences. James's younger brother, then aged 15, appeared in the Children's Court on Tuesday, 11 March 2003. At the time, he was facing sixty-six charges for stealing cars and motoring crimes, criminal damage, assault, larceny, public order and trespassing.

Judge Miriam Malone said that she was concerned that he had not adhered to bail conditions set down by the court. The offences, which went back over fourteen months, involved nineteen gardaí from six Dublin stations. Many of the offences had been committed while the boy was on bail from both the Children's Court and the High Court.

In earlier High Court proceedings, he had been released on bail to take part in a health-board-run programme. However, since then, the situation had deteriorated greatly and the boy had picked up more charges. Judge Malone said that the boy was 'a risk to himself and others and out of control', and remanded him to the Trinity House Detention Centre. The case was later put back until 21 March when a further court date would be set for a full afternoon sitting of the Children's Court dedicated to hearing the evidence of the boy's crimes.

Meanwhile, his older brother, James, was facing thirty-one charges, not including the awful attacks on the man and woman in Maryland.

These included five charges for joyriding or travelling as a passenger in a stolen car, as well as several charges for drink-related public order offences, attacking a garda, skipping court, theft, handling stolen goods and possession of implements for use in larcenies.

As it turned out, the two brothers were to be dealt with on the same day, 2 April 2003. James was the first to appear before Judge William Early. The judge heard how the long-time out-of-school teenager had been stopped driving stolen cars numerous times and, in one escapade, had trespassed into the sorting room of a post office and stolen an official An Post postman's delivery bicycle. He had also been caught pushing a delivery motorbike which had been stolen outside the Domino's Pizza restaurant in Rathmines. He had punched a garda in the face when he was stopped driving a stolen car, while drunk, and had become violent at the station when he was asked to provide a urine sample.

He had been arrested numerous times for engaging in threatening and abusive behaviour and for being intoxicated in public places. Judge Early heard that shortly before the court case, James had been taking part in a FÁS training course but had left after a row with his course supervisor.

Many members of his family had difficulties with the law, the court was told. Until that day, he had no previous convictions as the numerous charges on which he had been on bail had been running separately until a decision was made to put them all together and deal with them at once. Judge Early imposed a 15-month sentence in St Patrick's Institution and banned James from driving for four years.

Later that day, the younger brother came into court for a two-hour hearing. Judge Early heard evidence relating to the sixty-six charges and he heard lengthy evidence on the boy's persistent re-offending over the previous year.

He had been arrested for stealing CDs and Playstation games from HMV on Grafton Street, was caught carrying a screwdriver on several occasions, was found with a stolen TV/video combi set which had been taken in a burglary, was arrested for carrying a bolt cutters and an iron bar. Evidence was also given that he had been stopped driving stolen cars, broken a shop window in a drunken row with a security man, smashed in a pub window with a brick, engaged in violent and insulting behaviour to gardaí and members of the public when intoxicated and was once caught trespassing in a hospital.

At a flat complex in Dublin 8, he was abusive to residents and hit one over the eye with a stick, leaving him badly cut. He had spat at staff at St James's Hospital when they asked him to leave the grounds, and, while drunk, he had also kicked and punched a garda who had arrested him.

On another occasion, when drunk, he had criminally damaged an antique sword and display cabinet, in the St Stephen's Green Shopping Centre, and had become abusive to staff and customers there when he was asked to leave the premises. Gardaí had also caught him drunk and dancing on the bonnet and windscreen of a car. A garda told the court that the boy had interfered with gardaí who had been dealing with a public order problem. He had blocked the garda car from moving and, when directed to leave the area, he had punched an officer.

In addition, he had been caught driving a stolen moped, without a helmet, a licence or insurance, and while carrying a passenger. Judge Early heard that the teenager had been the subject of ongoing High Court proceedings for a suitable residential placement. Furthermore, the boy had also been repeatedly in breach of curfews imposed on him and had broken his bail several times.

Having read volumes of reports on the boy's behaviour, Judge Early detained him for two years in Trinity House, where, the judge said, he needed to 'get all the help he could obtain'.

Like his older brother James, this boy had no criminal convictions until that day when all charges were finalised. Together the brothers had amassed ninety-seven criminal convictions between them. Their father was present for the proceedings but did not offer any enlightenment as to what had gone wrong with his children. The younger brother would finish juvenile years in custody with about eighty criminal convictions.

Meanwhile, detectives were still preparing their case against James and his two friends over the Maryland attacks. James's role was outlined on 14 April. In addition to the charge of assault during the alleged burglary, James also faced charges of violent disorder, burglary, and endangering the lives of two people with a spade, a two-pronged fork, a knife and a pot of boiling water.

In an account of the evidence, Judge Early was told that James 'beat the male visitor for an hour with a spade and then stabbed him from the top of his head to his ankle.' The garda giving evidence continued, 'It is also alleged that the boy poured boiling water over him.'

The court also heard of the attack on the woman in which she was held by James against the sitting-room wall where he poured lighter fluid over her and set her on fire. When the fire was put out, he then poured boiling water over her.

A stunned silence hung like a pall after the garda described the attacks. Judge Early ruled that James should be tried on indictment in the Circuit Criminal Court due to the seriousness of the allegations. James was granted strict bail until the following June, pending the preparation and service of the book of evidence in the case. On 17 July 2003, both he and Christine were sent forward for trial to the higher court, which is empowered to give longer sentences than the Children's Court.

Christine would await trial in custody as a result of threats against the elderly woman who had once taken care of her and who owned the house where the attacks had taken place. Later, the woman told Judge John Coughlan, at the Children's Court, 'If you let her out, my life will be in danger; she is going to kill someone.'

Christine had brazenly returned to the woman's house and threatened her not to give evidence. During this incident, Christine, along with two women and a man, had entered the house, held a knife to the woman's throat and demanded money. Having stolen €90, they had left. 'She said that she would burn me, bury me in the garden and then collect my money from the post office and no one would miss me,' the woman said nervously. The woman was so afraid that a religious order had employed a security guard to stay at her home with her every day—at a cost of €144 a day.

As Christine had broken bail conditions which stated that she was forbidden to go to the elderly woman's house, Judge Coughlan remanded her in custody to Mountjoy Prison.

Later that year, James was released into the community, having launched an appeal at the severity of the sentence he had received for his earlier thirty-six crimes. A spate of new offences would follow. On 3 October 2003, he was detained for one year and banned from the roads for sixty years for breaking into and attempting to take two cars. Judge John Coughlan made the order at the Children's Court after James, now aged 17, had pleaded guilty to two counts of unlawfully interfering with the mechanism of cars and two counts of criminally damaging them—to the value of €1,300. The court's ruling meant that he was forbidden from holding a driving licence until the year 2063, when he would be 77 years old.

In mitigation, the defence counsel told Judge Coughlan that James came from a family in which many of his siblings had been involved in crime and heroin abuse and said that he had pleaded guilty to the offences. The teenager had a drink problem, he said, and was intoxicated at the time of the offences but would be prepared to compensate the car owners for the damage he had caused.

However, Judge Coughlan put an end to matters having heard that the teenager had not brought any money to court as compensation for the victims. 'People who steal cars go to jail,' he said and he imposed a one-year term in St Patrick's Institution. Saying that he never wanted to see the boy behind the wheel of a car again, the judge imposed one of the lengthiest road bans in the history of the Children's Courts, to which the boy shrugged indifferently and retorted: 'I wasn't going to be driving anyway.' One of his older brothers, an adult who had been sitting in court, jumped up at the end of the case and said to him, 'Sure don't worry; just get some good food into you when you're in there [St Patrick's Institution].'

Robert, the youngest of the trio to be involved in the burglary and related attacks in Maryland, was another repeat offender, with a similarly troubled background. By that New Year's Eve, Robert, though still aged only 14, had become notorious among gardaí in Dublin's south inner city and had numerous charges pending. Yet despite the growing number of offences, he was still on bail.

He was first brought before the courts when he was 13 years old for not going to school. When he had attended school, he had been extremely disruptive and was eventually expelled because his teachers were afraid of him. His learning difficulties were later assessed in the National Remand and Assessment Centre. However, the findings were inconclusive because it could not be determined whether his educational and behavioural problems had been caused by his lack of schooling or by learning difficulties.

In one of his earlier offences, on 26 April 2002, he had held a garda by her throat and elbowed her in her face in an effort to stop her from arresting one of his friends. Having jumped between them and tried to prise them apart, Robert had grabbed the garda by her throat and restricted her breathing when he tightened his grip on her collar. At the time, he was extremely intoxicated and his 'eyes were rolling in his head', the Children's Court was later told.

Robert had educational problems which had not been addressed and there seemed to be little family control over his increasingly chaotic behaviour. He spoke little and always seemed to have the same facial expression, a smile.

On 10 April, the garda investigation into the Maryland attack had been completed and Robert was now facing more charges: violent disorder, burglary, endangering the lives of the man and woman. It was alleged that Robert had attacked the man with a knife and a crutch, while the disabled woman was covered with lighter fluid and set on fire. When the fire was put out it, Robert poured a pot of boiling water over the woman.

Judge Thomas Fitzpatrick ruled that the case was, 'much too serious to be heard in the Children's Court', and directed that Robert, like James and Christine, should be tried on indictment in the Circuit Criminal Court. Robert was released on restrictive bail until June, pending the preparation and service of a book of evidence.

In the meantime, he was sentenced to a year's detention in the Finglas Child and Adolescent Centre, in connection with his earlier offences, as well as others committed after the Maryland attack. However, on 5 June, when he was due to appear in court again he had absconded.

Judge John Coughlan issued a bench warrant for his arrest and, within eleven days, he had been brought back to court, where it was claimed that during his time in the centre he, as the ring leader, had led two other 14-year-olds on a rampage. It was said that they had caused €10,000 worth of damage to the juvenile institution during a stand-off where they had allegedly barricaded themselves into a room and refused to come out.

For two hours, efforts were made to negotiate with them, but eventually the door had to be removed from its frame and gardaí wearing riot helmets for their own protection got into the room and succeeded in containing the situation.

A senior official from the Finglas Child and Adolescent Centre said that he was prepared to take only two of the boys back to the facility. Judge Murphy remanded Robert in custody to Trinity House instead. Sending him to that detention centre meant that: 'the biggest problem in relation to peer influence had been removed.' On 17 July, at the Children's Court he was furnished with the book of evidence and returned for trial to the Dublin Circuit Criminal Court for the Maryland attacks.

A few weeks later, he was also detained for two years over the attack on the garda, which had taken place over a year before. Other offences to which he admitted included being in breach of the peace, skipping court, trespassing in an inner-city school and travelling in stolen cars, all of which had occurred over the previous twelve months.

Robert had been out of education from an early age and for his welfare his parents wanted him to be held in custody. Judge McBride imposed a two-year sentence in Trinity House and ordered that he be given psychological and psychiatric counselling, behavioural therapy and an education, while in custody.

Before he was sentenced and nearly three months after the Maryland attacks, Robert had been involved in another frightening incident for which he would be detained in September 2003. Now aged 15, he had violently mugged three teenagers and threatened to harm or kill them. During this case it was said that his learning problems were also illustrated by the level of naiveté shown in his crimes because he was easily identified by his victims, two of whom knew him personally. Over a four-week period, Robert mugged three teenage boys aged 13, 14 and 15, and stole their money and mobile phones.

When arrested, he made a statement admitting the theft of the 14-year-old victim's personal belongings, together with two items of sportswear from a shop in Blackrock. His parents were still anxious that he remain in the detention centre, the court heard.

A child-care worker from Trinity House told Judge Murphy that Robert had been undergoing drug abuse and anger management counselling and that there were signs of some progress. Communicating by nodding or shaking his head, Robert agreed that his behaviour was unacceptable and indicated that he would not be happy if one of his younger siblings were attacked in the same way as he had mugged his victims.

Judge Murphy described him as 'acting like a bully', and strenuously advised him to cut offending behaviour out of his life and to heed the assistance that was being afforded to him by staff at Trinity House. He was detained for two years and now had seventeen criminal convictions.

Things did not run smoothly, however, and he later managed to escape. On 5 April 2004, gardaí received a report of a burglary at a house at Windmill Lane, in Dublin. When they arrived at the house, they found Robert in an upstairs bedroom, with his bulging pockets full of stolen jewellery. He had broken into the house through a first-floor rear window. It had been clear that the residents were not at home because there had been no cars parked outside the house.

In a ruse to hide the fact that he was on the run from Trinity House, he gave gardaí a bogus Christian name after he was arrested. His mother, who had come to the garda station, also vouched for this misleading name. However, gardaí soon established that the name was false and that he was at large from the detention centre.

On 2 July, he pleaded guilty at the Children's Court to taking part in this burglary. His solicitor told Judge Anne Watkin that he had been returned to Trinity House, where his sentence was nearing an end. She asked the court to adjourn the case to monitor his step-down from being in detention to his release into his family's care. She said that the boy would turn 16 shortly and knew that if he were not co-operative in the meantime he would face a certain custodial sentence in St Patrick's Institution, for the burglary. Judge Watkin agreed to adjourn the case until later that year to monitor the boy's development prior to and after his release.

However, on 19 October, Judge Watkin heard that since July, when he had been given an opportunity to turn his life around, Robert had fallen in with the same group of people who had been involved in his earlier offences. Although he knew that there was a sentence hanging over him, he had been caught travelling as a passenger in a stolen car and had mugged a man for his mobile phone.

Imposing six-month sentences for the burglary and phone-theft charges, Judge Watkin took into consideration Robert's guilty plea, the evidence that most of the stolen property had been recovered, and the fact that he had not used violence or intimidation in his latest offences. She ordered that the terms would run concurrently and not one after the other.

Following tense silence after he had been repeatedly asked whether this was how he planned to spend the rest of his life, Robert answered 'no' in a staccato voice, three times. Meanwhile, he had yet to face the Dublin Circuit Criminal Court over the Maryland attacks.

Christine was the first of the trio to be dealt with by the Dublin Circuit Court. She pleaded guilty to two counts of assault causing harm and one count of violent disorder. She also owned up to the later burglary at the elderly woman's home and the connected witness intimidation incidents, as well as yet another burglary at the same house on 28 May 2003.

Judge Yvonne Murphy was told that, until her involvement in the attack, Christine had no previous convictions. She had lost her parents and brother early in her life. As she lay on her death bed, Christine's mother, who was suffering from terminal cancer, had pleaded with the elderly woman to watch over Christine and make sure she went to school. But that had proved an impossible task.

In the aftermath of her ordeals, the elderly woman had moved away from the area. 'Her basic wish is to be left alone by these people,' the court was told.[1]

In mitigation and pleas for leniency, Christine's counsel said that she had fallen in with company known to gardaí, had many emotional problems and abused drugs as a means of escape. He said that she was now starting to accept responsibility for what she had done and asked Judge Murphy to put sentencing back to another date.

Judge Murphy said that Christine had done the honourable thing by pleading guilty and she ordered her to undergo psychological treatment. Later, she sentenced Christine to four years in prison. However, the final year of the sentence was suspended on condition that she enter into a good behaviour bond.

In October 2005, James, then aged 19, and Robert, by then 17 years old, came before Judge Desmond Hogan in the Dublin Circuit Criminal Court. Robert and James both pleaded guilty and both were sentenced to five years' detention. Judge Hogan suspended the final two years of Robert's detention and one year of James's on condition that they enter into good behaviour and probation bonds for four years following their release. At time of writing, both are still in custody.

V. VICTIMS

21 | THE BUTTERFLY EFFECT

Although young offenders frequently tend to be victims of their own upbringing, environment and circumstances, minor offences committed by them can often have a greatly disproportionate effect on a victim. The boy at the end of Chapter 15 was involved in two offences, one minor and fit to be dealt with in the Children's Court, the other extremely serious and which because of its nature was sent to the Central Criminal Court. There was a massive difference in degrees of seriousness of the crimes but a much lesser disparity in the scale of trauma inflicted on the victims.

In the more obviously serious cases, which tend to be sent to higher courts, the effects on victims become known and are generally more apparent. Not so for the victims of minor offences committed by juveniles. The offenders also have the benefit of receiving help from the state in the form of the Probation and Welfare Services. Victims very often have no one to whom they can turn.

Scientists have used the term 'the butterfly effect' in reference to the fact that the wind flutter from a butterfly may ultimately have a domino effect that, over time, creates a typhoon in China, six months away, 3,000 miles away. The theory was excellently explained by the thirteenth-century English nursery rhyme:

For want of a nail, the shoe was lost; For want of a shoe, the
horse was lost;

For want of a horse, the rider was lost; For want of a rider, the
battle was lost;

For want of a battle, the kingdom was lost; All for the want of
a horseshoe nail.

Similar unexpected consequences can be triggered by what are
classified as minor offences. On 28 May 2004, a man told the
Children's Court that he had lost his job, home and fiancée, and
had then suffered a nervous breakdown—resulting from an incident in which he had been attacked by a 14-year-old schoolboy.

The 41-year-old man told Judge Angela Ní Chonduin that,
about a year previously, he had gone out with friends and family
to celebrate his fortieth birthday. Having spent the evening cele-
brating in a pub in Tallaght, he went to a chip shop to get some
food for his party.

When he came out of the take-away, he rested the bag of chips
on a car parked nearby, while he gestured to his group, who had
been watching from the pub. As he signalled to his party that the
food was ready, the 14-year-old boy snatched the bags and handed
them to two girls who ran away with them. An argument followed
and the man told the boy to 'stop messing' and to get his food
back for him. The boy, who was aged 15 by the time of the hearing
of the case, swung a karate kick aimed at his groin, which the
victim managed to block with his forearm. He grabbed the boy by
his collar and was attacked from behind by other teenagers who
kicked and punched him. His son and another local man ran out
from the pub, at which point the group of teenagers dispersed.

As a result of the kick, the man's wrist was broken and a bone
in his hand was crushed. This, he said, had forced him to give up
work for three months, leaving him at a loss of €10,000. The
financial strain had caused difficulties between him and his
partner, and the relationship had ended soon after. 'My arm was
in plaster for five-and-a-half weeks and then I had to wear a brace
for two months to help the bones knit in my hand,' the man said.
'I was a taxi driver and the financial loss led to a break-up with my

fiancée. There was a lot of pain and I ended up having a nervous breakdown. I lost my home and family.' He also told Judge Ní Chonduin that, a year later, he was still in constant agony and had been told by his doctor that he would suffer arthritis in his hand.

The defendant, a schoolboy, had pleaded not guilty to attacking the man, causing him harm. The victim's adult son gave evidence that he had seen the teenager kick his father, although he admitted that when he initially made a statement to gardaí he had stated that his father had been punched. The man's former partner also said that she saw the kick land on him.

The teenager denied instigating the fight. He said that the two girls had taken the man's food, while he was in the chip shop. He said that when he came out, he saw the victim screaming. He claimed that the man punched him first, leaving him with a lump and bruising over his eye. But he admitted that he did not make a complaint to the gardaí. He told the court that when he found out that the man had made allegations against him, he too wanted to lodge a formal complaint but was told that it was too late.

Judge Ní Chonduin convicted the teenager, who had no previous convictions. She ordered a probation report on the teenager to be furnished to the court and adjourned the case. She indicated that if the report were favourable and if the boy had not come to further garda notice, he would be given the Probation Act and therefore would not have a criminal record.

The teenager was sentenced on 14 October 2004. The judge noted that the probation report was positive and that the boy had not been in trouble since. His counsel said that the incident was not typical behaviour for the boy. Judge Ní Chonduin noted that the boy planned to start an apprenticeship and agreed to be lenient with him. Accordingly, she gave him the benefit of the Probation Act, telling him that he was lucky and that if he got in this kind of situation again, he would be detained. 'I feel sorry for the injured party; I think his nerve is pretty well gone,' she said as the case ended.

On the evening of 6 February 2004, a man was walking home through south Dublin with his wife. Casually, they made their way along Pleasant Street—perhaps not so aptly named, given the events about to unfold. The man was set upon by a gang of teenage boys and beaten. The culprits were charged with robbery.

However, on 14 April 2005, when the case came to court, the devastating consequences of the mugging were revealed. The four teenagers, who pleaded guilty to the offence, were supported in court by their parents, and remained silent throughout the hearing, with one sitting face downward as the evidence was given.

Judge Cormac Dunne heard that the teenagers had ganged up on the man as he had been out walking with his wife, who was pregnant at the time. A garda from Pearse Street told the court, 'The man saw the five youths coming towards him and his wife. The man and his wife crossed the road to avoid them; they approached and asked him for a Euro. The man said that he did not have money; they surrounded him and started pushing him. He stayed in front of his pregnant wife to protect her.'

The man was then pushed to the ground and kicked on the head. He got back up and tried to push the teenagers away, but they punched him from all directions and then one of them 'threw a flying kick hitting him on his chest'.

The man then got back onto his feet and chased the teenagers away. The group fled along Camden Street where they were arrested shortly afterwards. The man was left bleeding and bruised following the incident and his wife was extremely distressed; she suffered a miscarriage the following day.

'This case will not be completed until medical evidence is furnished to the court as to what extent this contributed,' said Judge Dunne. 'None of us here are medical people, but the law of coincidence would imply that it was not a coincidence.'

Judge Dunne remanded the teenagers on bail until the following May to allow the gardaí to ascertain whether the woman's miscarriage was a result of the ordeal. He also said that the information would be of benefit to the defendants if it were established that the miscarriage was a result of non-related factors.

The court had heard that the one of the teenagers was in full-time employment. His solicitor said that the boy's family was taking the matter very seriously. The boy had drunk a naggin of vodka on the day of the incident.

The three other co-defendants were all taking part in training courses and had the support in court of their family.

The case was again adjourned, pending an obstetrician's report.

On 9 June, the case was finalised, with all four being detained for three months. Judge Dunne said that it had not been medically possible to determine whether or not the miscarriage was linked to the incident. He continued: 'Recently, in this country, this type of behaviour has been attributed the misleading title of "anti-social behaviour". That is a misleading misnomer and masking conduct which is barbaric, brutal battery.' He described this conduct as intimidation of vulnerable people. 'And what is more vulnerable than a husband and wife, a pregnant lady, walking our streets and being set on.'

Commenting on the effects the incident still had on the husband and wife, a year and four months later, he said: 'They have lost confidence in traversing the streets at day or night. They feel vulnerable, they feel at risk. The wife, whose privacy I wish to protect, is totally uneasy. She cannot relax until her husband comes home because she is terrified something will occur to him.'

None of the defendants had previous convictions but the judge said that their conduct had 'drastically changed the lives of decent people'. However, there had been nothing forwarded in court to explain why they had committed the offence, other than that one of them had drunk a 'naggin' of vodka on the day of the incident, which the judge held to be an aggravating factor. 'No other individual has mitigated any facts that could assist the court in considering mitigating factors.'

He said that a custodial sentence was in the interests of the teenagers, as well as these of the public and the victims. The teenagers remained silent during the sentence hearing. All were supported in court by family members, who appeared genuinely upset.

Judge Dunne sympathised with the parents, saying, 'No parent rears a child to go out on the streets and do what happened here. Rearing children has never been an easy task throughout civilisation but in recent years has become an enormous task for parents with all the temptations pervading society.'

The actions of a 13-year-old Romanian girl turned the lives of two pensioners upside down. The girl, who had been living with her family in Ireland since 1999, had never gone to school. On 27 November 2004, in Dún Laoghaire, which was several miles from where she lived, she arrived at the house of a 63-year-old woman. The woman opened the door to find the girl on her knees, begging on the doorstep.

The woman gave the girl €1.50 at which she then asked for a plaster, claiming that she had a sore finger. The woman went back inside to get one, returning a minute later and nervously handing out the plaster through the doorway. The teenager then asked the woman to put it on her finger. Suddenly the girl started to push the door as the terrified elderly woman tried to force it shut. Another person with the defendant, a girl believed to have been aged 11, joined in and wedged her foot in the doorway to prevent the woman from closing the door.

Meanwhile, the 13-year-old girl was pressing her shoulder against the door in an effort to overpower the woman. Eventually the woman managed to close the door and she called the gardaí. The girl then went to a neighbouring house, which was the home of an 80-year-old woman. This woman opened her front door to find the girl on the ground, saying, 'please, my sore finger' and she then started to 'inch her way in the door'.

The girls forced their way into the house and pushed the woman into her sitting room where they tried to take her handbag. The woman had a panic button which she used to alert the gardaí, at which the girl and her accomplice left.

On 18 July 2005, now aged 14, the girl pleaded guilty at the Children's Court to trespassing with intent to commit burglaries at the women's homes. The girl had a huge entourage of family and friends to support her at court that day. As she had earlier entered a not-guilty plea, in order for the prosecution to proceed, the victims were required to come to court also, to give their evidence. This added greatly to their trauma and sense of fear of the girl and her family.

However, the girl changed her plea minutes before the hearing, making the victims' journey to court pointless.

The court heard that the incident had had a significant impact on both women. 'This has had a huge effect on her. She does not trust people any more. Every night she checks everything six or seven times before going to bed and she is very jumpy,' a garda from Dún Laoghaire Garda Station said in relation to the first woman.

Of the 80-year-old woman, he said: 'The injured party is struggling to cope; she is on medication and regularly visits the doctor and is afraid to leave her home. She was a keen gardener but rarely goes to her garden any more.'

Judge Ní Chonduin remanded the girl in custody to allow time for a probation report on her to be furnished to the court. The girl then started screaming and begging to be released and had to be brought out of the court. There were similar scenes among the girl's family who had gathered in large numbers outside the courthouse.

A passing tourist, an English woman, noticed the commotion, and came over to speak to the girl's relatives. Having received a garbled account of how the girl had been taken into custody, she became indignant at the version she had heard, and demanded entry into the court to find out why the child had been taken. Gardaí explained to her that she could not enter the building. 'It's not right taking a young girl like that,' she protested and then began a monologue about how the girl and her family were being treated unfairly. Finally, when a garda managed to get a word in, he pointed to the two elderly victims trying to leave the court-house and said: 'It's her victims that I feel sorry for.' The woman saw the two elderly victims who were still obviously distressed. On hearing what the girl had done, she stood slack-jawed and speechless for a couple of minutes, and sullenly left.

A week later, a probation report on the girl was furnished to the court. 'The matter that is of concern is that she does not seem to realise the seriousness of the offence,' said Judge Miriam Malone, having read the report. The girl was held in custody for another night. The next day, she was brought before Judge Ní Chonduin for sentencing. 'The parents are responsible for this child and her actions and I am going to make them feel that responsibility,' the judge said as she ordered them to compensate the victims. Judge Ní Chonduin directed the family, all of whom were on social welfare, to collect €600, through a 'whip-round', which was to be divided between the two victims.

She said that she would give the family until the following October to pay the compensation, but the money was produced there and then when a youth entered the court and handed over a wad of money to the girl's father. The girl was then given conditional release and banned from going out in public unless she was in the company of her parents. She was also forbidden to go to the Dún Laoghaire area.

Judge Ní Chonduin ordered a probation bond and bound the teenage girl to the peace for one year, stressing that if she re-offended within that time, she would be detained for two years. She ordered the girl to co-operate with the Probation and Welfare Service, saying that she wanted efforts to be made to get her into the education system. She also said that she was concerned for the victims who had been badly affected by the incidents.

A similar crime was committed by a 14-year-old Dublin girl who preyed on elderly people living in remote areas along the Wicklow–Kildare border. The girl, who lived in a halting site in west Dublin, had been working at the direction of adults, and the burglary was one of a number that occurred in the same area at around that time.

On 17 November 2005, the Children's Court heard that the girl had been let out of a car with a young male and had approached a woman's house looking for change to allow her to get a bus. When the door was opened, the pair forced their way past the 72-year-old woman. However, the burglary was stopped when a garda detective arrived at the scene and caught the girl.

The young man who had been with the girl escaped but she was arrested and later admitted to gardaí that she had gone to the house with the intention of taking money.

A garda from Blessington Garda Station said that the victim lived in a remote area on the outskirts of Ballymore Eustace and there were not many houses nearby.

He said that she was left terrified by the ordeal. 'We believed that they were working from a car that drove the accused and the young man to the scene. Adults directed them to do this; it is a typical ploy that young people are brought to these houses.'

In mitigation, the girl's solicitor pleaded for leniency, saying that the girl was aged 14 at the time and had been under the influence of an older boy whom she had been seeing. The girl, who was in tears during the case, was said to be remorseful and now understood that she had committed a very serious offence. A one-month detention term in Oberstown Girls' Centre was imposed, with the judge describing the girl's crime as 'extremely serious.' The girl was told that had it not been for the fact that she was so young at the time and had pleaded guilty, she would have been detained for two years.

Apart from the sometimes serious effects of minors' offences, they can also be the source of unexpected consequences. One teenager's simple phone snatch led to a garda getting a savage beating which put him in a coma.

As throngs of GAA supporters were leaving Croke Park following a 2001 All-Ireland Hurling semi-final, a man pulled out his mobile phone. It was immediately snatched by a boy who ran off with it.

Unknown to him, two off-duty gardaí were also in the crowd and saw what had happened. They then gave chase and followed the boy to Sean O'Casey Avenue where they caught him and recovered the phone. The boy put up a struggle and a group of youths pounced on the gardaí as the boy was being arrested. The youths attacked both gardaí and one ended up in a coma, although he subsequently made a full recovery.

On June 2003, the phone thief was released on a six-month probation bond. The judge had been told that the teenager was making good behavioural progress and had not got into any more trouble.

In May 2004, a 17-year-old boy from Ballyfermot pleaded guilty to an attempted car-theft charge, one of the most common offences that come before the Children's Court. The charge sheet read that, on 26 November 2003, he: 'unlawfully interfered with the mechanism of a mechanically propelled vehicle, without the consent of its lawful owner, at Cherry Orchard Avenue.' He also admitted a charge of criminally damaging the car.

Superficially the case looked run of the mill. But evidence showed that it was quite different. The 17-year-old youth and another man, aged 19, had gone to a neighbour's driveway at Cherry Orchard Avenue, in Ballyfermot, and had been trying to steal his car.

The youth, who was an alcoholic, had got into the car and tampered with the steering wheel and its locking mechanism. He was trying to hot-wire it, when the owner, a father of two girls and three boys, aged from seven to early teens, came out of his home and disturbed the attempted theft. He was fatally stabbed by the 19-year-old, in front of two of his children. The following day, the youth presented himself at Ballyfermot Garda Station and was detained for questioning.

Since the incident, he had been involved in a dangerous driving incident, in February 2004. Gardaí on mobile patrol on the Blackditch Road were alerted by a taxi driver to a car that had been driving dangerously.

The gardaí observed the car in question and witnessed how it had failed to yield right of way at a roundabout and had been taking turns without using its indicators. When the squad car's sirens and lights were activated, the youth stopped the car, which he then explained belonged to his sister. As he was being cautioned to produce his driving licence and insurance details at a garda station, another motorist arrived and reported the youth for colliding with her jeep.

After the crash, he had failed to stop at the scene of the accident to exchange details. Having heard the woman's account of the accident, the gardaí arrested the teenager for dangerous driving, driving without a licence and for not having motor insurance.

When the hearing concluded, the teenager was remanded on bail pending a pre-sentence probation report. The report showed that the teenager had developed a lackadaisical attitude towards the prosecution. He did not believe that meeting the probation officers was a positive process and he had not made any progress.

Since the youth had been given bail, he had been arrested twice for breach of a number of conditions. He had broken a curfew and had been arrested in the early hours of 14 and 24 July. 'He was intoxicated on these occasions and was arrested in the Ballyfermot area,' the court was told.

Gardaí felt that the youth's parents had no control over their son. Communicating through his solicitor, the youth repeatedly told Judge Ní Chonduin that he would not co-operate with the probation services in future.

Judge Ní Chonduin said that she was considering imposing a custodial sentence but that the youth had seemingly not considered that he could face custody. 'I am willing to give a last chance to co-operate with the probation services and in that time I want him to think about custody as an alternative. I do not want to put him in custody unless I have to,' the judge said. 'I'm going to give an opportunity; what is saving him is that he presented himself to the garda station; the facts in that case were very serious,' she said.

Eventually the teenager agreed to be more co-operative in future and was released on bail until that September, pending an updated probation report. In September, he was warned that he had four weeks to get a job or else he would be detained. He was again released on bail and given another 'last chance', having been warned that his non co-operation with the Probation and Welfare Services could result in a custodial sentence.

On 7 February 2005, he was given a two-month suspended sentence for the murder-related attempted car theft and more suspended sentences for thirty-four other charges. All sentences were suspended for two years. Fines totalling €875 were also imposed by the court and the youth was given a five-year road ban.[1]

On 21 June 2005, a young English tourist was making her way along Parnell Street, when a 17-year-old boy, with two teenage cohorts, attacked her viciously. The woman was dragged down an alley, where she was punched in the face and kicked in the stomach.

Adding to the ordeal, the teenager bit the woman's arm as his accomplices hit her. They had tried to take her handbag but were unsuccessful and left her badly bruised and cut. When the case came before the Children's Court in early 2006, the teenager pleaded guilty to a charge of attempted robbery of the 23-year-old woman.

The out-of-school and unemployed defendant, who was supported in court by his father, already had thirteen previous convictions for assault, robbery, theft, handling stolen goods and skipping court. He had left school and for a while had taken part in a training course. However, that had ended and, before the case came to court, he had been attempting to find a place on a new training course.

He also had a history of disruptive behaviour. Once in August 2004, when he was held in the Finglas Child and Adolescent Centre, he had stood on the roof of the centre and thrown bricks at a patrol car, causing shards of broken glass to cut a garda. As a result of that incident, he had been detained for one year.

After he pleaded guilty to the mugging of the English woman, he was remanded in custody to St Patrick's Institution, pending a victim impact report. On 7 March 2006, he was given a one-year sentence.

The young woman was clearly left with psychological as well as physical scars. A detailed victim impact report recorded how the young woman now felt about life, Ireland and Dublin, as a result of the ordeal. She was not present for the case but in her statement, she said: 'I can count on one hand the number of times I have gone out since that night. If I see a teenager now, I cross the road to avoid him. I would not come back to Ireland on my own again and I would not set foot in Dublin in particular in a million years.'

22 | ALAN

Just outside the UCI cinema complex in Coolock on Saturday night, 12 October 2002, schoolboy Alan Higgins had just kissed his girlfriend goodnight. They had spent the evening together after Alan had arranged to meet up with her and some of her friends. They had played pool for a while and had fun as she and her friends took turns on the dance machines.

Meanwhile, a trio of north Dublin teenage boys, Jonathan and Rory, both aged 16, and their 'leader', 15-year-old Stephen, had been on the rampage in the same area. They had spent the day drinking cans of beer on a GAA pitch and smoking cannabis joints. The first victim they encountered, sometime after 8 p.m., was a 16-year-old. This young boy had also been at the UCI complex along with two female friends. As they walked towards McDonald's, the three youths set upon the boy who luckily escaped into the UCI complex for protection. He was chased into the building by the 15-year-old ringleader who was armed with an umbrella.

The staff of the complex finally removed the 15-year-old from the building. But just a quarter of an hour later, a 14-year-old boy was attacked by the three. This boy, who was with his 11-year-old brother and a 12-year-old friend, was sitting on a wall near a bottle bank outside the UCI. The three youths came towards the boys and asked them for the time. Having demanded money from them, the youths then stole €10 and a wallet. The 14-year-old victim was hit in the face.

Just after 9 p.m. that night, another 16-year-old fell prey to the trio; he was robbed of a haversack that contained cans of lager and was told that he would have to fight to get it back. A scuffle ensued during which the victim managed to get away with his bag.

An hour-and-a-half later, another 16-year-old boy was in the vicinity with two female friends when the trio approached. One of the trio had a white plastic pole in his hand and used it to hit the victim on his head. Another had a knife. The youngster fled, chased off by Stephen of the attacking youths.

Minutes later, the trio confronted Alan Higgins who was now on his way to catch his bus home. He had to be at work the following day at McGuirk's golf store in Malahide, and hoped to catch the last bus home.

He too was set upon, but was less fortunate than the other victims. In addition to being mugged by the trio, he was stabbed three times by Stephen. Two of the cuts were superficial but the third went deep into his lung, causing massive internal bleeding. He staggered back to the front of the cinema, bleeding and coughing up blood. His white French Connection T-shirt was ripped down the front and was heavily bloodstained. At 11.21 that night, an ambulance arrived and Alan was rushed to Beaumont Hospital where doctors were on standby. He was immediately taken to theatre but he had lost a huge amount of blood and suffered three heart attacks. A doctor later said, 'There was blood oozing from every cut.' During the robbery, Alan's mobile phone had been stolen and about €115 in cash was also taken. As surgeons worked tirelessly to save Alan, his distraught girlfriend received a text message from his stolen phone. Despite attempts to resuscitate him, Alan was pronounced dead at 3.10 a.m. on 13 October 2002.

On Tuesday, 15 October, the three teenagers were brought to the Children's Court to be charged over Alan's killing. The three boys nervously made their way into the tiny courtroom where they were also in the centre of the media spotlight which would remain fixed on the case throughout its duration. This murder had caused public revulsion more than most. A young man had been cut down at an age when he had his entire life before him. And worse, three teenagers, younger than he, were to blame. The youngest of the trio, Stephen, was charged with the manslaughter of the schoolboy.

Twelve journalists were present to cover the case. At the start of the proceedings, Judge James Paul McDonnell said that although the press had a right to report from the court, the presence of a dozen reporters could be 'oppressive' for the defendant and his parents. He ordered the members of the press to choose three from their number to sit in the court who could then pass on to their colleagues and the public the matters of interest in the case. Three reporters, the author, Mick O'Toole from the *Irish Daily Star* and RTÉ crime correspondent Paul Reynolds, were chosen and the case then proceeded.

Stephen, who had tightly cropped black hair and was wearing Nike runners and a dark-coloured tracksuit, returned to the courtroom and took his place while the detective read out the particulars relating to his arrest. Stephen had been arrested in the early hours of that morning. At 1.53 a.m. the boy had been charged and made 'no reply' when cautioned. He had then been released into the custody of his parents.

Stephen was accompanied to court by both his parents who stood up and spoke to confirm their son's date of birth. They also accepted the court's offer of free legal aid for their boy. Stephen was released on bail subject to certain conditions which included signing on daily at Coolock Garda Station and complying with a curfew that required him to be at home every night from 10 p.m. to 7 a.m. Judge McDonnell told his parents that they must make sure that their son abided by his bail conditions. He added that gardaí were entitled to call to their home at any time after 10 p.m. and would ask for the boy to 'show his face'. Stephen was released on bail.

The second defendant, Jonathan, then aged 16, out of school and unemployed, was charged with stealing a mobile phone and a wallet. He had been arrested the previous night and made 'no reply' to his caution. Accompanied to court by his father, the boy was granted free legal aid to appoint a solicitor. He was remanded on bail until 12 November and ordered to sign on daily at Coolock Garda Station. A curfew from 10 p.m. to 7 a.m. was also imposed. The court heard that because of the 'complexity of the investigation', directions from the DPP might not be available by 12 November, but the judge said that a further adjournment could be sought at that point.

The last of the boys to appear before the court was 16-year-old Rory. He was also charged with robbery of a mobile phone and a wallet. He had been arrested at 1.11 that morning and charged nearly an hour-and-a-half later. In reply to a caution, he also had had nothing to say. With tight-cropped hair and wearing a dark-coloured jacket and beige jeans, he sat with arms folded. His mother, who was in court, said, 'I don't know any solicitor.' He too was remanded on bail with the same conditions as his co-defendants. This boy was the only one of the three who spoke in court, to confirm that he understood the bail conditions. His mother was also advised to take an interest in her son's compliance with his bail conditions. He too was remanded on bail until 12 November.

Three more adjournments were to follow before there would be more progress in the case. On 6 February 2003, Rory and Jonathan were further charged with manslaughter. Stephen also had a new charge put against him for theft of the mobile phone and wallet. At their next court appearance, Judge Geoffrey Browne heard that the DPP had decided that the case should be sent forward to the Circuit Criminal Court. A state solicitor applied for a further adjournment to allow for the preparation of books of evidence on the case. The boys were further remanded on conditional bail.

However, on 20 March, the charges were upgraded from manslaughter to murder, meaning that the trio would now be facing the Central Criminal Court and the possibility, if convicted, of life sentences. They were remanded in custody for a week. They would later be released on High Court bail. On Thursday, 22 May 2003 the prosecution was given a final six-week adjournment to serve books of evidence on the three teenagers. Any murder file represents a tremendous amount of paper work for arresting officers and their staff; putting this one together was a huge task.

Explaining the delay in preparation of the books of evidence, a state solicitor told Judge Mary Collins that the case was extremely complicated, involved over 200 witness statements and that more time was needed. Judge Collins granted a final adjournment and ruled that the case would be 'peremptory against the State' to have the books of evidence ready by 3 July, which meant that if the books of evidence were not ready by that date, the case could be struck out. The book of evidence was completed and served on 3 July. Stephen, then aged 16, and Rory and Jonathan, at this point aged 17, were returned for trial to the Central Criminal Court.

At the outset of the trial in October 2004, Rory and Jonathan pleaded guilty to a lesser charge of manslaughter. Their pleas were accepted, but Stephen went to a full trial for murder before Mr Justice Henry Abbott and a jury of eight men and four women.

The jury would hear that Alan Higgins had died from 'haemor-rhaging and shock due to a stab wound to the chest'. State Pathologist Marie Cassidy said that Alan had 'suffered considerable blood loss, so much had been lost that he developed a blood clot and blood was flowing from his wounds.' He had also suffered 'a blunt force trauma to the head and arms' and his wounds suggested that he had 'received a few punches to the face'. The position of the fatal wound was in an 'area normally protected' by the arm. 'This suggests he had his arm raised in self defence when he was attacked,' the State Pathologist testified.

A day after Alan Higgins was fatally stabbed, Stephen had admitted to stabbing him, telling investigating gardaí, 'I just stabbed the bloke. I am very sorry; it wasn't meant to happen that way.' Accompanied by his father and mother, he had voluntarily given a statement to gardaí, in which he confessed: 'There was three of us and I did the stabbing with the steak knife.' His statement continued: 'I got the knife out of my own house. I didn't get the phone; myself and Rory got the wallet; there was about €115 in it. We took €50 each and spent it on smokes and drinks that night.'

'I was drunk at that stage,' Stephen admitted. He had drunk six cans of beer and smoked a cannabis joint. The three had been thrown out of a fastfood restaurant in the UCI complex at 9.30 p.m. Regarding the earlier incidents with the other victims, he said, 'I wanted to get my mates to take them on again. They wouldn't come back. I went into my house and got out two knives.'

Stephen also said in his interview that he had given Rory one of the knives. They had then taken a piece of white piping from a skip and broken it in two.

In relation to the fatal attack on Alan, Stephen said:

A bloke came up the path towards us, it was dark, he bumped into me. When I turned he was looking at me. I called the bloke a dope; the other guy said nothing. As he turned to walk away, we jumped him. The two of us fell to the ground, he was on top of me. I couldn't get him off me; he was bigger than me. I reached into my pocket and pulled out the knife. I stuck him with the knife and he rolled off me. He cried out 'ah'. I stuck him again. I stabbed him in the side. I felt the knife go in. Rory was holding him down as well. I found the wallet in his front jeans pocket. He walked towards the cinema holding his stomach and limping. That's the last time I saw him.

After the stabbing, Rory and Stephen were in a further fight. Rory, according to Stephen, had a 'busted lip' and bleeding nose. The two then split up the spoils of the fatal stabbing. As surgeons were trying to save Alan's life, Stephen and Rory were going through his wallet. There were 'loads of cards' in it, including a provisional driving licence, bank cards and a Movie Magic card, according to Stephen. 'We dumped everything except the cash,' he said. 'I still had the knife, I put it back in my back pocket.' The bank cards were strewn on the road near where the attack had taken place.

Following a 10-day trial, Stephen was found guilty of the murder of Alan Higgins. The jury deliberated for just over three hours before reaching its unanimous verdict. He was also found guilty of stealing Alan's Nokia 3310 mobile phone and the cash he had on him on the fatal night. Stephen was remanded in custody, pending sentence. In December 2004, Alan's mother read out a heartrending victim impact statement, to a hushed court. It read:

My name is Miriam Higgins and I am the mother of Alan and Caitriona Higgins. I appear before the court today on behalf of my daughter Caitriona, Alan's sister, family, friends and myself, to represent Alan. More than anything else I do this to respect and honour him.

On 23 March 1985, my son was placed in my arms for the first time, just minutes after he took his first breath. He was so precious, his face so flawless, his skin so soft, I whispered I love you for the first time. He was born into this world innocent to be taught right from wrong by his parents.

In August 1989, Alan was diagnosed with leukaemia at four years of age; his existence for two years was being in hospital or at home isolated from his friends and family because of infection. He never moaned and took his illness in his stride and was extremely brave throughout. Every night I kissed my son goodnight and told him I loved him, as I never knew if he would survive this serious illness as his chances were slim. But against the odds he fought his illness and miraculously survived.

On 12 October 2002, I was brought to an emergency room where my beautiful son lay; this time his face was not flawless, his skin was not soft only cold and very pale. His frightened beautiful brown eyes looked up at me as I told him I loved him; he asked me to 'stop fussing' and hold his hand. Little did I know that this would be the last time my son would look at me, talk to me and hold my hand.

That Saturday started like any other. I got up early with Alan and we collected his friends Jamie and Adam and I brought them to play golf in St Anne's Golf Club. After golf, Alan was collected by Jamie and Adam's parents. They all went to help their aunt move house. He came home after 4 p.m. where he practised his play that was coming up in school, we watched a video, had something to eat and then he got ready to go out with his girlfriend Tanya.

They had arranged to go to the UCI complex. Like most parents, I was glad that his friends were law-abiding and responsible. I said goodbye to him that night not realising that it would be the last time I would see him happy.

At approximately 11 p.m. my life changed by receiving a phone call. The person informed me that Alan had been beaten up and was on his way by ambulance to hospital. He had got a lot of orthodontic treatment done on his teeth and my first thought was that they were damaged. How wrong I was. When I entered casualty the seriousness of Alan's condition was made known to me. I went through a range of emotions that night but never once thought that Alan would not survive.

At 3.30 a.m. on 13 October, Dr Adrian Ireland came to see me in the waiting room; he informed me that Alan had died at 3.10 a.m. A part of me died too, knowing that no one person or one thing could ever fill that piece of my heart.

Words seem trite in describing what follows when you find out that your child has been murdered. It took my identity, it took my security of knowing that when I passed on Caitriona and Alan would have each other for support and comfort. It took my innocence, it took my rest, it took my happiness, it took my peace and it took my ability to enjoy anything. His murder gives me sleepless nights, nightmares and night terrors. It gave depression and a struggle to simply find the reason to survive each day.

It gave me tears upon tears, pain upon pain, it covered my world in sadness, pain and anger. It continues to destroy my health a little at a time.

There is not one second of the day that I don't see Alan alive in the emergency room followed by seeing him in his coffin. There is not one second that I don't long for him. He is my first thought when I wake and my last thought before sleep. And all my thoughts during the day. The hardest thing for me is knowing the pain and terror he suffered at the time of his murder.

When I eventually returned to work I could not go straight home knowing that Alan was not going to walk in the door from school. I had no favourite dinners to cook for him, his chair empty at the table, none of his washing on the line, his golf balls around the garden that would never be played with again. So many times I wished I could die too just so I could see and touch my son again and above all know he was all right.

I avoided going home, I sat in coffee shops alone, plucking up the courage to turn the key in the lock, knowing the house would be silent. Wishing I could just hear his voice or see him. People avoided me in public because they didn't know what to say to me. I felt I had leprosy or that I had done something terribly wrong for them to avoid me.

When Alan was 15 years old, his sister Caitriona went to Glasgow to follow her dream to study to become a veterinary nurse. When Alan was taken away from her, so too was her dream. She returned home unable to cope with the loss of her brother. A mother's instinct is to protect her child from the cruelty and pain of society. I could not take her pain away, I could not make her feel better, I could not bring back Alan, her brother, whom she stood by over all his years of illness. I felt so helpless, all I could do was comfort her with a hug and tell her how much I loved her. I knew in my heart that was all I could do.

I had not only lost my son but also had to watch my other child suffer the most horrific pain that could ever be inflicted on her.

[The killer] not only stabbed Alan but us too, for we carry that knife pierced in our hearts that cannot be removed.

Alan was a loving and caring young man with a heart as big as the world. His murder took a son, a brother, half brother, grandson, nephew, cousin, boyfriend and friend. In the past two years and two months since his murder I have watched helplessly as his relatives and friends have struggled with their pain, anger and grief.

We never know as family and friends what sound or sight is going to trigger in our minds a memory. And while the memories of Alan are so cherished, with them comes the realisation that he is gone. Each time that realisation hits our hearts it is devastating. Especially family gatherings where we see an empty space where Alan's presence used to be. We have been robbed of all that and the void is so loud. He loved to have his family around him especially his younger cousins and half sister, where he had so much patience drawing cartoons and playing with them. He has one more cousin now, Colm, who Alan will never have the opportunity to give his love and attention to.

When Alan was six years old and Caitriona eight years old, their father and I separated. The three of us were very close and they both had a lot of respect for me as I worked to keep the mortgage paid and the food on the table. They did not have a lot of material things like other kids but what they were taught was respect for other people and knew right from wrong in our society.

Caitriona and Alan were my life and I was always so proud of them. I did a good job with them being reared in a one-parent family. In later years they both got part-time jobs to help financially and also helped pay for their dental treatment.

Alan had borrowed a sum of money from his uncle to pay the final bill; he was paying him back in instalments. That Saturday he withdrew a large amount to pay back his uncle after work on the Sunday.

Alan held no grudges despite his years of illness. He was a grade A student and worked hard at his ambitions to be an architect. He was generous in his thoughts to all of us in his life. He had caddied for his uncle from an early age and at the age of 13 he joined St Anne's Golf Club as a juvenile member and also worked part-time in McGuirk's Golf Shop. I always knew that Alan had a select amount of friends both in school and outside. One thing I discovered in talking with them was that he touched a lot of lives.

Having thanked the Garda Síochána, bereavement counsellors and general public for their support, Alan's mother concluded her statement:

I ask you, your honour, on our behalf, will you take into consideration the following facts:

1. That Alan's age be taken into consideration, he was only 17 years old. 2. Alan was given a second chance of life when he survived leukaemia. 3. Alan was not a bully, he did not entertain the three accused on the night he was stabbed; apart from the clothes he wore, he only had in his possession his phone and wallet. 4. The fact that Rory and Jonathan participated with Stephen in his actions to hurt Alan; they could have stopped the stabbing if they had any consciences. 5. That I as Alan's mum and Caitriona as Alan's sister had to hear in a public court after two years details of what happened to Alan that night is taken into consideration. 6. After 21 years in my home I had to move as the accused and his family lived not far from us. 7. My health is suffering badly and I have aged well before my time. No prescription can be got to mend a mother's broken heart. 8. Whilst the three accused will be behind bars their families can visit and talk to their sons—we won't be able to see, hear or touch Alan again. 9. The fact that I as Alan's mum took responsibility as a parent to bring up my children with respect towards others and to obey the law in our society. 10. None of the accused or their families has shown any remorse to us for the murder of my son.

All children are born equal into this world, innocent to be guided by their parents. Sadly some parents fail to do this and blame society for their children's actions, instead of themselves. This is an easy cop-out as society did not bring them into the world—the parents did.

A life sentence does not mean life in prison for the accused. But Caitriona and I will serve a life sentence without appeal or parole, having committed no crime.

The sentence hearing was on 20 December 2004. Mr Justice Henry Abbott was led into a packed courtroom in the Four Courts by his usher Gerry Whelan and escorted to the bench where he proceeded to deal with the trio. The then 17-year-old convicted murderer, Stephen, was sentenced to thirteen years with four suspended for the robbery of the mobile phone and sum of cash. Stephen's accomplices, Rory and Jonathan, were sentenced to ten years and eight years respectively for the manslaughter of Alan. Rory, then aged 18, had seven years of his ten-year manslaughter sentence suspended by Mr Justice Abbott. Jonathan, also aged 18 at this point, had six years of his eight-year manslaughter sentence suspended. Both were also given lesser and concurrent sentences, with portions suspended, for robbing Alan and the other young victims on that night.

Detective Kevin Fields told the court that Stephen and Rory had committed crimes since Alan's death.

Stephen's senior counsel read a letter written by Stephen's parents. It said:

Dear Mr and Mrs Higgins, writing this letter is very difficult, we can't imagine what it must feel like to lose a son. That our son is responsible for his death is very difficult to accept. I hope you and your family can accept this apology. You will always be in our prayers.

Mr Justice Abbott heard lengthy submissions from Stephen's counsel for two days before he proceeded to sentence the teenager. The defence counsel unsuccessfully requested the court to treat Stephen as a child under the 2001 Children's Act.

But Mr Justice Abbott held that for the purpose of sentencing, Stephen was 'not a young person'. Mr Justice Abbott took into consideration the robberies of up to five other teenage boys by Stephen when sentencing him to thirteen years, with four suspended, for mugging Alan. Meanwhile, awaiting his fate on the murder charge, Stephen held his mother's hand as his sister wept.

The judge referred to Stephen's behaviour on the night of the stabbing as 'absolute banditry'. 'If there was a cameo for an ideal young man, one could hardly get a more normally successful picture than that of Mr Higgins,' Mr Justice Abbott said, adding that this idyllic image had been 'destroyed by this robbery'.

Stephen, the judge said, had caused 'mayhem, destruction and tragedy' that night. He also added that the boy did not 'seem to have got the message that crime doesn't pay', referring to the fact that Stephen had been convicted of more offences, committed after the murder. 'For that reason, [Stephen] must spend a considerable amount of that thirteen years in detention,' the judge said in regard to the sentence for the robbery. For the brutal murder of Alan Higgins, Stephen was sentenced to life.

VI. WHERE TO?

23 | WHERE TO PUT THEM

The issue of spaces, or lack of them, in either detention facilities or care units, has been a core issue in the juvenile justice system and a topic that has been raised several times in the cases of troubled or out-of-control young offenders. The problem exists among the centres that specifically hold under 16-year-olds—Trinity House, Oberstown Boys' and Girls' Centres, Finglas Child and Adolescent Centre[1] and the National Remand and Assessment Centre.[2]

MAY 2002. The parents of a troublesome teenage boy asked to have him remanded in custody. Their 15-year-old son had already failed to appear at a hearing for a criminal damage offence. And during that week he had been arrested again for criminal trespass. Other new charges were also mounting. Judge William Early heard that the boy's mother, who was present in court, wanted her son to be remanded in custody and not sent home because it was too difficult for her to prevent him from getting into trouble. In an effort to stop their son from getting out of their home, the boy's parents had taken the handles from the doors and windows of their house to keep him indoors. But he was still managing to break out. Initially Judge Early said he would remand the boy in custody due to his failure to appear at his earlier hearing. However, enquiries made by gardaí to Oberstown Boys' Centre and Trinity House revealed that there were no remand places available. Judge Early said it was 'grossly unfair' to the boy's parents that he would have to grant bail, but given the circumstances he was compelled to do so.

JUNE 2002. Judge Clare Leonard directed that the case of a 14-year-old homeless boy should be taken to the High Court to vindicate his constitutional rights to care and protection because there were no remand places available for him and the health board could not help. The boy had been living with his father, a recovering drug addict, on the streets, having been thrown out of a B&B. After that, the boy and his father had been 'living out of bags' in friends' homes. There were no remand places available and only temporary emergency hostel accommodation could be recommended by the health board.

A garda said that the boy had broken his bail by entering an area from which he had been previously barred by the court. He applied to have the boy remanded in custody but said that the two institutions he had contacted had no places available. The case was put back three times that day to see if a place could be made available in a detention centre or in a care unit through the health board. Judge Leonard said that the emergency accommodation was not sufficient in this 'urgent' case.

The teenager eventually moved in with a very supportive uncle but continued to present major policing problems through petty offending. By the time he turned 18, he had accrued sixty-eight criminal convictions, by which stage there were plenty of places available—in St Patrick's Institution.

SEPTEMBER 2002. An out-of-control 15-year-old girl was sent to a care unit in Co. Fermanagh, in Northern Ireland, for an assessment. There was nowhere in the state to hold the girl whose mother would not take her home.

The mother told the court that her daughter was out of control and pleaded for her to be taken into custody. The previous April, the girl had been arrested after a complaint that she had attacked her mother with a knife. A garda had gone to the girl's room where he had seen the knife on the bed. When he had reached to pick it up, the girl had grabbed it and he had received a slight nick on one of his fingers. The girl had been sent to live in foster care for a month but had been allowed home at the request of her mother. The girl's mother had later said that the only reason she had made the complaint against her daughter was that she needed help with her. She had been trying to get therapeutic help for her teenage daughter for three years.

Over the previous year, the worn-out mother had gone to a social worker over 100 times, with issues involving her daughter. The incidents were becoming more serious and the social worker feared that someone would be seriously injured or killed if the girl remained in the home. 'It is getting to the stage where I cannot take her home; I swear to God she has got out of control,' the mother pleaded with the court. The court heard that there were still no places for the girl.

SEPTEMBER 2002. Another boy with behavioural problems had begun appearing in court on a regular basis. Highly intelligent and articulate, he had been one of the best students in his school. Suddenly, while in his early teens, he had gone out of control. At the age of 15, he was thrown out of home; his parents did not want him living there because they could not cope with his behaviour. They wanted a psychological assessment of their son to be carried out, but because there were no places for the boy that would not be possible.

The teenager was then put into voluntary care of the health board and was utilising 'out of hours' services whereby he could stay in a hostel, depending on vacancies. However, the boy turned up late on some occasions and could not get a bed.

He started disappearing onto the streets of Dublin. His mother could no longer rein him in and needed him placed in a secure unit for his own welfare, it was believed.

In what was called by a judge a 'recurring scandal' of the criminal justice system, the homeless boy had returned to the streets because the state had no facilities to accommodate him and he refused to go back to his family. A couple of days before his court appearance, the boy had been remanded in custody to

Trinity House for the weekend. He left the facility to go to court on the morning of 16 September; his case was finished at 1 p.m. but, in the intervening period, his place had been taken.

There were no other places for the boy in either Oberstown House or the Ballydowd Special Care Unit, and he had to depend on hostel accommodation. Judge William Early said that it was to the 'frustration of the court' that once again it was facing 'this predicament'. Judge Early was told that the boy was charged with stealing €2 worth of sweets from a shop. More charges were pending for public order and criminal damage offences. The boy's solicitor said that the health board had a duty to provide care for the boy. However, counsel for the health board said that there were no places available in care facilities.

Judge Early ordered that efforts should be made again to see if a place was available in Trinity House, but they were not successful. He referred to it as 'the common situation of having no where to place him' and said that because of the criminal justice system, this 'young man of 15' was 'back on the streets'. He remanded the boy on bail until 23 September and urged him to try to reach a reconciliation with his family. The boy was told to turn up in court the following week by which time it was hoped there would be a place to hold him, 'somewhere'.

But the teenager then went missing for a couple of weeks. The next time he showed up, a fortnight later, was after gardaí found him wandering around Mountjoy Square in the early hours. In court, he was again turned out on to the streets because the state had no remand places to accommodate him. Gardaí were still looking for a remand in custody but because there were still no places for the boy, the judge had no other option but to grant bail.

A week later, a judge ordered that a decision must be made within the next week on when a place in the Ballydowd Special Care Unit could be provided for the teenager. But a week later there was still no place available and the boy was sent to a special sporting unit in Northern Ireland to await a decision on Ballydowd.

The health board with authority for the Ballydowd Special Care Unit believed that the boy was not suitable to be sent there.

The Northern Area Health Board disagreed. It took months before he was finally admitted to the centre.

After his term there ended, he rarely came before the Children's Court again.

FEBRUARY 2003. An out-of-control 14-year-old boy, then facing twenty-six charges, was released on bail because there were no suitable places in the state's juvenile institution to hold him.[3] The case was put back for a week when there was still no place to hold him.

Two months later, Judge Michael Connellan said that he held the Government responsible for the situation. The executive, he said, was to blame for the shortage of secure detention facilities for young offenders, which saw them released on to the streets where they committed further crimes. He had heard that a homeless 15-year-old boy, who had been charged with a number of offences including larceny, breaches of public order, handling stolen goods and burglary, needed to be held in a secure facility but none was available.

Following a six-week assessment in the National Remand and Assessment Centre, in Finglas, staff there concluded that in view of the boy's homelessness, he should be detained in a secure centre such as Trinity House.

However, Judge Connellan was told that neither Trinity House nor the Oberstown Boys' Centre had a long-term sentence bed. The judge said that the boy needed to be detained in a secure facility for his own welfare. He made the point that young offenders often end up back on the streets where more crimes are committed. 'The courts get blamed for releasing them but it is not their fault,' he said. 'The Government is not doing anything to provide places.'

JUNE 2003. A solicitor for a troubled teenage boy who was in need of a 'secure therapeutic educational environment' initiated High Court proceedings to compel the State and Oberstown Boys' Centre to provide a place to hold him. The 16-year-old boy needed an appropriate placement but none was available and the only alternative was to detain him in St Patrick's Institution which could serve to criminalise him. It was submitted that by being placed in Oberstown Boys' Centre he would benefit from the institution's educational and training facilities.

He had earlier been detained in Oberstown but officials there were against taking him back because he had head-butted a staff member after he was sent off in a football match. The staff member received three stitches to his head. The teenager had smashed up a video recorder following a row with another detainee at Oberstown. He had spent two weeks on remand in St Patrick's Institution on these charges because there was no where else to detain him.

However, St Patrick's Institution had been deemed an unsuitable place in view of the teenager's needs and psychological problems. The boy had massive anger management problems and an earlier assessment had recommended that he should be held in a 'secure therapeutic environment'.

Since he was aged 13, his parents had tried in vain to find a suitable placement where their son could be helped. He had spent a year in a unit run by the health board. He was looked after by psychiatric nurses there and had managed to complete his Junior Certificate. Having been turned away from Oberstown Boys' Centre, he was released from state custody and took part in a vicious attack over which he would later receive a lengthy detention term from the Dublin Circuit Criminal Court.

Efforts had been made to have him placed in the Hassela Gotland Unit in Sweden[4] which works with young people with social and behavioural problems, but the case in the Circuit Criminal Court overtook the boy and rendered these plans mute.

SEPTEMBER 2004. The state's juvenile detention facilities had no place to hold a 14-year-old boy who had come to garda attention after his father threw him out of their home.

The boy from west Dublin had been arrested for missing a court appearance in relation to other charges. He had left home several months previously. However, he told the court that he hoped his father would take him back home shortly if he stopped smoking cannabis.

The teenager had been staying in different hostels from night to night. Despite having a social worker appointed to him through the hostels, his long-term accommodation arrangements had not been advanced. The court was told that there were no remand places available in Trinity House, in Oberstown Boys' Centre or in the National Remand and Assessment Centre. Judge Michael Connellan said that given the boy's young age, his irregular accommodation arrangements and the fact that he was taking drugs, he had to make an order to remand him to Oberstown, although he had been told that the facility had no remand places.

He said that his 'hands [were] tied' and that he had no choice. He advised that if the boy were taken to the centre and turned away, the case should then be brought to the High Court. He again said that he was 'sick' of this situation, and he held the Government responsible. He also said the he wanted the child's father to be in court when the case was back the following week. He believed that the father was not taking responsibility for the boy.

OCTOBER 2004. A couple of weeks later, the same issue continued to dog proceedings. On 6 October, a Wednesday afternoon, Judge Connellan was confronted with the same problem for the second time that week. A 14-year-old boy who needed to be placed in a secure unit was sitting on the defendant's bench. He had also been deemed unsuitable for a placement in the Ballydowd Special Care Unit. There was no place to remand the boy either in Oberstown or in the National Remand and Assessment Centre.

Despite this, Judge Connellan ordered a remand to Oberstown. He said that he could not grant bail in case something happened to the boy. 'He could be killed or injured or start taking drugs on the streets,' the judge said. He told the boy's solicitor to bring the case to the High Court if the boy was turned away from the door of Oberstown Boys' Centre.

NOVEMBER 2003. A violently dangerous teenage boy was given two years' detention. However, the 15-year-old boy still walked out of court and could not be put in custody because there were no places in any of the juvenile detention facilities which dealt with his age group. Judge Mary Collins imposed the order but had to let the boy free, ordering him to come back to court the following Monday to see if a spot had been found for him.

She said that she had 'serious worries about this person not being in a very secure environment.' She was in no doubt of the danger the boy posed to others.

On 19 August 2003, a social worker from the Northern Area Health Board, who had been assigned to work with the teenager and his family, had been held in their home for twenty-five minutes until gardaí freed him. When the social worker had arrived at the house, in Skerries, north Co. Dublin, the teenager had tried to attack him with a bottle. The boy had grown increasingly agitated and had broken the bottle and held it to the social worker's neck while making threats to kill him if he tried to leave the house. However, the social worker had managed to make a phone call to one of his colleagues who had alerted gardaí.

Since the incident, it had been deemed unsafe for any social workers to visit the teenager's home.

The boy had also been involved in violent assaults on gardaí in the courthouse. On 2 September, while in custody in the court-house's holding cell, he had lashed out and hit one garda. A short time later, as he was being escorted to the courtroom, he had punched another garda in the face.

The youth pleaded guilty to assaulting the social worker and the two gardaí and to possession of an offensive weapon, the bottle. He also admitted public order violations where he had been caught in breach of the peace, and he was facing another charge for damaging his mother's home.

Referring to the lack of placements provided by the state for juvenile offenders, Judge Collins said: 'Are they to wait until there is a fatality before there is any facility made available?'

Before these incidents, the boy had been held in the Ballydowd Special Care Unit by order of the High Court. But Judge Collins was told that during his stay there he had 'wrecked' the facility. After that, he had been moved to a residential care home for troublesome young offenders but had stayed there for only two days. Since then, the High Court proceedings to find a secure placement for him had been dropped.

At the same time, his brother was being held in Oberstown and the facility's authorities were against holding both of the boys in their custody even if they had the space, Judge Collins was also told.

High Court proceedings on behalf of his brother were taking place to provide him with a place in a care home. If these efforts were successful, this might free up a space in Oberstown for the boy. Judge Collins ordered two years' detention in Trinity House but the youth had to be freed temporarily until a place for him there became available. This happened the following Monday and the boy was detained.

24 | THE PROFILER

On 22 May 2003, a young boy appeared in the Children's Court following his arrest for indecent exposure. These cases are not uncommon, with the court frequently hearing about incidents where young people got drunk and 'flashed' for a prank. This case, however, was to be completely different and the boy's actions were found to be symptomatic of deep sexual problems which he could not control. He walked hurriedly into the courtroom, followed by his mother. While sitting on the defendant's bench, he stared intently around him, his expression like that of a rabbit caught in car's headlights. This demeanour would remain with him throughout the many court appearances that were to follow. The charge before the court related to an extremely disturbing incident. He was also suspected of having committed a random sexual assault on a young woman in a park. An investigation into this incident had been launched and it would later lead to another prosecution. It was also believed that he had been behind a series of garbled sexually explicit letters which had been sent to a woman in his neighbourhood whom he was stalking.

Judge Mary Collins heard that there had been a number of complaints about a youth exposing himself to women in a lane way. When a garda from Dundrum went to investigate the reports on the morning of 7 October 2002, the 15-year-old boy was already standing in the lane way. The garda got permission from a local resident to keep the area under surveillance from his sitting room. He then covertly took up position at the window and waited. A few minutes later, he saw the teenager undo his trousers but hold them by keeping his hands in his pockets.

Shortly afterwards, two unsuspecting little girls, aged around 10, came along the lane way, on their way to school. As they got closer to the boy, 'he dropped his trousers and started to masturbate in their direction,' the garda said. The two frightened girls started to scream and ran away. The garda dashed out of the house and called to the girls but, not realising who he was, they kept running. Meanwhile, the boy had pulled up his trousers and grabbed his school bag, and was trying to escape, but he was caught and arrested.

The court heard that the boy had personal difficulties which were caused by domestic problems. He had already started going to counselling before this incident. In April 2002, his GP had referred him to a counsellor but the boy had been able to go to therapy only occasionally. Judge Collins said that the boy was in need of 'urgent therapeutic intervention' and adjourned the case pending a psychological report and one from the Probation and Welfare Services. She was also told that the teenager's mother had given an undertaking not to let him go near the lane way again and had said that she would drive him to school every morning.

The psychological report was to identify 'complex issues' and recommended referring the boy to Temple Street Hospital for specialised psychological counselling for children who have committed sexual offences. Judge John Coughlan agreed, on 3 July, to adjourn, after he was told that the boy was prepared to co-operate with any measures recommended in helping him. In the meantime, two further charges had been brought against the teenager for more serious offences. He had been arrested for an indiscriminate sexual assault on a woman in late 2002 at St Enda's Park in Rathfarnham, during which he had grabbed the woman's breast. Around that time, he had also been arrested for a more serious sexual assault where he had dragged a 14-year-old schoolgirl into a bush, held her against a wall, then forced his hands into her underwear and molested her genital area. The girl had broken free at which the boy had threatened to do the same to her younger sister if she did not acquiesce. A few days later, he again sexually assaulted the same girl in similar circumstances.

On 23 February 2004, now aged 16, he was back in court, twitching nervously. Judge Collins told him that he needed to get psychiatric counselling. 'There is a difficult road ahead and a very serious one, which concerns me,' she stressed. 'I will direct a psychiatric report. You are to do your best to hear what you are being told and to use it to help yourself. You have got to stay out of this type of trouble and take every help you can get.'

She also noted that it had been becoming increasingly difficult for his mother to monitor him. The case was then adjourned twice more until the following September when it was revealed that he had again been arrested for similar offences. These latest events had had an even more worrying effect on his victims and their families.

A garda told the court: 'The impact on the latest victim would be substantial; it happened twice. There would be a nature of profiling involved which would be worrying for her and her family.' The latest incidents allegedly occurred near his school, the court was also told.

Judge Mary Collins said that she was concerned over the efficacy of his current treatment. The case was adjourned until October to allow the teenager time to instruct his solicitor in relation to the new charges. The teenager's mother told the court that in future she would collect her son from school each day and bring him straight home in an effort to prevent any further incidents.

In early 2005, there was no sign of any progress and efforts were made to find a treatment centre in England for the now 17-year-old boy. Judge Collins was told that there were no facilities in Ireland that could help him, and the complexity of his problems and magnitude of the pattern of his offending had even made it difficult to identify a suitable facility overseas. One treatment centre in England focused on children with similar problems but tried to help them when they were as young as 13.

Another therapeutic centre, also in England, had been approached. It helped teenagers involved in abnormal sexual behaviour. Judge Collins heard that an assessment was to take place in the coming weeks, during which experts would meet the boy and his family. One of the major issues to arise was who would fund the placement. Judicial review proceedings were brought to the High Court, in the course of which the boy was described as living in a 'sexual fantasy inner world'. During the proceedings, Mr Justice Henry Abbott urged the HSE several times to agree to have the boy assessed for a placement in the English treatment centre. However, the HSE repeatedly opposed the moves to facilitate the placement.

A detailed account of a later incident was given to the Children's Court in April 2005. The court heard how, on 18 March 2003, the teenager, 15 years old at the time, had followed two young girls, aged about four, and exposed his penis to them. These victims had not suffered any long-term trauma as a result but their parents had changed their routine to make sure that the girls were brought to and from school via different routes.

There was more to come and it was getting closer to home. Evidence was heard of how, on three separate occasions, the boy had repeatedly exposed himself to a young girl who lived next door to him. 'On 13 December 2003, he came out his front door and walked onto his front lawn. He pulled down his pants and walked over to his next-door neighbour's wall. He then stood on his front lawn and exposed himself to the young girl inside the neighbouring house who was watching television,' the court heard.

Eight days later, there was a similar incident. While standing in his front garden, he again exposed himself to the same girl. The girl then went to a neighbour's house. On her return home later that day, the boy was standing at the front of his house and he exposed himself again. Three weeks later, the girl was in her sitting room watching television when the boy started to expose himself from his front garden. When she moved to a different seat in the room, he walked closer to the dividing wall between their houses so that she would be able to see him again.

In the final incident, seven months later, the girl was in her back garden, and the boy was in the kitchen of his own house. He stood on the kitchen sink and exposed himself to her. Judge

Collins was asked to adjourn the case pending further efforts to convince the HSE to allow funding for assessments to determine whether the boy would be accepted by a therapeutic centre in England.

Judge Collins said that the initial four-week assessment would cost £3,000 to fund which was significantly less than the HSE had paid in legal fees to fight the case in the High Court. She described the case as being 'one of the most serious' that she had seen in many years. 'There is need for serous intervention, but he has been totally ignored out of hand for the last two years. They are going to ignore this situation as they have done for the last two years even though there are no services available to him,' she said.

She granted bail and adjourned the case to allow the boy's legal team to continue in its attempts to secure a commitment from the HSE.

As the case was adjourned, the judge commended the boy's mother for her tireless efforts to monitor her son and prevent him from re-offending. 'I do not know how she has managed to survive; it is quite astonishing, he needs such intensive hands-on supervision all of the time,' she said.

The beleaguered mother's daily routine was dedicated to keeping a watch on her son. She had become like a prison guard and surveillance detective rolled into one. He had to be monitored 24 hours a day. He was escorted by his mother to and from school daily. When he returned home from school, he remained there under her supervision. Her health suffered as a result and she feared that she could not continue to keep up this level of supervision but she was still afraid that her son's offending could escalate.

His behaviour was described as grossly abnormal and there were fears that if he were detained, this would merely allow him to associate with sex offenders. At this point he had little life outside home and school. Notoriety attached itself to him like a limpet, and in his community, he had no friends or hobbies and he had been jeered in public; there were fears that he could be attacked as a result of his behaviour.

In December 2005, the boy was detained for three months on the indecent exposure charges. Meanwhile, he had to await sentencing for the sexual assaults. On 3 April 2006, now aged 18, he was given a five-year sentence and a three-year concurrent sentence by Dublin Circuit Criminal Court for the sexual assaults on the young girl. Four days later, he was given a concurrent one-year sentence, again by the Dublin Circuit Criminal Court, for the sexual assault on the woman in Rathfarnham, when he was aged 15. Pronouncing sentence on the first of these two cases, Judge Con Murphy said that the boy had 'obvious deep psychological health problems which [had] not been dealt with'.

25 | HASSELA GOTLAND:
THE FUTURE?

Cut off from the Swedish mainland by 100 km of the icy choppy waters of the Baltic Sea, Gotland island is a mythical setting, with broody moors, high cliff faces and a coastline bounded by white beaches. The Vikings believed Gotland to be an enchanted place that would evaporate in daytime to reappear once darkness had settled. Laden down with treasures from across Europe, they used Gotland as a hideout and a secret repository for their loot.

For the past twenty years, Hassela Gotland has operated as a working community, educating young people with social problems. About sixty students of both sexes, with problems including criminality and drug abuse, are helped at three communities on the island—the Klintehamn Centre, Hassela Vange and Tors Gard. Most of the students are under the age of 20 but, in exceptional cases, older students are admitted as well. Some 100 staff members are employed to run the communities' programmes which are tailored to suit individual needs. Every student has the opportunity to complete secondary school and gain the marks required to go on to higher education. Social interaction is important, and through various activities and trips, within Sweden and abroad, students are exposed to different environments and encouraged to find new interests without being under the influence of drugs.

About half of the young offenders who are sent to Hassela are Swedish and the rest come from all across Europe, as well as from war-torn countries such as Iraq and Afghanistan. The majority have turned their backs on crime and anti-social behaviour by the time they return home.

Meanwhile, in Ireland, about half of teenagers who are held in the state's most secure unit for young offenders under the age of 16, Trinity House in Lusk, in later years end up in adult prisons, or in health-board care, or are homeless within a short time after their release.

The success of the Hassela Gotland community is attributed to its central ethos of offering every child the opportunity to experience a normal life in a structured environment, where they are motivated to take responsibility for their lives and learn to give back to their community. The children live in comfortable apartments with their minders while they are on the island, which is run along the lines of a kibbutz. A strict daily routine starts early every morning, when everyone gathers at the main house for breakfast. And there is no mollycoddling—if you turn up late, you go without and wait until the next meal.

The students attend school or work to earn their keep in the centre's local businesses, which include a bakery, a zoo and a carpentry workshop. The community has a wide range of evening activities, like football and boxing, as well as other fun or creative pursuits such as dancing and acting.

Students are forbidden to consume alcohol, and the local community plays a role in enforcing this rule; if it is broken, calls will be made to report the youngsters.

Sniffer dogs kept at the centre serve as friendly pets but also make sure that drugs are kept off the premises. Escape attempts from the island are almost impossible.

Teenage drug addicts who relapse are sent to a special detox centre in another part of the island where they receive the best treatment. They also receive ongoing therapy and are watched over by child specialists when they are back at the community. Good behaviour is rewarded with skiing trips and sun holidays.

The dearth of care facilities for Irish teenagers with severe emotional, psychological and behavioural problems has been a significant factor in a number of the cases that have come through the juvenile justice system. The problem became personified in the cases of two highly disturbed boys. In these cases, the state was shown to have little to offer, leading to both boys being sent overseas for help, and for them salvation was to lie on the shores of Hassela Gotland.

On 10 November 2003, a 17-year-old boy appeared in the Children's Court in connection with a number of crimes, including handling €850 worth of stolen computer games and DVDs, criminal damage to a cell in a garda station and possession of a weapon—a sharpened screwdriver.

The court heard that Brian's nature had suddenly and inexplicably become hostile and violent. This had later been attributed to the sexual abuse he had suffered at a young age, at the hands of an uncle, when they took trips together. Judge Sean McBride heard that there was no suitable care facility in Ireland to help deal with his complex psychological problems. For years he had been shunted around various detention facilities as well as the health board high-support unit.

He was held in custody for fourteen months in the National Remand and Assessment Centre, pending fruitless efforts to find a suitable placement for him in the care system.

In 1998 the High Court recommended that he be moved into the health board run high-support unit, Newtown House, in Co. Wicklow. That facility had a regime of using force to restrain troubled children who could be held in solitary confinement for twenty-three hours each day.

One of his fellow residents, who was also one of his closest friends, committed suicide while in the care of the unit, and this had a profound effect on Brian. The unit was closed down following a complaint by Brian's parents and a subsequent investigation.

The deeply troubled boy was then moved to the National Remand and Assessment Centre, but staff there could not cope with his behaviour. He was then put into the more secure Trinity House Detention Centre until his release. His parents had continued to fight to find an appropriate therapeutic placement for him, but the state could offer nothing.

Eventually, social workers in the East Coast Area Health Board investigated the possibility of sending him to the Hassela Gotland therapeutic centre. Social workers deemed that this facility would be suitable for Brian, and it was planned that he would spend two years there.

Judge McBride adjourned the case, pending an answer on when the placement would start. He said that if Brian were accepted by the Swedish authorities involved, he would impose a suspended sentence and bind him to the peace for two years.

On Friday, 12 December 2003, Brian was given an eight-month suspended sentence on condition that he be sent to Sweden for treatment. Judge Angela Ní Chonduin heard that as a result of the suspended sentence she imposed, Brian would be free to go to Sweden on the following Tuesday, with the placement being open to him for up to two years.

Two months later, the treatment was going well. 'He is a changed person now,' his solicitor told Judge Mary Collins. 'As a result, the funding for the second phase of his stay there has been secured by the health board,' she added.

Brian stayed at Hassela Gotland for over a year and came back to Ireland and his family a new person, equipped with a new outlook on life. When he had been locked up in Ireland, he had felt institutionalised and was almost encouraged to break the laws, whereas in Sweden he had felt he was being treated as a human being, with equality and respect.

'When you did something wrong, you weren't kept in a room where you just feel threatened, but you were sent on a long walk, with staff, to clear your head and think about what you had done,' he said after his return.

'Although I learned a lot in Sweden—a new language and a different culture—sending young teenagers abroad, away from their families, isn't the answer. We need to have facilities like Hassela here, not the outdated detention centres we have, where kids learn to be criminals.'

It was Thursday, 22 September 2005. The Children's Court was hearing how masked gunmen claiming to be members of the Continuity IRA had raided the house of a troubled 14-year-old boy and threatened him and other children in his family over perceived anti-social behaviour in the area. Judge Angela Ní Chonduin was told that four men had entered Simon's Dublin home, wearing balaclavas and armed with guns and baseball bats. Guns were pointed at his mother and young sisters and he was threatened by the men.

Simon was facing charges for assault and a breach of the peace. He was being held on remand in a detention centre for young criminals because there was no suitable care home environment in which he could be placed. Simon had been held in Oberstown since July that year, pending efforts to have the HSE source a suitable residential and therapeutic care placement for him.

Commenting on the situation, Judge Ní Chonduin said that it was wrong to keep a child in a detention centre over welfare issues but added that she could not grant bail to him either because he would end up homeless. Simon's mother gave the court an outline of the difficulties she had encountered in trying to get help for her son. She also said that she and her family had had to move house following the gunmen's raid on their home.

Simon's solicitor also said that he had been remanded in custody over welfare issues, which were outside the jurisdiction of the Children's Court which deals with criminal matters.

An assessment of Simon had found that he needed to be in a secure placement for at least six months. However, the Ballydowd Special Care Unit, a secure therapeutic facility, does not take children for that long. It had also refused Simon on the grounds that he was 'doing well in his current placement', in Oberstown.

At that day's hearing, the HSE did not appear in court to outline its proposals to find an appropriate placement for Simon but it was aware that the case was being heard.

Simon's mother quietly explained to the court that her son had first exhibited behavioural problems when he was two years old and had shown signs of an unusual level of hyperactivity. At the age of six, he had been made subject of a care order which had led to placements in three care homes in Dublin. 'He has not had much of a home life,' Judge Ní Chonduin interjected, to which Simon's mother replied, 'He has not had much of a life.'

Following his placements in the three care homes, he was sent home and prescribed the drug Ritalin, for people with ADHD. Heavy anti-psychotic and anti-depressant medication followed. 'It was like they tried every one and then they said they had made a mistake and could not find anything wrong with him,' she continued.

At the age of eight, Simon suffered a mental breakdown and had to be sedated. 'They put him in care for six weeks and never gave him back.' When Simon was nine, the health board moved him to a care facility in England in the hope that there would be a breakthrough in his therapeutic treatment.

However, his mother had concerns for his safety there, because he had run away from this unit. 'He was spending time on the streets of London, drinking on the streets with the homeless in London.' Simon was then brought back to Ireland and put into care until April 2005. Shortly after Simon returned to his family home, they were visited by men claiming to be from the Continuity IRA. 'There were four men in the house and I think four outside. They had guns and baseball bats and were wearing balaclavas. They put guns into the faces of the girls and threatened him [Simon]. We have moved and since then he went into custody. My other children can't sleep and wet the bed.'

When Simon's mother approached social services again, looking for assistance, she was told by them to have her son arrested so that help could be found through the criminal justice system. The boy's solicitor described this situation as a 'disgrace and a shocking indictment of the HSE'. This advice had followed an incident in which Simon had set fire to a room with three children in it.

The prosecuting garda in the case agreed that the arrest and prosecution were based on an effort to get assistance for Simon and added that there was no objection to bail.

Simon's solicitor told Judge Ní Chonduin that the child was being held in a detention facility on welfare grounds. She submitted that the court and she 'were being forced to address issues in the absence of the HSE taking responsibility to provide alternative placements in the event of Simon getting released on bail.' The HSE had not come up with a proposal for an appropriate placement for her client and if he were bailed he could end up homeless or, at best, be relying on hostel accommodation.

His mother said that she would take her son home but did not feel she could manage him, and there were concerns for his safety arising out of the earlier incident with the gunmen.

Judge Ní Chonduin refused to grant bail and adjourned the case for a week. She ordered that a guardian be appointed to Simon and further directed that representatives of the HSE attend the case to explain how they intended to address the issue of the teenager's future accommodation and welfare.

Counsel for the HSE told Judge Ní Chonduin on that day that there had been considerable social service involvement in the boy's life and his case presented difficulties in terms of providing suitable accommodation. He said that efforts were under way to find an appropriate placement for Simon overseas, in particular the Hassela Gotland unit in Sweden. The case was adjourned, pending the outcome of these latest efforts. Later, the issue of bail was raised again. Judge Ní Chonduin said that she did not want to keep Simon in custody but remanded him to Oberstown Boys' Centre for another week as suitable alternative accommodation was not available.

Arrangements were made to organise an assessment to see if he was suitable for a placement in Hassela Gotland.

On 21 October 2005, Judge Timothy Lucey amended the existing court order holding Simon in custody to allow him mobility to leave the jurisdiction to travel to Sweden. Three days later, the teenager was flown out to take part in the two-day assessment for a placement in the Swedish centre. He was accompanied by two members of staff from Oberstown, two social workers and his parents. When he came back from Sweden, he returned to Oberstown.

Simon was accepted by the Hassela Gotland community. On Thursday, 3 November 2005, he left Ireland to commence his placement, becoming the second Irish child to be sent there. The length of time he would spend in the Swedish unit was not yet established but Simon was agreeable to the placement and his parents were pleased with the plan. He was accompanied on the journey by two members of staff from the Swedish centre.

On 31 January 2006, he was flown back for his trial, having pleaded not guilty to the charges before the court. Judge Catherine Murphy applied the Probation Act, leaving Simon without a criminal conviction for the offences.

The court was told that Simon could stay at the Hassela Gotland unit until he reached adulthood, which would be nearly three years later. When asked by the judge how he felt about his placement in Sweden, Simon said cheerily, 'I like it.'

APPENDIX I
THE SYSTEM

THE GARDA JUVENILE DIVERSION PROGRAMME

The Garda Juvenile Diversion Programme is part and parcel of the 2001 Children Act's concept of Restorative Justice as a way of dealing with juvenile offenders. It allows the offender and the victim to be brought together so that victims have a chance to say how crimes affected them, and it poses a new challenge to the offender who must now confront and deal with the harm caused. The offender is given the opportunity to take some action that will, in some way, attempt to restore things to as they were before the offence was committed. This action may take the form of an apology, compensation or a specific undertaking. Offenders may then enter into a plan designed to help them to move away from the possibility of re-offending.

Upon detection, young offenders may be either prosecuted or diverted from prosecution under the Garda Juvenile Diversion Programme, by means of cautioning or a decision that no further action is deemed necessary. Almost two-thirds of referrals to the programme are dealt with by a caution rather than a prosecution in court. The decision to caution is based on the admission by the child of wrongdoing, the nature of the offence and the juvenile's criminal history. Those prosecuted are deemed unsuitable for the scheme due to their denial of responsibility for the alleged offence.

Figures published in 2005 showed that alcohol-related offences were the most common among the young people referred to the Juvenile Diversion Programme in the previous year. The highest proportion of offenders, 27 per cent, were aged 17, while 25 per cent were aged 16; 19 per cent were aged 15; 12 per cent were aged 14; 8 per cent were aged 13; 4 per cent were aged 12, and 4 per cent were under 12.

In 2004, about 250 children aged below ten years were referred to a Garda Juvenile Diversion Programme. In total, about 17,000 children aged between seven and 18 years were referred to the scheme for offences which included burglary, criminal damage, theft, drink-fuelled public order violation offences and motoring offences. Nearly half the youngsters referred to the programme received an informal caution; 7 per cent got a caution but also received further guidance from the scheme. Just 17 per cent were not deemed eligible for the programme and were taken to court to face prosecution instead, in the Children's Court. The rule of thumb is that each young person, if eligible, gets three chances at the diversion programme.

CRIMINAL RESPONSIBILITY

The much-vaunted Children Act 2001 raised the age of attaining adulthood from 17 to 18 years and also raised the age of criminal responsibility from seven to 12. But amendments to the Act have been drafted to allow for prosecutions of children between the ages of 10 and 12 in situations where it is alleged that the child committed a serious offence, such as murder, rape or sexual assault.

For children over 14 years, the process is straightforward. Following their arrest, they must be released into the custody of a parent, guardian or responsible adult. Generally, unless custody is sought immediately, they are released from the garda station and given a date to appear in the Children's Court. On their first date in court, a garda gives details of the teenager's arrest. A remand is usually sought to allow the child to take legal advice. The teenager is assigned a solicitor and the vast majority are granted free legal aid, which is a reflection on their family's financial circumstances. Normally, they are released on bail to allow them consider what plea they want to enter. In more serious cases, objections to bail may be given and, if the judge accepts the reasons cited, the teenager faces a remand in custody.

BAIL

Strict bail conditions are frequently sought, mostly by the gardaí but sometimes by the children's parents, and normally involve a curfew compelling the youngster to be indoors, at home, between certain hours, mostly nocturnal ones. They may also be given a ban, for the duration of the case, from entering certain areas, where they have repeatedly come to garda attention. Bans are often imposed on the juveniles, preventing them from being in contact with individuals who are deemed to be bad influences. And bans on alcohol and illegal drug use are also regularly made conditions of bail. In Dublin, a practice has evolved where judges forbid teenage defendants to come to the Children's Courthouse area, except for dates when they are required to appear there. This came as a result of fears that the youngsters were coming to the courthouse to support their friends who were facing prosecutions of their own. Frequently gangs of tracksuit-clad teens descended on the environs of the courthouse to swap stories and to wait for their friends who were being dealt with inside. Court began to take on a social element. Anxieties grew that, paradoxically, the court itself was actually, and inadvertently, allowing the younger and more impressionable defendants come under the influence of more experienced teenage offenders. Allowing them to loiter around the area was viewed as counterproductive and unlikely to divert them from crime.

Bail terms imposed on the defendants can prove problematic; breaches of the conditions lead to arrests and sometimes a custodial remand. However, judges differ on how they treat the bail breakers. Some judges give them numerous chances before choosing to order a remand in custody. Meanwhile, others keep the rule simple, such as one judge who often tells the erring defendant, 'If you break the bail, you go to jail.'

OFFENCES

The most prevalent type of offence comes under the Road Traffic Act, for motor theft, followed by public order violations such as breach of the peace or being drunk and disorderly. The third most common type of offence for young offenders is theft.

Minors who deny the allegations against them must face a hearing, just like an adult, where the state must establish beyond reasonable doubt that the defendant was guilty. Some more cunning juveniles employ a clever ruse to beat the prosecution. They will deny charges even when they may have been caught red-handed, and a date for a full hearing of the evidence is set. If, for example, a youth is charged with a motor-theft-related offence and the case against him strong, he can naturally still plead not guilty. This requires the owner of the vehicle to come to court for the hearing to give evidence that he or she was the legitimate owner of the car and that the defendant had no permission to take it, travel in it, criminally damage it, and so on. Similarly the requirement of an injured party to give evidence is required in all cases where a defendant denies involvement in an offence against a person or property. Often, the injured parties cannot take time off work to go to court or they simply might not want to. In this event, the defendant walks free from court. But if the victim does come to court, the defendant may decide to leave the court just before the hearing is due to commence. This means that a new hearing date will have to be set and the victim will have to come back to court again. And the next time, the victim might not bother. This is a process of wearing down the prosecution's case and it often succeeds. And the ploy has often been best used by teenagers who have been out of the education system for years.

CHILDREN UNDER 14 YEARS

The law also makes a differentiation between older and younger children. Prosecutions against children under 14 years are not as straightforward as those brought against older juveniles. There is the presumption, called *doli incapax*, that a child under this age is incapable of committing a criminal offence. However, this can be challenged by the prosecution producing evidence, not just of the crime itself, but of the criminal capacity of the accused. The presumption of *doli incapax* can be rebutted if the prosecution proves beyond reasonable doubt that the child knew that he or she was doing what was not merely wrong, but what was gravely, seriously wrong, and thus a criminal offence.

These types of Children's Court hearings often prove the trickiest for the prosecution, especially if, in the course of the investigation of the offence, the child was not, as often happens, questioned by gardaí with special training in how to interview children to get insight into their reasoning. And if the court finds that the presumption has been rebutted and the child has a criminal capacity, that ruling does not apply to other charges that may have been brought while the child was still in the same age bracket. For example, if a child under 14 has been found to have the criminal capacity to commit a theft, and is facing a separate charge for another offence, such as burglary, the same process must be gone through at a separate hearing.

If the court finds that the prosecution has failed to show that the child suspect understood the difference between an act of mischief and a crime, the case is dismissed. On the other hand, if the judge rules that the child understood what a crime was, the prosecution proceeds and eventually, if convicted, which might take yet another hearing to establish that the child actually committed the offence, the youngster faces the same process as older juveniles. Children under the age of 14 enjoy the right to this process no matter how many times they have been charged.

PARENT OR GUARDIAN

Most of the children who appear in the court are accompanied, if at all, by their mothers, and in many cases a distinct absence of paternal guidance can be seen. Section 91 of the 2001 Children Act says:

> Where the parents or guardian fail or neglect, without reason-able excuse, to attend any proceedings to which *subsection (1)* applies, the Court may adjourn the proceedings and issue a warrant for the arrest of the parents or guardian, and the warrant shall command the person to whom it is addressed to produce the parents or guardian before the Court at the time appointed for resuming the proceedings.

> Failure by the parents or guardian, without reasonable excuse, to attend any such proceedings shall, subject to *subsection (5)*, be treated for all purposes as if it were a contempt in the face of the court.

However, children frequently turn up for their court appearances without a parent as required by the law. Often this results from children not telling their parents of the impending court date.

Much of the time it can be attributed to parental apathy. And bench warrants for the arrest of the absent parents are rarely issued by the court.

DEMEANOUR

The demeanour of the young defendants varies, with some entering the court demurely while others, desensitised to the seriousness of their situations through frequent previous appearances, swagger in and even greet the judge happily. Some are taciturn and prefer to communicate through their legal representatives. Others have bouts of loquacity and suddenly pipe up to make their representations to the judge, sometimes going as far as to take over from their lawyer. As dress codes go, a pair of jeans and a jumper are regarded as smart attire. Most of the defendants use the stereotypical young offender uniform: a tracksuit, hooded top, runners and the optional baseball cap.

Around the courthouse, the atmosphere, depending on how big the day's list is, can be tense and hostile. Arguments break out involving not just the juveniles but the parents as well.

The courtroom is tiny, a reflection on the fact that only the defendants, gardaí involved in the cases, the lawyers, the probation officers, the judge and court staff (and also bona fide members of the press) are allowed inside for the *in camera* proceedings. One doorway leads in from the public area. Another leads from the courtroom itself to the courthouse's four cells. In the Children's Court, unlike other courts, the judge does not sit on an elevated bench. The bench is on the same level as the lawyers, gardaí and also the defendant, to promote the concept of equality. Judges don't wear formal attire in the Children's Court.

THE JUDGE

Judges must determine guilt or innocence where prosecutions are contested. They are compassionate and patient. Their role is to strike a balance between being tough and fair and, on conviction of defendants, the judges must decide the best and most appropriate recourse. There is an obligation to seek a Probation and Welfare Service report on the background of the convicted teenager before proceeding to sentence. These evaluations are valuable in indicating whether or not the child is likely to re-offend. They can also make recommendations for the child's welfare, such as education and training courses, anger management counselling or alcohol and drug addiction therapy.

THE PROBATION ACT

The Probation Act, meaning no resulting criminal record, is often applied for first-time offenders who did not commit a crime between time of arrest and the date of their sentence hearing. Fines are frequently imposed but have to be realistic, having regard for the defendants' and their families' financial circumstances. However, a loop hole in the 2001 Children Act leaves no effective default penalty for failure to pay a fine. Adults receive fines in lieu of custodial sentences. If the fines are not paid, they are jailed. But if a juvenile does not pay a fine, the only recourse open to the court is a community sanction, such as community service or a curfew. If the child does not adhere to this penalty, no other sanction can be imposed.

Probation bonds are often imposed to release the offender to be of good behaviour for a specific time period. This sanction also allows young people to receive further assistance from the Probation and Welfare Service after their case has ended.

THE 2001 CHILDREN ACT

Guiding the juvenile justice system throughout the process is the 2001 Children Act. Its key aims are to promote the welfare and rehabilitation of the child involved in criminal proceedings, and it provides for family action plans involving defendants and their parents. Significantly it removed the Children's Court's power to order the health services to attend cases of juvenile defendants who have been placed in their care to explain what steps they are taking to promote their care and welfare. Penalties set out in the act are: an order that the child pay a fine or costs, an order that the parent or guardian be bound over, a compensation order, a parental supervision order, an order that the parent or guardian pay compensation, an order imposing a community sanction. The legislation's central ethos—detention—must be used as 'a last resort'.

DETENTION

The main detention schools for boys under 16 are: Finglas Child and Adolescent Centre, Finglas West, Dublin, incorporating the National Remand and Assessment Centre, formerly known as St Lawrence's Institution and St Michael's Institution; St Joseph's Special School, Clonmel, Co. Tipperary; Trinity House School, Lusk, Co. Dublin, which is the most secure centre for offenders under 15; and Oberstown Boys' Centre, Lusk, Co. Dublin. These centres focus more on the education and rehabilitation of the child offender.

Most young offenders over the age of 16 are sent to St Patrick's Institution, an environment which is closer to that of an adult prison. Locking children up in St Patrick's, which holds young men up to the age of 21, is in clear contravention of international treaties which prohibit the detention of juveniles alongside adults. In 2005, 174 young people aged from 16 to 18 were placed in adult detention centres such as St Patrick's Institution, Cloverhill and Limerick prisons.

Girls under 17 years are sent to Oberstown Girls' Centre, Lusk, Co. Dublin. But 17-year-old girls, though still regarded by the law as children, are held in the Dóchas Centre, the women's unit of Mountjoy Prison, with adults. Again, this is in violation of international treaties that are against the detention of juveniles with adults.

It is this very practice of detaining children with adults that gives credence to the concept of the 'college of crime'. Youths, who should be rehabilitated, often end up even more criminalised by being locked up with older and more hardened criminals who have a lot to teach them.

APPENDIX II
NAME AND SHAME: THE LAW AND THE NAMING OF MINORS

Normally children brought to the court for committing a crime are shielded from notoriety by legislation which bans the news media from identifying them. The case of the teenagers who had been in the car which crashed into the taxi driver Robert McGowan (chapter 14) became a legal landmark in that it was the first criminal prosecution where a court held that the news media had a right to identify a juvenile offender in certain circumstances. Section 93 of the 2001 Children Act states that:

> In relation to any proceedings before the court against a child or in relation to a child no report shall be published or included in a broadcast which reveals the name, address or school of any child concerned in the proceedings or includes any particulars likely to lead to the identification of any child concerned in the proceedings, and no picture shall be published or included in a broadcast as being or including a picture of any child concerned in the proceedings or which is likely to lead to his or her identification.

Accordingly during the two boys' sentence hearing in the Dublin Circuit Criminal Court, the judge made an order prohibiting the identification in the media of the two boys. But an application made by three media groups challenging the direction resulted in Judge Desmond Hogan doing a U-turn on his earlier order.

Following legal submission from senior counsel Eoin McCullough, Judge Hogan agreed that he did not have the power to make such an order under provisions of the Children Act 2001. 'This court and any court has power to make an order only when it is given that power,' Mr McCullough said in his application on

behalf of Independent Newspapers and Examiner Publications.[1]
The application was also supported by RTÉ.

Judge Hogan had made the order at the outset of the sentence
hearing on the application of barristers for the two defendants, on
the basis of provisions contained in the Children Act 2001 dealing
with prohibition of identity of a defendant under the age of 18 years.

However, Mr McCullough submitted that the provisions of the
Children Act referred only to 'any proceedings before the Court'
and that the Act defined the 'Court' as 'the Children's Court'. He
submitted that the legislation clearly distinguished between the
Children's Court and the other courts and its provisions did not
apply to the Circuit Criminal or Central Criminal Courts.

'It is clear that this court, the Dublin Circuit Criminal Court,
cannot be in any circumstances the Children's Court,' he said.
Mr McCullough replied, 'Yes', when Judge Hogan asked if he was
to understand that counsel was submitting that 'a child' as defined
by the Children Act could not be identified in media reports from
the Children's Court but could be in Circuit Criminal Court
proceedings. 'It is not open to the Circuit Criminal Court to make
any order banning identification,' he added.

In reply, one of the defence barristers argued that an order,
which had been made in the Children's Court, relating to the
accused who was defined as 'a child' in the legislation, carried
through to the end of the proceedings.

But Judge Hogan said that he accepted the submissions made
to him that he did have the power to make the prohibition order.
He said that he was being asked to accept that the original order
applied to any proceedings before the Dublin Circuit Criminal
Court, and that such an order should be continued by him, but his
answer to that proposition was 'No'.

Judge Hogan agreed with the defence senior counsel that his
decision showed a dichotomy in the law which allowed for the
protection in the Children's Court of the identity of a 'child' from
the age of seven to 18 as defined in the Act but didn't provide for
that in the Circuit Criminal and Central Criminal Courts.

In other words, the legislation contained a gaping loophole.
Thereafter, juveniles who came before the higher courts facing

criminal offences could be named, while those whose cases were retained in the Children's Court still enjoyed their anonymity.

In the aftermath of Judge Hogan's rulings, the debate arose again in almost every case involving a juvenile who appeared before either the Circuit or Central Criminal Court. Each time this interpretation of the legislation was tested, but the letter of the law was clear and, on each occasion, it was held that the media had the right to identify juvenile offenders who appeared before these courts. Any remaining doubts about the matter were dispelled by the High Court judgment of Ms Justice Elizabeth Dunne who shored up the argument that the news media had the right to identify juvenile offenders in the higher courts.

This interpretation of the law, while probably pleasing to the average person on the street, has been criticised by experts in juvenile justice systems and children's rights advocates. A report published by the Law Society of Ireland, entitled *Rights Based Child Law*, has recommended that the Children Act, 2001, be amended to extend to other courts the anonymity afforded to children appearing before the Children's Court.

The Irish Youth Justice Alliance (IYJA), coalition of children's rights groups, cites as its objectives:

> To work towards reforming the Irish youth justice system by promoting practices that are in line with international human rights standards; To advocate for the full and immediate implementation and adequate resourcing of the Children Act, 2001; To facilitate networking, research and information-sharing on issues related to youth justice between organisations and individuals throughout Ireland.

It has raised concerns over threats to the juvenile's right to privacy which could be affected by plans to introduce Anti-Social Behaviour Orders (ASBOs). In response to proposed amendments to the Children Act, the IYJA has said that:

> Under the amendments, section 93 of the Children Act, 2001, which prevents the media from publishing or broadcasting

details as to the child's identity, has been amended to provide for such publication where 'it is in the public interest to remove or relax these requirements' and where the child is the subject of an order under section 273 (an ASBO) whose enforcement requires these provisions to be dispensed with. The requirement on the court to explain the reasons for its decision in open court has been retained. It is thus proposed in certain circumstances to remove or restrict the child's right to have his or her privacy protected when an Anti-Social Behaviour Order has been made. This involves an amendment to the right to privacy which children enjoy when before the Children Court and represents a weakening of children's rights as set out in the Children Act, 2001.[2]

There are various provisions in international law that provide for the rights of juveniles, who face prosecution, to protection of their right to privacy. Article 40 of the Convention on the Rights of the Child, ratified by Ireland in September 1992, which sets out the minimum protection and safeguards to which every child is entitled, has often been cited as an argument against identification of young offenders. In an analysis of the subject of media coverage of juvenile's cases, Dr Ursula Kilkelly, Faculty of Law, University College Cork, wrote:

The most important general principle is set out in Article 40 (1) which provides for the right of every child charged with or convicted of infringing the penal law to be treated in a manner consistent with the promotion of the child's sense of dignity and worth, which reinforces the child's respect for the rights and freedoms of others, and which takes into account the child's age and the desirability of promoting the child's reintegration and the child's assuming a constructive role in society. According to this standard, children convicted of a criminal offence have the right to have measures taken that are in their best interests and that promote the chances of their successful rehabilitation and reintegration into society. The release to the public of information revealing the identity of a young person convicted of crime would undoubtedly run counter to this principle and would arguably breach the standards set down by the Convention to which Ireland is a party. This is confirmed by the requirement set out in Article 40 (b) (vii) that juveniles have the right to have their privacy respected 'at all stages of the proceedings'. To suggest that this protection should end when the proceedings are concluded is to fail to read this provision together with the general principle set out in Article 40 (1) of the Convention.[3]

Similarly, the issue is covered in the UN Standard Minimum Rules for the Administration of Juvenile Justice, the Beijing Rules, adopted by General Assembly Resolution 40/33 in 1985. Its Rule 8 advocates that the juvenile's right to privacy be respected at all stages in order to avoid harm being caused to him or her by undue publicity or by the process of labelling. It also requires that no information that could lead to the identification of a juvenile offender be published. Rule 8 explains the importance of protecting the juvenile from stigmatisation and the damaging effects resulting from permanent identification of a young person as criminal. It also highlights the negative effects that may follow from the publication in the media of the names of suspected or convicted young offenders. Rule 17 of the Beijing Rules provides that the wellbeing of the juvenile will be the guiding factor in the consideration of his or her case.

The Beijing Rules are non-binding, but they are regarded as representing the international consensus and a best-practice model for justice systems' treatment of juveniles before the criminal courts. According to Dr Kilkelly:

The fact that section 93 of the Children Act, 2001 makes provision for the protection of the privacy rights of children tried by the Children Court indicates support for this principle in Irish law. Recognition of the negative impact that publicity may have on the trial of a juvenile is also clear from Article 6 of the European Convention on Human Rights which provides that the press and public may be excluded from all or part of the trial where the interests of juveniles require.

The principle to include protection from undue or negative post-trial publicity is also set out in the cases of John Venables and Robert Thompson, probably the world's most notorious young offenders, who were convicted by an English Crown Court of the murder of toddler James Bulger, in 1993. They were just ten years old when they abducted the two-year-old from a Liverpool shopping centre before torturing and killing him. The trial judge chose at the time to reveal their identities to the press, but later an injunction was granted to limit the information the media were allowed to publish. That injunction ended on their eighteenth birthdays. They were released from secured accommodation in June 2001; Judge Dame Elizabeth Butler-Sloss awarded them anonymity for life.

An application was made for indefinite injunction to forbid publicity of their identities. This was granted by Dame Butler-Sloss, President of the Family Division, on 8 January 2001, with the support of the Attorney General and the Official Solicitor (*Venables and Thompson v Newsgroup Newspapers Ltd*, QBD, 8 January 2001). In granting the order, Dame Butler-Sloss was convinced by the abundance of information that the pair were uniquely notorious and at serious risk of attacks from members of the public, as well as friends and relatives of the murdered child. It was this danger that led to the decision to give the pair new identities on their release from custody. Having found that the pair's lives and welfare required protection, the judge then held that the provisions of the European Convention on Human Rights could be extended to protect individuals who would be at serious risk of injury or death if their identity or whereabouts became public knowledge. Consequently the court had authority to grant the injunctions to ensure their protection. While the importance of supporting freedom of expression and the rights of the press were taken into consideration, it was considered necessary in that case to grant indefinite injunctions restraining the media from disclosing information about the identity, appearance or addresses of Venables and Thompson, on their release.

Dame Butler-Sloss's ruling has been seen as an attempt to undo the damage done by the decision of the original trial judge to reveal their names.

Dr Kilkelly concludes:

While a similar case can be made here for the right of the media to publish this information, it is clear that withholding that information at the current time would be a preventive measure aimed at protecting convicted juveniles and their families from exposure to harassment, intimidation and abuse of their rights by the media or the public. It would also improve the chances of them reintegrating into society upon their release from custody, which international law clearly requires.

Plans have been drafted to amend the legislation to extend the reporting restrictions to any court in which a child is tried— including the Circuit and Central Criminal Courts. But a new exception has been introduced which could still allow the courts to lift the protection on the child's identity if such a move were deemed to be 'in the public's interest'. This is to apply to all courts, including the Children's Courts.

APPENDIX III

(A) CRIMINAL RECORD OF GARY IN CHAPTER 9: TWO BROTHERS

2001

15 December, at Virgin Megastore in the Liffey Valley Shopping Centre, stole €577 worth of computer games.

2002

17 March, at Mountjoy Square, obstructed a garda in the execution of his duty.

7 May, at Marathon Sports in the Ilac Shopping Centre, D.1, criminally damaged an Ireland jersey.

7 May, stole jersey worth €45 from Marathon Sports in Ilac Shopping Centre.

7 May, unlawful carriage in a stolen vehicle in Summerhill.

3 June, at Temple Street, D.1, failed to comply with a garda's direction having been cautioned under the Public Order Act.

7 June, unlawful carriage in a stolen vehicle in Summerhill.

9 July, at Champion Sports on Henry Street, stole a pair of Nike runners worth €130; also charged with handling stolen goods.

17 July, skipped court.

29 July, attempted car theft at Morning Star Avenue, D.7.

29 July, attempted theft of another car at Morning Star Avenue, D.7.

25 July, breach of the peace on Parnell Street, D.1.

10 August, drunk and disorderly at Dorset Street, breach of the peace, assaulted a garda at same location.

30 August, drunk and disorderly, breach of the peace, obstruction of a garda at Sean O'Casey Avenue, assaulted garda in Store Street Garda Station.

31 August, breach of the peace and assault of garda, damaged a garda's shirt at Store Street.

9 September, at Gardiner Street, possession of implements for use in connection with theft offence.

12 September, trespassed on a property with intent to commit an offence.

25 September, skipped court.

28 September, assaulted two gardaí at Mountjoy Square, drunk and disorderly, breach of the peace.

15 October, unlawful carriage in a stolen vehicle, at Sean McDermott Street.

25 November, unlawful interference with a car at Talbot Street.

26 November, criminally damaged the ignition and steering lock of a car.

29 November, skipped court. Criminally damaged a car, possession of a screwdriver for use in a car theft, unlawful interference with a car, on North Great Charles Street, D.1.

3 December, obstructed a garda.

2003

9 January, skipped court.

2 February, criminal damage to a car window at Buckingham Street, unlawful interference with the car on same date.

17 March, breach of the peace.

3 December, skipped court.

9 December, driving without insurance and a licence, failed to produce documents to a garda station.

23 December, at North Great Clarence Street, handled a stolen mobile phone.

Christmas Day, driving illegally.

2004

12 March, assaulted a man in a sports clothing shop on Henry Street, D.1.

12 March, criminally damaged a tracksuit belonging to same shop.

12 March, breach of the peace at same location.

24 May, skipped court.

5 April, at Lourdes Church, D.1, obstructed a garda during a drug search.

22 April, handled a stolen jersey worth €90, from a shop on Liffey Street.

22 April, criminally damaged same jersey worth €90.

21 May, intoxicated to such an extent he was a danger to himself and others in Summerhill, contrary to section 4 of the Public Order Act.

21 May, engaged in a breach of the peace.

21 May, assaulted a garda at same location.

21 May, assaulted a second garda at same location.

(B) CRIMINAL RECORD OF MARK IN CHAPTER 18: DEVOTED TO CRIME

2004

2 January, in Ballymun, obstructed a garda executing his duty.

5 January, skipped court.

8 January, skipped court.

28 January, skipped court, caused a breach of the peace and assaulted a garda in Ballymun.

11 February, trespassed on a property in a Ballymun flat complex with intent to interfere with property there.

15 April, skipped court

4 May, refused to comply with a garda's direction under the Public Order Act, in Ballymun.

2003

2 January, caught handling stolen goods, a bottle of perfume, on O'Connell Street.

17 January, stole a T-shirt worth €79 from a shop on Talbot Street. On the same date, was caught in possession of the stolen T-shirt.

21, 27, 29, 30 January: escaped from detention centre four times.

26 February, trespassed in a house in a manner likely to cause fear in another.

3 March, skipped court.

2 April, at Boots in Jervis Street, stole aftershave valued at €40.

25 April, breach of the peace at a Ballymun flat complex.

29 April, refused to comply with a garda's direction having been cautioned under the probation act that his presence was likely to cause a breach of the peace.

14 June, at Lower O'Connell Street, attempted to steal a mobile phone.

14 July, stole €3,500 in cash from a kiosk in the Stephen's Green Shopping Centre.

14 July, skipped court.

7 August, stole an orange drink from a shop on O'Connell Street.

30 October, stole €610 in cash from a mobile-phone retailer on Grafton Street.

13 November, skipped court and on that day stole a pair of runners worth €60.

27 November, skipped court.

9 December, caused a breach of the peace at Henry Street, and on same day assaulted a woman there.

11 December, caught in possession of a stolen T-shirt at Henry Street.

16 December, stole a jumper worth €160 from a shop on Talbot Street.

2002

15 April, was arrested for dangerously driving a moped while not wearing a helmet and also charged with driving without insurance, tax and a licence in connection with same incident. Had also failed to stop the moped when signalled by pursuing garda.

16 April, at a flat complex in Ballymun, refused to comply with a garda's direction having been cautioned under the probation act that his presence was likely to cause a breach of the peace.

1 June, unlawfully driving a stolen vehicle in Finglas.

16 July, refused to comply with a garda's direction having been cautioned under the probation act that his presence was likely to cause a breach of the peace.

29 July, skipped court.

5 August, unlawful carriage as a passenger in a stolen vehicle.

6 August, stole a leather wallet worth €155 from a shop on Grafton Street.

10 August, arrested in Glasnevin, for trespassing on private property where he attempted to take a vehicle unlawfully, and for being in possession of a bolt-cutters for use in a motor theft at the same location.

3 September, skipped court.

26 October, skipped court, stole DVDs worth €335, from Virgin Megastore in Liffey Valley Shopping Centre.

9 December, damaged the security tag on an item of clothing at sportswear shop in Mary Street.

NOTES

1: Why? Parallel Lives (PAGES 3–17)

1. Irish Association for the Study of Delinquency.
2. Pól Ó Murchú in interview with the author, 11 April 2006.
3. Founder of Dublin-based charity, the Arrupe Society, which provides support services to young people experiencing homelessness. These hostels are especially geared to those who do not meet the regulations of many other hostels which stipulate that residents must be employed or attending a course. In particular, he has sought to help those thought by other agencies to be too difficult to deal with.

3: Severe Psychiatric Problems: Circumstances Verging on the Unique (PAGES 25–39)

1. Sarah Molloy in interview with the author, 3 February 2004.

6: Three Brothers (PAGES 61–71)

1. One national newspaper included Judge Connellan's comment in its top ten quotes of the week section.

10: Lost Cousins (PAGES 100–106)

1. See Chapter 4.

12: Car-Crime Addicts (PAGES 121–8)

1. At time of writing, this case is still pending.

13: In the Line of Duty (PAGES 129–40)

1. *Irish Independent*, 18 April 2002.
2. Ibid.
3. *The Irish Times*, 19 April 2002.

14: Another Motoring Outrage (PAGES 141–6)

1. *Irish Examiner*, 23 October 2003.

15: Sex Crimes (PAGES 147–59)

1. Tomás Mac Ruairí (CCC news agency), article, 6 March 2006.
2. Quotes from Circuit Court hearing from article by Sonya McLean (CCC news agency), 25 November 2004.

3. Sonya McLean (CCC news agency), article, 12 May 2006.
4. CCC news agency, 27 January 2004.

16: An Armed Robber (PAGES 163–74)
1. Bronagh Murphy (CCC news agency), article, 28 July 2005.

17: Out of Control (PAGES 175–86)
1. In suicide by cop, an individual behaves so as to provoke police officers into attempting to disarm him, sometimes killing him in the process.

18: Devoted to Crime (PAGES 187–93)
1. Now known as the National Remand and Assessment Centre.
2. See Appendix I, page 279, for text of Section 91 of 2001 Children Act.

19: Girl Trouble (PAGES 194–207)
1. Sonya McLean (CCC news agency).

20: Christine (PAGES 208–19)
1. Quotes from Circuit Criminal Court hearings from articles by Bronagh Murphy (CCC news agency), 25 July 2005 and 6 October 2005.

21: The Butterfly Effect (PAGES 223–34)
1. Darren Rogers (then aged 21), of Elmdale Park, Ballyfermot, Dublin, was sentenced to life imprisonment, having been found guilty at the Central Criminal Court of the murder of 43-year-old Thomas Farrell.

23: Where to Put Them (PAGES 251–9)
1. Formerly called St Lawrence's Institution.
2. Formerly called St Michael's Institution.
3. See the case of Mark in Chapter 18.
4. See Chapter 25.

24: The Profiler (PAGES 260–65)
1. Bronagh Murphy (CCC news agency), 3 April 2006.

Appendix II (PAGES 283–9)
1. Tomás Mac Ruairí (CCC news agency), article, 22 October 2003.
2. The Irish Youth Justice Alliance (IYJA).
3. Dr Ursula Kilkelly, Faculty of Law, University College Cork, in interview with the author, 19 January 2005. Further material from Dr Kilkelly on this area of law can be found in her excellent work, *Youth Justice in Ireland: Tough Lives, Rough Justice*.